CHILDREN OF GLOBAL MIGRATION

# CHILDREN OF GLOBAL MIGRATION

## Transnational Families and Gendered Woes

RHACEL SALAZAR PARREÑAS

STANFORD UNIVERSITY PRESS

*Stanford, California*

2005

Stanford University Press
Stanford, California

Printed in the United States of America on
acid-free, archival-quality paper

Library of Congress Cataloging-in-Publication
Data

Parreñas, Rhacel Salazar.
Children of global migration : transnational
families and gendered woes / Rhacel Salazar
Parreñas.
p.   cm.
Includes bibliographical references and index.
ISBN 0-8047-4944-2 (cloth : alk. paper)
ISBN 0-8047-4945-0 (pbk. : alk. paper)
1. Children of alien laborers—Philippines—
Attitudes.   2. Parental deprivation—Philippines.
3. Family—Philippines.   4. Alien labor, Philip-
pine—Foreign countries.   5. Filipinos—Employ-
ment—Foreign countries.   6. Philippines—
Emigration and immigration.   I. Title.

HQ792.P5P37 2005
306.85'09599—DC22

2004016220

Original Printing 2005

Last figure below indicates year of this printing:
14   13   12   11   10   09   08   07   06   05

*In memory of Lola Udi*

# CONTENTS

ACKNOWLEDGMENTS

I could not have written this book without the cooperation of the transnational family members who participated in this study. I thank all of them for their willingness and openness to share intimate stories about their family life with me.

My family in the Philippines, including my brother Rolf and his wife Sharon and my cousins Lourdes Jerusalem, Alan Pagunsan, and Angelo Pagunsan, greatly eased my transition into the field. This book could not have been completed without their assistance. My family in the United States, particularly my sister Rhanee, also lent much emotional support. My sister Cerissa, who co-authored an earlier version of a chapter in this volume, gave me much intellectual stimulus in our discussions of migration and the law. My sister Celine Shimizu also provided plenty of solid advice.

Various sources provided material support that enabled me to complete this project. They include the University of California President's Postdoctoral Fellowship Program (1999–2000); the Ford Postdoctoral Fellowship for Minorities (2001–2002); the Office of the Vice Chancellor for Research and the Dean's Office of the Division of Humanities, Arts, and Cultural Studies at the University of California, Davis; and the Graduate School and Women's Studies Program at the University of Wisconsin, Madison.

I am grateful to the individuals and academic communities that provided a forum for me to share ideas during the data analysis and writing stages of this project. I received valuable feedback from lectures that I delivered at Cornell University, Hunter College, and Pomona College. Conferences held at Duke University, New York University, and the University of Arizona provided another forum for my ideas. For providing me with these opportunities to share my work, I am grateful to Lourdes Beneria, Miranda Joseph, Mario Salazar, Lok Siu, Pamela Stone, Hung Thai, Joan Tronto, and Robyn Wiegman.

I also had the opportunity to share my work at various professional meetings. They include the American Anthropology meeting, Chicago, Illinois (2003); the American Sociological Association meeting, Atlanta, Georgia (2003); the Association for Asian Studies meeting, New York, New York (2003); the Sociologists for Women in Society winter meeting, Tempe, Arizona (2001); and the Association for Asian American Studies meeting, Toronto, Canada (2001).

Various intellectual communities of which I have been a part aided the development of this project. They include the FemSem series of the Sociology Department at the University of Wisconsin, Madison; the Empire in Transition working group at the University of Wisconsin, Madison; and the Ford Foundation-sponsored workshop on the Meanings and Representations of Work in the Lives of Women of Color. I thank Myra Marx Feree, Victor Bascara, and Evelyn Hu De Hart respectively for inviting me to join these groups. I also acknowledge Myra Marx Feree and Aili Tripp for their mentorship of my academic career while at the University of Wisconsin, Madison. At the University of California, Davis, I appreciate and benefit from the collegiality of Nicole Fleetwood and Gayatri Gopinath.

Comments from anonymous reviewers as well as friends and colleagues who read earlier versions of different chapters helped me hone my arguments and ideas, including Eileen Boris, Nina Eliasoph, Pierrette Hondagneu-Sotelo, Grace Hong, Kevin Johnson, Richard Kim, and Leith Mullings. Deserving of mention are the long discussions I had with Lok Siu, who helped sustain me through the writing stage of this project and challenged me to think about transnational families more as gender paradoxical entities.

I worked on this book a great deal in the company of Ethelene Whitmire as well as Sherene Cherrard, who during my time in Madison, Wisconsin, met with me every Friday morning at one of the many coffee shops in town. I also acknowledge Mary Beltran, Grace Hong, and Lisa Nakamura, who later joined us in our "women of color coffee hour." I am also grateful to Michael Cullinane, an expert extraordinaire on the Philippines, for giving my scholarship such unrelenting support.

In the Philippines, friendships with numerous individuals provided me with many welcome distractions. They include Jaylin Salazar, Art Tajanlangit, Jr., Ellen Tajanlangit, and Bernardine Tiongco. For providing me with an academic community in my field research site, I thank Jigger Latoza. I gratefully acknowledge my friends in the Trappist abbey in Guimaras Island for welcoming me into their community. I especially thank Brother Stephen Peralta for his hospitality. In the United States, my friendships with Sherry Apostol and Fernando Gaytan helped sustain me through the writing process.

This book also benefits from the invaluable support of my editors at Stanford University Press, Pat Katayama and Kate Wahl, its production editor, Tim Roberts, as well as the assistance of Carmen Borbon-Wu. At the University of California, Davis, the office staff support provided by Kathy Entao, Tina Tansey, and Ben Wang was invaluable to the production of this book. I thank Winnie Tam for completing the index.

The research assistance of Jason David, Luisa Gonzaga Maricel Lesondra, Sauro Solis, and most especially Ella Liu were invaluable to this project. I am additionally grateful to Ella Liu for being such a supportive interlocutor. Her patience allowed me to work through many of my ideas. While many individuals aided me in the process of writing this book, all the errors are mine.

Last, I wish to give recognition to the staff at Loma Linda Hospital's Intensive Care Unit. Without their care during the twelve days I spent there in April 2002, I could not have completed this book.

R.S.P
Berkeley, California

# Gender and the Transnational Family

Femininity is imposed for the most part through an unremitting discipline that concerns every part of the body and is continuously recalled through the constraints of clothing or hairstyle. The antagonistic principles of male and female identity are thus laid down in the form of permanent stances, gaits, postures which are the realization, or rather, the naturalization of an ethic.
—Pierre Bourdieu[1]

The view that gender is performative sought to show that what we take to be an internal essence of gender is manufactured through a sustained set of acts, posited through the gendered stylization of the body. —Judith Butler[2]

The task of "measuring up" to one's gender is faced again and again in different situations with respect to different particulars of conduct. The problem involved is to produce configurations of behavior *which can be seen* by others as normative gender behavior. —Sarah Fenstermaker, Candace West, and Don Zimmerman[3]

*Lalake yan o baba-e yan?* ("Is that a man or is that a woman?") is a question that I frequently heard passersby utter out loud when I walked by. Some people gawked, others pointed, and the rest just looked at me in perplexity. I stirred gender confusion everywhere I went in the Philippines including city streets in Manila, beach towns in the provinces, a hallway of the Presidential Palace, the neighborhood where I lived, even the sports facility where I went running every day, and finally the malls I frequently visited to escape the sweltering heat outdoors. I was born biologically sexed as female with XX chromosomes, and before doing the research for this project in the Philippines had never questioned my gender identity to be other than that of a woman.

Prior to my return to this country where I was born and from which I was uprooted at the age of thirteen, I had not once thought that I would

1

cross gender boundaries when clad in a dress, defy gender normativity with my floral hairclips, challenge gender norms with my red lipstick, or violate gender categories when strutting in high heels. The gender trouble over my identity and the gender confusion I stirred left me aghast and quite offended at first, then troubled, and finally puzzled. What is it about me that instigated "gender trouble" in the Philippines? Moreover, why did people not hesitate to vocalize their gender confusion over me? In other words, why did they have to box me in a sex category? Finally, why did they need to place me within a set gender category that discretely embodies cultural notions of masculinity or femininity?

In the Philippines, I was often assumed to be a man, or more precisely a transgender woman, a *bakla*.[4] Ironically, I am a heterosexual woman. At my field research site, a group of friends, I heard, had wagered a bet of a case of beer over my sex. Once, after a lecture, I was approached by a woman from the audience. In the middle of lauding me she could not help but suddenly blurt out, "Oh, my . . . you fooled me! The whole time you were talking to us, I thought you were a real woman." The "gender trouble" embodying my everyday life in the Philippines is not mirrored in any other country I have visited in Asia, Europe, or the Americas. Thus, I often left the Philippines to take a break from my gendered woes and seek the comfort of gender recognition that welcomed me in another country. To be categorically defined as a woman, with all of its labels, stereotypes, and assumptions, became a welcome break from my gender ambiguity. Categorization, I learned from experience, brings comfort.

Because of my ability to escape the cultural terrain that placed me in an ambiguous gender location, I do not think that the confusion over my gender had been due to my physical appearance. Moreover, I do not believe that I have biological attributes that could predispose one to assume that I am biologically male. For instance, I do not have an Adam's apple. I do not wear a moustache or sport any other facial hair. I happen to have curves. I may not have the biggest chest, but one could see it is not flat. At 5′4″, I am taller than most women in the Philippines but not taller than most men. I may have muscles, but they are not large enough to bulge on their own. I also wore my hair long in the Philippines, and often wore skirts. Despite all these physical attributes and my choice to manufacture a gendered female stylized body, I was still, perplexingly, labeled "biologically male."

In my bewilderment over the gender confusion provoked by my physical presence, I asked my friends and family to identify the distinguishing markers that labeled me as male. When I asked how I could be *mistaken* for a biological male, almost all gave the same response: *galaw*, or movement. This one word captured what I would have to transform to fit prescribed gender categorizations in the Philippines. It is not what I do or the way I look but the way I move that labels me as biologically male. But where I learned to be a woman shapes how I move as one. I had conformed to femininity not in the Philippines but in the United States, not as part of a majority but as a racial minority, not in a suburb but instead in the inner city housing projects, and not in a neighborhood known for its safety but instead one associated with crime. Thus I learned femininity in a space that cultivated in it toughness, which emerges in my quick-paced walk, my purposeful gait, and my tough exterior. The everyday practice of my femininity violated the system of knowledge and discourse of femininity prescribed to women in the Philippines. Accordingly, most Filipinos placed me in the biological category of male.

In vocalizing their confusion about my gender, people did not leave me in a space of gender ambiguity but often forcibly categorized me as one who is biologically male and gendered female. Yet, my choice to be gendered female as one assumed to be biologically male was often met with resentment and resistance. Waiters frequently greeted me "sir"; store clerks directed me to the men's and not the women's room; and airport security reprimanded me for being in the wrong line for the required body check of passengers. In the Philippines, my gender determined my sex.

In the perspective of most, I had to accordingly succumb to my prescribed categorization. As feminist sociologist Judith Lorber similarly observes, "The norms, expectations and evaluation of women and men may be converging, but we have no social place for a person who is neither woman nor man. A man who passes as a woman or a woman as a man still violates strong social boundaries, and when transsexuals change gender, they still cross a great divide."[5] The same can be said for a woman who in her actions passes quite well, even if only inadvertently, as a man; she is seen to violate social boundaries by not behaving like a man. In my socially situated experience, practice and not biology had determined not only my gender but also my sex. A reconstitution of my everyday practices would have accordingly placed me in a gender and sexual category familiar to the discursive construction of masculinity and femininity in the Philippines.

My contestation of gender terms did not elicit transformation, however, but forced my conformity via my categorization. Including ascribedly male traits in my performance of femininity was not greeted by a welcome expansion of gender terms from most. My insistence to be labeled as a female who includes in her self-presentation ascribedly male gender characteristics was met with resistance. Women blocked me from entering their rest rooms, and airport security detained me for not moving out of the line designated to women into the line for men. Thus, biology did not entitle me to be included in the social spaces of women, but my membership required the conformity of my behavior according to the gender terms in the Philippines. In other words, my performance of gender had to abide by the rules, the prescribed practices of the gender order, and the recognizable actions that would deem me worthy of the label of "Filipino woman."

## Gender and Transnational Families

These gender lessons in the field emphasized to me that deeply embedded norms and expectations distinguish the daily practices of men and women. These distinctions, while arguably social creations in their maintenance, uphold gender boundaries that create social order via the proper behavior assigned to men and women. The prescription of "normative gender behavior" attends to the most minute actions, gestures, and behavior of individuals. As I had encountered, society continuously enforces gender boundaries to uphold norms through the monitoring of daily practices. A person's crossing of socially inscribed gender definitions is often met with dismay and faces obstacles, as shown for instance by my being prevented from entry into women's public spaces in the Philippines. I did not have to be biologically female, or just physically ascribed to be a woman; instead, to be allowed in these spaces I had to behave like a woman. Experiencing the Foucauldian assertion that society is a panoptic machine, I faced the coercion of gender conformity through the surveillance and policing of my actions and behavior.[6]

My experience raises the question as to the other ways that society may similarly attempt to control the reconstitution of gender—not just for those with transnational lives such as my own, but also for women who participate in the labor market, those affected by the disjunctures brought by the penetration of "ideoscapes" and "mediascapes" and other dimensions of cultural flows in globalization,[7] and finally those forced to reconstitute their households due to migration. In this project, my concern is with the constitution of gender in the formation of migrant transnational households, meaning households located in two or more nation-states.

An estimated 7.38 million Filipinos work and reside in more than 160 countries.[8] This makes them one of the largest groups of migrant laborers in the global economy. Notably, a great number of migrant Filipinos are parents—mothers or fathers who have had to migrate to provide for their children economically but who must at the same time leave these very same children behind in the Philippines. The increasing number of transnational families marks an institutional rupture to the order of gender in the Filipino family, as the maintenance and constitution of such households call for a redistribution of the traditional gender division of labor in the family. The formation of transnational households threatens cultural parameters and institutional norms marked by material inequalities between men and women as well as ideology. Thus, transnational families in their institutional arrangement invite gender transformations in the level of interaction.

This is the case in transnational families maintained by both migrant mothers and migrant fathers. For instance, in the case of migrant mother–based households, we see social change invited by the complete removal of biological mothers from the physical confines of the home, as well as by the increase in women's earning power in the household. In the case of migrant father–based households, we see the geographic inconvenience that fathers experience in maintaining their male-ascribed responsibility of disciplining children when they relocate to work across national boundaries.

In Anthony Giddens's concept of structuration, structural constraints potentially disable practices so as to prompt social transformations.[9] If so, we should expect to see the emergence of social transformations from the formation of Filipino transnational families. As social theorist of gender Robert Connell states, "To describe structure is to specify what it is in the situation that constrains the play of practice. Since the consequence of practice is a transformed situation which is the object of new practice, 'structure' specifies the way practice (over time) constrains practice. . . . But practice cannot escape structure, cannot float free from its circumstances (any more than social actors are simply 'bearers' of the structure)."[10] According to Connell, structural conditions control but do not predetermine the gender outcome of the practices that constitute institutions. The reproduction of the social order depends on the constitution of practices. Disagreements in practices that emerge from internal contradictions in structural constraints may in fact subvert structures.[11] This perspective suggests that actions potentially transform institutional orders and structures.

Actions that depart from the reproduction of normative conceptions thus enable "countervailing processes of resistance, challenge, conflict and change."[12] As Judith Butler notes, "The possibilities of gender transformation are to be found precisely in the arbitrary relation between such acts, in the possibility of a failure to repeat, a de-formity, or a parodic repletion that exposes the phantasmatic effect of abiding identity as a politically tenuous construction."[13] Transnational families open the door for the reconstitution of gender by rupturing the structural constraints that encourage the "normative gender behavior" more appropriate to patriarchal nuclear households.

Indeed, transnational families are significant because they pose a challenge to the maintenance of the ideology of separate spheres as well as the traditional gender division of labor in the Filipino family. As noted, these challenges include the removal of biological mothers from the domestic sphere, the increase in the income power of women, and also the parodic performance of mothering and fathering that is prompted by its recital over distance. An example of "parodic performance" is the need for migrant fathers to portray themselves as exaggeratedly domineering authorities as their way of adjusting to being denied by geographical distance to perform their gender-ascribed duty as the disciplinarian of the family.

Although following "normative gender behavior" is not at all convenient in transnational families, I found that patriarchal traditions are more often sustained than contested by the actions that maintain these families. In other words, the institution of the transnational family reifies more than it transgresses conventional gender boundaries. Notably, the maintenance of gender does not only occur via the occupational segregation of most migrant mothers into domestic work. Instead, as I will illustrate, the various ways that migrants and their kin adapt to their reconstituted households enforce gender boundaries. Moreover, the integration of transnational families into the Philippine public sphere imposes a pressure to uphold gender norms via the public sphere's rejection and society's disapproval of this household structure.

By illustrating that actions in transnational households maintain "normative gender behavior," I establish that actions do not necessarily succumb to their situated context or give in to structural constraints and organizational pressures. The reenactment of conventional gender norms in the transnational families of migrant mothers and fathers in the Philippines is testament to actions defying the potential subversions offered by the physical absence of mothers and fathers from the home.

As the actions that maintain transnational families do not always abide by their institutional and structural context, I found that a gender paradox of reifying and transgressing gender boundaries limits the potential for gender transformation in Filipino transnational households. More specifically, I observed that while the structural arrangement of transnational households sometimes forces the unavoidable transgression of gender norms, for instance via the incomes earned by women, the performance that maintains these families also upholds "normative gender behavior." I found that migrant mothers indeed provide care from thousands of miles away, whereas fathers continue to reject the responsibility of nurturing children. Additionally, migrant fathers insist on disciplining from a distance. Finally, mothers left behind at home by migrant fathers perform a parodic version of intensive mothering in response to the ultimate breadwinning achieved by migrant fathers. Resistance to the forced crossing of gender boundaries secures for transnational family members their self-identities as gendered male or gendered female. It should come as no surprise that both mothers and fathers insist on defying the gender transformations instigated by the reorganization of their households. They resist gender ambiguity and conform to gender boundaries.

In summary, this book establishes that a gender paradox defines transnational family life in the Philippines, from the incorporation of these families in the public domain to the actions that maintain them. It also illustrates the reifications and transgressions of gender norms that occur in transnational households. These conflicting processes of gender are the base from which I examine the experiences of children in transnational families.

## Methodology

The primary research site for this project was a city located in an area of the Central Philippines that is composed of six provinces with an approximate population of 6 million.[14] I chose this city as my field research site because of the high concentration of colleges and schools in this small geographic area. Based on my previous research on migrant Filipina domestic workers, I assumed that many children left behind in transnational families would be represented in institutions of higher learning, because the attainment of education for one's children is a central motivating factor for labor migration.[15] I also chose this site because it has a medium-range scale of migrant labor outflow and thus offers us a perspective on transnational families from a community that is equally divided between those directly and those not directly affected by emigration.

I spent eighteen non-continuous months between January 2000 and April 2002 doing field research for this project, with the first round of data gathered between January and July 2000 and the second round from May 2001 to April 2002. For my primary data, I conducted one- to three-hour in-depth and open-ended tape-recorded interviews with sixty-nine young adults who grew up in transnational migrant households. I supplemented these interviews with open-ended interviews with thirty-one of their guardians.

I identified most of the participants in this study with the cooperation of schools in the area. I solicited volunteers to participate in this study in four of the largest schools, but I also diversified my sample by seeking research participants outside the school setting through the use of informal networks of family and friends. Altogether, I interviewed thirty children with migrant mothers, twenty-six with migrant fathers, and thirteen with two migrant parents. The parents are scattered globally, working in Asia, the Middle East, the Americas, and Europe. Some of them worked on cargo ships. My interviews with young adult children focus on their family life, relationships with their parents and other relatives, feelings about parental migration, and finally their goals and aspirations in life. With only an intermediate knowledge of the local dialect, I conducted these interviews in Tagalog, the national language of the Philippines. Most interviewees responded in Tagalog, but some used a combination of Tagalog, English, and the local dialect. I fully transcribed and then translated these interviews into English. A research assistant aided me with translation of passages in the local dialect into English.

Interviews were conducted in a private and quiet setting, usually my residence in the city center, since many of the interviewees resided in crowded student boarding houses or did not feel comfortable enough to talk openly about their transnational family life in their own homes amidst kin. To protect the anonymity of informants, I have used pseudonyms for all interview-ees. I collected an unsystematic sample of research participants by using snowball referrals that began in four of the largest schools in the area. I identified interviewees by making classroom announcements and visiting business establishments that students frequent near school grounds. I collected interviews in both public and private school settings so as to generate a sample that is representative of diverse class backgrounds. To further ensure the diversity of my sample,

I also identified interviewees using nonuniversity-based networks of friends and relatives in the area.

From May 2001 to April 2002, I returned to the field to conduct follow-up interviews with the children as well as open-ended and in-depth interviews with their guardians. I interviewed thirty-one guardians of twenty-eight children in my study and an additional five guardians of young children. I located the guardians with the help of a research assistant, who had to travel to quite a few remote destinations. We were able to locate only fifty-six of the children originally interviewed. Of these children, two denied our requests to speak to their guardians. Of the children who gave us permission, ten of their guardians declined our request for an interview. Most gave the reason of being too busy. We were unable to interview as many guardians as we would have liked as many were also geographically inaccessible. We conducted the interviews with guardians not necessarily to check the validity of the information we gathered from our original sample, but to gain an understanding of the roles and contributions of other members of the family in transnational household maintenance.

In order to include the perspective of younger children in my data, I supplemented my interviews with a survey questionnaire of 228 elementary and high school students from transnational migrant families. I conducted this survey in two public school districts and one private school in the area. The survey expands our perspective on the changes in family life initiated by migration, the role of extended kin in transnational household maintenance, and the emotional state of younger children growing up without at least one migrant parent. Two research assistants helped me complete the survey, which we conducted in all of the public elementary schools in one district in my research site and in one public high school and one private high school in the area.

Finally, to gather information on the community perspective toward transnational families, I conducted focus-group discussions with members of local organizations and support groups for migrant workers and their families and interviewed guidance counselors, priests, and representatives of nongovernmental and governmental organizations. I also gathered secondary research materials in Manila, particularly surveys and census reports released by governmental and nongovernmental organizations on the state of migration, the labor market, and the status of women in the Philippines, as well as media reports on transnational families.

In summary, I look at transnational families from the perspectives and experiences of those left behind by migrant workers in the Philippines. My readings on the constitution of gender in transnational family life come from the perspective of individuals whose narratives are accordingly shaped by their gendered expectations of the family, their gender ideologies, and their notions of "normative gender behavior." In my analysis of the constitution of gender, I do not ignore the assumptions that shape the narratives that I had collected for this study but deconstruct and identify them in my reading of transnational family life. While I was mistaken as a *bakla* in the field, I do not believe that my perceived sexuality influenced the contents of my interviews. *Bakla*s are far more integrated in the Philippines than they are in the United States. At most, I believe my interviewees probably talked about my mistaken sexual identity after I had left and commented on how deceptively good I looked as a woman.

## Organization of the Book

As noted, this study establishes the paradoxes of gender that define the maintenance of transnational households. By this I mean that I illustrate the disruptions and perpetuations of "normative gender behavior" in Filipino transnational migrant families. I begin my inquiry into the constitution of gender by situating these families in a political framework that explains their formation from the gendered lens of the global economy. I explain in Chapter 1 that transnational families form in the context of the macroprocess of *care resource extraction*. This macro-process occurs via two mechanisms—(1) the labor migration of women as domestics and nurses and (2) structural adjustment policies that enforce the reduction of state welfare provisions in lieu of servicing the foreign debt.

In Chapter 2, I shift my focus to the integration of transnational families in the Philippine public domain. I argue that public reaction to transnational families highlights their dysfunctions vis-à-vis dominant perceptions of the proper order of gender in Philippine society. In so doing, the public inadvertently hides the dysfunctions of the Philippine economy by placing these problems in the shadow of migrant women's disruptions of gender conventions. Then, in Chapter 3, I move to establish how gendered care expectations of children define intergenerational relations in transnational migrant families. I establish that children's care expectations demand greater work from women than they do from men.

In Chapter 4, I begin my close interrogation of intergenerational relations in transnational families. This chapter focuses on the families of migrant fathers, which I establish to reflect heteronormative nuclear families. The only difference is the temporal and spatial rearrangement of the family: instead of routinely coming home during suppertime, the father comes home to his family every ten months. However, the maintenance of these families, which may seem to epitomize the patriarchal nuclear family, in actuality relies on the transgression of gender boundaries by the wives left behind in the Philippines.

In Chapters 5 and 6, I take a closer look at the transnational families of migrant women, which I show rely on the assistance of extended kin, unlike the more nuclear-family–based transnational households of migrant men. Chapter 5 establishes the contradiction between the reconstitution of gender by the institutional rearrangement of migrant-mother families and the perpetuation of gender norms by the care practices in these families. I look closely at the work of fathers, migrant mothers, eldest daughters (of which I interviewed fifteen young women), and finally extended kin, showing that each group reinforces gender boundaries in the caring work that they do for the family.

In Chapter 6, I examine the prominence of the discourse of abandonment among the children of migrant mothers. I establish that regardless of the care that they do receive in transnational families, the children of migrant mothers are more apt to describe their relationship with their mothers as consisting of abandonment. Moreover, their cries of abandonment increase the more their families deviate from the conventional gender scripts of the Filipino family.

Chapter 7 offers a look at the lives of children in families with two migrant parents. In this chapter, I address the issue of prolonged separation, which is a common experience but is not exclusive to this group of children. Notably, most children who endure prolonged separation have parents who are based in nations with liberal migratory regimes, such as the United States. Here, I address how the geographical destination of parents—in other words, the state policies of the receiving country of migration—shapes transnational family relations.

I conclude my study with a discussion of the persistence of gender in globalization. I emphasize how not even the complete removal of biological mothers from the home can threaten the stronghold of the ideology of separate spheres in the family. I end with some proposals on how ideological changes might lessen the difficulties confronting transnational households.

# CHAPTER 1

# The Global Economy of Care

A growing crisis of care troubles families in the developing world. By care, I refer to the labor and resources needed to ensure the mental, emotional, and physical well-being of individuals. This is the case in the Philippines, where parents must look to labor migration as a way of ensuring that they can send children to school, give them access to quality health care, and even provide them with just the basic food. On average, 2,531 Filipino workers, many of whom are parents, leave the country as overseas contract workers on a daily basis.[1] Indeed, the transnational family has become a norm in the Philippines, where according to representatives of local nongovernmental organizations in Manila, there are approximately 9 million Filipino children under the age of eighteen who are growing up without the physical presence of at least one migrant parent in the country.[2]

The phenomenon of the transnational family cuts across class boundaries. Migrant parents occupy not a few but many labor market sectors, from professionals to semiskilled workers to unskilled laborers. These workers are in various destination countries and occupy a vast range of occupations in the global labor market. They include engineers toiling in the oil rigs of Gulf region countries; nurses caring for the elderly and sick in Saudi Arabia, the United Kingdom, and the United States; domestic workers cleaning the homes of the affluent in Asia, the Gulf region, North America, and Europe; seafarers manning cargo ships the world over; and teachers safeguarding the classrooms of public schools in Texas and California. These are just a few of the occupations held by the parents of the children I met in the Philippines.

In this chapter, I explore the reasons why parents raise their children in transnational households. Not all parents who want to leave the Philippines are able to do so, and likewise not all who have the resources to leave do leave. Acknowledging the agency of migrant parents, I wish to point out that they seek migration as individuals and in so doing also opt to raise their children from great geographical distances. To raise children in transnational households is a decision that does not occur in a vacuum, of course. Social networks that are well in place in the Philippines control the selectivity of migrant outflows, enabling certain parents to turn to labor migration as a strategy of household maintenance, controlling the direction of their migration, and preventing those without access from doing so.[3] Moreover, a well-established program for exporting labor also opens the door to labor migration. Established in 1982, the Philippine Overseas Employment Administration (POEA) oversees labor contracts for temporary migrant workers, while the Commission for Filipinos Overseas (CFO) administers the departure of permanent migrants to countries such as the United States and Canada. Both of these government agencies work in close cooperation with recruitment agencies that identify and target markets facing labor shortages outside the country.[4]

In this chapter the discussion does not so much concern the selectivity of migrants and the institutional process of migration. Instead, I address the reasons why parents in the Philippines turn to labor migration as a strategy of household maintenance. In other words, I do not seek to explain how migrant parents leave but instead why they leave. Larger political-economic structural forces that dictate the access to resources of the working class, middle class, or struggling landowners in the Philippines control the decisions of parents. These forces include, first, the political economic inequality of global restructuring; second, the paucity of options for economic mobility available in an export-oriented developing nation such as the Philippines; and third, privatization by the state. To explain the formation of transnational migrant families, I consider how these factors jointly lead to the depletion of care resources available to families in export-oriented nations such as the Philippines. I establish that an increasing number of families seek the higher wages available outside of the Philippines to make up for the shortfalls of care imposed by a weak economy and a fragile welfare system.

Care inequities trouble the global economic landscape. By care inequities, I mean the disparities in both public (i.e., the state) and private (i.e., the family) care resources between nations in our global society. The lack of care resources in countries such as the Philippines should be seen as a result of global inequalities. More specifically, it emerges from the macro-process of care resource extraction, that is, the systematic withdrawal of care from poor nations to rich nations in the global economy. In this chapter, I explain the process of care resource extraction and then situate the formation of transnational families in this macro-process of globalization.

## The Political Economy of Care Inequities

> Philippine society is in crisis and the Filipino family, being the basic unit of social production, mirrors this crisis.[5]

To what crisis confronting Filipino society does the popular citizen watchdog group Ibon refer?[6] Mirrored in the family is the crisis of care in society. At the moment, many families have no access to the resources needed to adequately reproduce competitive members of society. To secure a variety of care resources for their family, fathers and mothers must seek the higher wages offered in other countries. Some leave to gain access to health care, while others depart to secure for their children better-quality health care. Others go in order to provide their entire extended family with a sturdier roof over their heads, while others leave to build a house for their nuclear family. Some set out to afford the college education of children, while more do so in order to send children to private schools.[7] Children in transnational families are usually not the poorest of the poor prior to the migration of their parents. Most were fed on a daily basis, but many did not have access to meat for every meal. Quality health care, a sturdy roof over their heads, good schooling, and abundant access to meat are some of the care resources sought by parents for their children when they migrate and leave these very same children in the Philippines.

While transnational families form because of the lack of resources in the global south, they also form because of labor market demands in the global north. In globalization these two economic realities are systematically tied. One way they are tied is through the macro-process of what I referred to earlier as care resource extraction. From the perspective of the Philippines, this macro-process occurs in two ways: first through the exhaustion of state care resources by structural adjustment policies that mandate the servicing of the foreign debt and second via the depletion of the labor supply of care workers from the global south as they move to the global north.

## The Foreign Debt and the Depletion
## of Care Resources

The first means by which care resource extraction occurs is through the systematic depletion of care resources by structural adjustment policies. Inadequate care resources plague families, although not uniformly. Still, in the Philippines the effect of depletion of care resources generally is to hamper the quality of life. To the detriment of families, the past few Philippine government regimes have not considered the development of the nation's infrastructure—such as schools, hospitals, and local businesses—to be as great a priority as keeping in good standing with foreign creditors. Obtaining the International Monetary Fund's (IMF) seal of approval, which is a prerequisite for obtaining more loans from foreign lending agencies, has been of greater concern.[8] From 1970 to 1998, the Philippines paid $77.6 billion in interest and principal to foreign creditors.[9]

Nevertheless, the government is not close to ameliorating its debt. At the end of 2000, the foreign debt of the Philippines stood at $52 billion.[10] What percentage of government revenues goes to servicing the debt? Under President Ferdinand Marcos, in the early 1980s, 50 percent of the country's annual export revenues (approximately $2.4 billion per annum) went to servicing debt interest; even so, his successor President Corazon Aquino still inherited $26.3 billion in debt when she came to power in 1985.[11] As recently as 2001, 20 percent of the country's expenditures went to servicing the interest on foreign debt, with more earmarked toward reducing the amortization of the principal of this debt.[12] This debt is unlikely to go away, as it has steadily grown since the government incurred its first debt in 1962, when the country faced a balance-of-payments crisis stemming from its campaign for free trade.[13] Entry into free trade in the global economy was further enforced with the implementation of the structural adjustment program (SAP) in the early 1980s, which granted a $200 million loan to the Marcos regime.[14]

In exchange for SAP loans, the Philippines was forced to open its doors to global competition via the development of export industries through the cheap manufacturing of goods. The economy had to abide by the stabilization program of the IMF, which stipulated that the government must withdraw subsidies for farmers and consumers, open the economy to foreign goods and services, reduce support for small producers, and privatize state utility services, the national railway, and social security pension funds.[15]

Moreover, the Philippines has had to enter free trade under the direction of export-oriented industrialization. As an export-oriented economy, the Philippines has had to abide by three basic policy elements: "(1) the rapid expansion of exports (rather than control of imports); (2) free international trade (rather than protectionist policies); and (3) open door for foreign companies."[16] Essentially, the emphasis on export-oriented industrialization has pushed the Philippine economy to create products to export, dictated by the needs of foreign direct investors, instead of products focusing on import substitution, keeping the Philippines heavily dependent on foreign markets. Illustrating the binding condition of unequal dependency between the Philippines and lending countries in the global economy is the fact that the United States, which purchases one-third of all exports from the Philippines, controls the market.[17]

With the foreign currency provided by the United States and other such lending countries, the Philippines in turn must purchase goods in foreign markets. Exacerbating the stagnation of the economy is the precondition attached to loans requiring the Philippines to patronize the products and services of lending countries. Bilateral official development assistance (ODA) in grants and loans rose by 322 percent in 1992 and amounted to $2.6 billion in 1996.[18] ODAs enforce the dependency of the Philippines to the lending country; for instance, more than 90 cents of every Japanese ODA dollar borrowed is used to purchase Japanese commodities or services.[19]

Opening the economy to global competition has not served the Philippines well. First, the economy's only basis of competition in the global economy is low-wage labor. Second, the power that foreign direct investors possess to dictate production limits the country's ability to diversify its products in order to provide goods that would generate revenue sufficient to purchase imports. Third, having to patronize the products and services of lending countries places the nation in a position of unequal dependency. Finally, local producers are not in a position to be competitive with the prices of foreign products, especially in the absence of economic assistance from the government. As political economist Rosario Bella Guzman notes, locally produced rice and corn cost much more than imports from Thailand and the United States. Additionally, meat from the United States, Canada, and Europe is cheaper than locally produced meat. Finally, garlic produced in Taiwan is one-third the price of garlic from the Philippines.[20] The high prices of locally produced goods eventually have led to stagnant production, a slow economy, and consequently a decrease in exports, a greater dependence on imports, and a balance-of-payments crisis. As Bella Guzman further explains, "The implication of slower exports, especially to an import-dependent economy like the Philippines, is tremendous. It means slower importation due to lack of dollar capital, thus slow consumption and production, which eventually translate to a sluggish economy. Thus, for a dollar-dependent economy like the Philippines, slower exports translate to more foreign borrowing."[21]

Purchasing products from foreign direct investors and developing an export-oriented economy have forced the Philippines to take on still more debt to pay for its existing debt. Not surprisingly, the government borrowed almost $2 billion to pay for debt interest in 1997.[22] Other debtor countries in the global south share this problem. On average, thirty-three of the forty-one highly indebted countries in recent years have been making $3.00 in debt service payments for every $1.00 received in development assistance.[23] There seems to be no end to the cycle of repaying the interest on debt by taking out new debt for the Philippines. Recently, the Arroyo government sought a $365 million loan from the World Bank and $300 million from the Asian Development Bank to maintain the IMF's "good housekeeping seal,"[24] Since the early 1980s, the Philippines has received ten SAP loans.[25]

The three elements mandated as "good housekeeping" by the IMF and other foreign lending agencies—liberalization, privatization, and deregulation—benefit transnational corporations. They are restructurings that fit the demands of those on top of the international economic order; they surely do not benefit families in the Philippines. Staying in good standing with foreign lending agencies means that the government must pour its revenues into debt servicing. Government expenditures in economic and social services are cut in order to cover foreign debt. The fiscal consolidation required by the IMF means increasing taxes, implementing a more comprehensive privatization, and finally limiting government spending. Where do these measures leave the average Filipino family?

Deregulation means lower salaries for rank-and-file public servants. Taxation of goods consumed by the majority translates to an increased cost of living. Limits on government spending compromise the quality of public services. The privatization of government shares in oil, steel, energy, and even the federal bank results in the monopoly control of prices.[26] All of these conditions, which are required by the IMF for the seal of good housekeeping, increase the vulnerability of the average Filipino worker and his or her family. Under the IMF, the basic conditions of life in the Philippines entail decreased wages and higher prices for goods. It is no wonder that more and more Filipino workers are leaving the country and seeking the stability of employment in nations that are benefiting from the global economic order.

## Migration and the Security of Care Resources

The instabilities imposed by the political economy of globalization on Filipino households force a great number of families to send an able-bodied member outside of the country. According to one report, "between 22 to 35 million Filipinos—34 to 54 percent of the total population—are directly dependent on remittance from migrant workers."[27] Workers migrate to provide their families with basic care resources that have been depleted by debt servicing. Stable wages abroad can reward their families with better-quality food, schooling, and health care.

Most Filipinos are aware that foreign sources control the quality of their lives. As Ida Montecilla,[28] a recent college graduate, whose father has worked as a seafarer for more than thirty years, explains:

We could probably afford those things [e.g., debutante balls] because of my father's salary. I do not think my mother's salary [as a teacher] could afford it. And probably because he is earning in dollars. Usually, when the dollar fluctuates, we [her family] follow. So, we are really not affected, unlike the people who earn in pesos. When the dollar [exchange rate] suddenly rises, then prices double and your salary stays the same. So your salary cannot cover the increase. But if you earn in dollars, you can adjust to the inflation. So you see there are a lot of secure families because they have family members outside the country.

Many Filipinos equate labor migration with stability. Moreover, the absence of quality public services in the Philippines mandates labor migration. As the citizen watch group Ibon reports, "The provision on the social service sector may appear to eat up a lion's share of the national budget. With a measly per capita share of P.53 for health, P11.33 for education, and P2.00 for social security, welfare, and employment on every Filipino on a daily basis, how can the budget help ensure decent living?"[29] The simple answer is, it cannot.

A solid education, steady employment, and quality health care are security, made available to many parents only by labor migration. Because quality education is not offered in public schools in the Philippines, parents turn to private education, which they can afford only with the security that comes from the higher wages offered in other countries. Illustrating the poor quality of public education in the Philippines, the budget of the Department of Education and Culture and Sports during the time of my fieldwork fell short of funding 45,080 teachers, 37,249 classrooms, and 22.3 million textbooks.[30] The low salaries of teachers further attest to the poor state of public education. Teachers on average earn only 200 pesos a day, not enough to feed a family. According to the Department of Labor and Employment, the daily cost of living for a family of six is 441 pesos a day and at least 506 pesos a day in Metro Manila.[31] Despite this fact, the IMF still called for cuts to the benefits allotted public school teachers, reasoning that pay increases would raise the budget deficit of the government by as much as 10 billion pesos.[32]

In light of the poor quality of public schooling, it should be no surprise that families send an able-bodied member to work outside of the Philippines in order to afford private education. For example, the sixty-eight-year-old matriarch Victoria Ilano[33] identifies education as the central motive behind her son's work as a seafarer: "My son has not saved for his retirement. Although he has not, he has invested in the education of his children. He will stop working once he has invested in educational plans for all of his children." To send children to decent schools, with hopes that these children would eventually land jobs that could support them through retirement, parents migrate. They simply cannot rely on the public educational system in the Philippines.

Arabela Gosalves[34] reinforces this view when she explains the educational gains secured by her four children from her husband's migration to the United States more than a decade ago:

If I look back and think what if he had not gone to the U.S., we can never educate the children with our salary, never. My children would have been pitiful. Like, maybe they would have gone to public school or a college that is not that good. My children all went to Assumption [an exclusive private school]. . . . If he had not gone to the U.S., do you think my children would have been able to receive an education like that?

For many families, securing a good education requires the strategic formation of split-apart households.

In my interviews, both parents and children took note of the necessity of migration for securing the education of youth. One of them was Rocil Relocio,[35] a twenty-three-year-old medical student whose mother migrated to the United Kingdom when he was less than ten years old. Explains Rocil:

There are two of us that they needed to send to school. So they wanted to send us to good schools. They needed the extra money and stuff. We were able to enjoy more than other kids who could not afford what we could afford. So my mom thought about that and decided it would be a good thing to work outside the country. But she knew that she had to leave us here.

Following the same logic is the now stay-at-home father Carmelo Ledesma,[36] whose wife provides his family with their primary income from the wages she earns as a nurse in Saudi Arabia. He similarly explains:

My wife and I talked about it. If we depended only on our sources of income here in the Philippines [as a military officer and a nurse] then it will be hard to raise our children, especially now that they are in college. Expenses are greater. Our income here would not have been able to afford their studies. Now, meeting their financial needs is not a burden. The income of my wife can support their daily expenses, their tuition fees, and their other school needs.

Exacerbating the struggle of parents to provide care for their children is the poor state of the labor market in the Philippines. Very few parents in my sample had been unemployed prior to migration. Moreover, only a handful were relegated to the informal labor sector. Many struggled with the limited salaries they earned, however, even as professionals. For instance, the salaries of Carmelo and his wife, though both are semi-professionals, were not enough for them to afford the cost of private schooling for two sons.[37] At most, Carmelo's wife could earn a monthly salary of only 9,000 to 15,000 pesos as a registered nurse in the Philippines, one-tenth of the going rate of 80,000 to 150,000 pesos paid to nurses in other countries.[38] Moreover, government workers in the Philippines, including military officers such as Carmelo and public school teachers, bear the brunt of budget shortages in the government; they sometimes have to work for months without pay. Even so, ironically, government employment is preferred in the country. More high paying than most private sector jobs, government employment provides better worker benefits and a more stable retirement package to the average semiprofessional and professional worker than private employment does.

In addition to education, the need for quality health care drives migration. In the Philippines, financial resources for health services remain quite limited, as government allocation for health care has decreased over the years while ironically the population has increased.[39] For instance, annual appropriations for health care declined from 3.71 percent of the total budget in 1991 to 1.78 percent in 2000.[40] How does this translate to the daily concerns of households in the Philippines? Most families do not have a cushion of financial savings for accidents and unexpected illnesses. Moreover, families are more likely than before to avoid or delay seeking appropriate medical treatment for illnesses and are more likely to engage in self-medication.[41]

Health care costs do worry parents in the Philippines. Arabela Gosalves, the earlier cited mother of four, who sees the affordability of health care as another benefit of labor migration to her family, states:

You know, to be frank with you, all the time that he [her husband] was not there, there was no time for loneliness to enter my brain. Because, most of the time, I was busy. When I went home, I was tired. So when I went to sleep, his absence was forgotten, even in my subconscious. The only times that I had been lonely, when I wanted his support, was when I had a problem concerning my children. I would tell him that that is his job. "I wish you were here. You, you just bring home the bacon, while me, I am the one dealing with all the problems with your children." Then, when the children get sick, I am there, but then I start thinking about the costs. There was a time that they all got measles, then mumps, then hepatitis, which sent all of them to the hospital. Who pays for the hospital? Him. If he were here, could we afford the hospital? No.

If not for the $1,000 monthly remittances sent by her husband in the United States, Arabela could not have covered the medical costs if her children fell ill. She is like most workers and retired workers in the Philippines: without health insurance benefits from either their private employer or the government welfare state.

This grim reality is of concern to many parents, who, if given the option, would migrate to give their children access to the better welfare benefits available in other nations. One of these parents is Josette Piedad,[42] who was raised in a two-parent-abroad transnational family but is now a stay-at-home mother of two. She speaks of her dreams to migrate to Canada to secure mobility for her children:

If worst comes to worst, we will migrate to Canada. If we could make do with our salaries here, then we would not seek the higher wages outside the country. [Her husband works as a marketing representative for a soft drink distribution company.] But I feel badly for my children. My child is very talented. She paints, then she is the national champion in Taekwondo for her age group, then she is an outstanding student. Her life would be wasted if we just stayed here in the Philippines. Because in the Philippines, you work and you work and you don't receive good remunerations, very low, almost nothing. So I said that it would be better if we migrate. *So Canada, because they have free education and free health care.* It's OK for me to do low wage jobs there because in the Philippines you can kill yourself working and nothing will come out of it. The rich will just get richer and the poor will just get poorer. [Emphasis my own.]

To secure a better future for her children, Josette is planning to pursue a job in Canada through the Live-in Caregivers Programme.[43] This program grants legal residency with the possibility of permanent residency to live-in migrant domestic workers who stay employed for two years with a sponsoring family.

The Philippines' structural adjustment policies have led to an unstable labor market, poor schooling, and inadequate health care for most Filipino families. The maintenance or achievement of middle-class status often requires the migration of a parent. In the field, I observed that the presence of a migrant parent in a family is often equated with the security of middle-class status. However, the fact that migration is a prerequisite for middle-class status indicates the limits in the care resources available to working families in the Philippines, a country where governmental spending on social and economic services has been diverted to debt servicing, thus promoting the formation of transnational families.

## The Export of Care

Coupled with unstable labor markets, inadequate public assistance in the Philippines has pushed families to meet labor demands in the global north, where low-wage employment offers greater stability than many professional jobs in the global south would bring. While migration partially solves the care crisis of working families in the global south, ironically, so too does it offer solutions to the care crisis plaguing working families in the global north. The majority of migrant workers from the Philippines are women, and the labor that they provide to the citizenry of other nations is mostly care work.[44] Approximately two-thirds of Filipino migrant women are employed as domestic workers, whereas the majority of professional women emigrants who leave as either contract workers or permanent migrants are nurses or entertainers.[45] In my sample, the majority of interviewees are children of care workers.

As I have argued elsewhere, women from the global south migrate to the global north in order to alleviate the care burdens of privileged women in the global north; at the same time, they leave the care of their children to women with less privilege in the global south.[46] The international division of caring work, meaning the three-tier transfer of care among women in poor and rich nations, is caused by gender inequities that keep the care of the family the responsibility of women, neo-liberal prescriptions that designate care as a private responsibility, and finally economic inequities between the global north and global south.

A global south to global north flow of domestic workers has emerged, with women from Mexico and Central America moving into the households of working families in the United States, Indonesian women to richer nations in Asia and the Gulf region, Sri Lankan women to Greece and the Gulf region, Polish women to Western Europe, Caribbean women to the United States and Canada, and finally Filipino women the world over.[47] A similar global south to global north movement of nurses has also arisen, in response to the shortage of 20,000 nurses in the United Kingdom and the anticipated need for 1.2 million nurses in the United States in the next ten years.[48] Migrants fill other labor shortages, and not only those related to the crisis of care in the global north. Filipino migrants also respond to the need for men willing to risk long separations from their families while manning cargo shipments the world over. They also fill shortages in traditional men's work in oil rigs and construction sites in Asia and the Gulf region. Compelled by the impact of structural adjustment policies on their daily lives, Filipino workers have in various ways responded to the labor market demands of the global north.

These workers from the global south benefit the economies of the global north. For instance, the manufacturing labor provided by men working in construction sites and economic trades helps economic production to flourish. Likewise, northern economies also prosper from the care work of women. Migrants, by freeing a large number of women from their care work in the family, allow these women to participate in the labor market. Regardless of the variety of labor market shortages filled by Filipino migrant workers, it seems that care is the labor in greatest demand of them in the global north.

In fact, care is now the largest imported product of the Philippines. The export of care is a legacy of colonialism, as it maintains an infrastructure of unequal dependency between the Philippines and richer nations in the global economy. As I noted earlier, the Philippine export-oriented economy is dictated by the demands of the global north. In the earlier years of colonialism, the core countries extracted raw materials, such as sugar, tobacco, indigo, hemp, and coconut, from the Philippines for their consumption.[49] Post–Bretton Woods, the highest volume of exports shifted to manufactured goods such as electronics and garments. Today, labor migrant remittances have surpassed manufacturing as the largest source of foreign currency for the Philippines. Migrant remittances generate at least $7 billion per annum for the Philippine economy.[50] With domestic workers and nurses constituting the majority of migrants from the Philippines, one can say that it is the export of care that sustains the economy.

## The Import of Care

Who benefits from the macro-process of care resource extraction, and whose quality of life is improved by the export of care from the global south? The Philippines meets the care work demands of the global north in two central ways. First, the Philippines has responded to the critical nursing shortage in industrialized countries, and, second, it fills the economic niche for domestic work. The reluctance of rich countries to invest in the reproductive costs of their labor force is much to blame for the nursing shortage. As Paul Ong and his colleagues describe in the case of the United States, "The United States has been reluctant to spend money on the training of health personnel, such as nurses, in a general effort at cost containment for health care. The ultimate goal is to reduce health care costs for capitalist employers by lowering the costs of their benefits packages. This policy creates a shortage of nurses in the United States and a demand for immigrant nurses."[51]

By not investing in the reproduction costs of nursing professionals, the global north passes on the burden of this responsibility to the global south. This works to the detriment of the global south, where taxpayers invest in the education of citizens who become labor migrants, arguably losing their best health care workers in exchange for the lesser gain of foreign remittances. For a minimal cost, the global north secures good health care, which is needed to maintain an able-bodied workforce for the greater production and consumption activities in their local economies. The global south arguably gains via the accumulation of remittances. As Catherine Choy observed, the migration of nurses is intertwined with the history of U.S. imperialism and the early twentieth-century U.S. colonization of the Philippines.[52] The professional nursing schools established in the Philippines during the period of colonization by the United States laid the groundwork for the establishment of trained nurses and for what continues today to be a ready supply of exportable skilled labor, which the local Philippine economy is unable to accommodate fully. Thus, the educational system of the Philippines seems to mirror its market economy: both are geared for exporting rather than designed to serve the needs of the local population.

However, much more than they do in hospitals and hospices, migrant Filipino women alleviate the care burdens in private households in the global north. Like women from the global south, women in the global north are entering the paid labor force in full force.[53] In various industrialized countries around the world, the number of gainfully employed women has climbed dramatically in the last forty years. For instance, in France, an additional 2 million women entered the labor force between 1979 and 1993, a 21 percent increase in the number of employed women.[54] Mothers are also increasingly likely to work. For instance, in the United States, three out of four mothers with school-age children are in the paid labor force, the majority working full-time.[55] In Italy, too, an increasing number of married women are in the labor force.[56] In Italy and Spain, women tend to keep their full-time jobs even when they have young children at home.[57] Even so, the division of labor in most families still does not reflect the increase in women's share of labor market participation.[58] For instance, a recent survey of dual wage earning families with children in Canada found that in 52 percent of households women were still responsible for all of the daily housework.[59]

The rise in women's share of labor market participation, as it has not initiated drastic changes in the traditional household division of labor, has instead caused a dwindling supply of care labor in the family. Although more fitting of households with a stay-at-home mother and breadwinner father, the work of care—feeding, cleaning, dressing, and watching over young children—is still performed by women much more than by men.[60] Yet, the "double day" indicates more than gender inequalities in the family. It also demonstrates that state welfare support for the family has not adequately responded to the changes brought by the entrance of women, particularly mothers, to the labor force.[61] For instance, in the United States, government assistance for the childcare needs of dual income households remains inadequately restricted to an income tax credit, keeping childcare a private rather than a public responsibility. This situation is mirrored in many countries in Europe, where cash subsidies for private care threaten the funding of public care institutions.[62]

Looking at the migration patterns of migrant Filipina domestic workers, the more that countries keep the care of the family a private responsibility, the greater the reliance on the low wage work of immigrant care workers. This seems to be the case in the Americas and Europe, where the presence of migrant Filipina domestic workers is more strongly felt in the countries with the least adequate welfare provisions. A heavy recipient of migrant care workers, the United States has the fewest welfare provisions of all rich nations in the global economy; U.S. families are without access to universal health care, paid maternity and parental leave, government-provided childcare, or family caregiving allowances.[63] The lack of communal responsibility for care in the United States is reflected, for instance, in the care of the elderly. Studies have shown that family members, usually women, provide approximately 80 to 90 percent of elderly care, without any formal assistance from the government.[64]

Although boasting more democratic welfare regimes than the United States, European nations are not immune to the growing trend of privatization. Domestic workers are present in European countries such as the United Kingdom, where markets have assumed a greater role in welfare regimes; countries such as the Netherlands, where single mothers are forced to seek paid employment and have no choice but to pay lower-paid workers for the care of their children; countries in the Mediterranean region such as Greece, Italy, and Spain, where dual wage earning families do not have market options for care; and finally nations such as France, where the universal care for children by the state is not mirrored in provision for elderly care.[65]

Ruth Milkman and her colleagues note that economic inequities direct the flow of domestic workers: they found that the urban centers with the greatest economic inequities in the United States have the highest rate of domestic service employment.[66] I would add to their observation that social patterns of welfare provision also influence the direction of migratory flows of foreign domestic workers. Nations with very low welfare provision—that is, nations that keep the care of the family a private responsibility, particularly the United States and southern European nations such as Spain, Greece, and Italy—have a greater presence of foreign domestic workers. In contrast, countries with social democratic regimes such as Sweden, with a universal benefit system and large-scale institutional support for mothers and families, are less likely to rely on foreign domestic workers. Thus, it seems that the less public accountability there is for the family, the greater the need for the labor of foreign domestic workers. This conclusion suggests that a movement against a neo-liberal state regime would lead to a greater recognition of the high worth of care and a decreased burden on women in the labor force. It would also mean less need to devalue—that is, commodify as low-paid labor—the caring work required in the family.

The implementation of a public family welfare system, as feminist scholars have argued, would not only benefit doubly burdened women in the labor force and give greater value to the work of privately hired care workers; it would also translate to the good of society as a whole.[67] As economist Nancy Folbre asserts, public responsibility for parental support would optimize the care of children and consequently increase the likelihood of their healthy and productive labor force participation in the future.[68] This translates to the greater ability of children to physically care for us in the future and pay the taxes needed to cover the social security benefits we are working for today.[69] As had been recognized with the implementation of universal public education in the nineteenth century, the optimal care of children promotes the welfare of society as a whole.[70] It cuts to the core of democracy, helping provide equal opportunity for children to succeed, so that they may contribute the most to the economy.

The inadequacy of welfare support for dual income families goes against the principles of democracy and against universal educational opportunities for children. As political theorist Joan Tronto further argues, individual accountability for children increases competition between mothers and families and concomitantly decreases the ethic of care.[71] Hiring private domestic workers, tutors, and other care workers increases the disparities between families. Those with private care workers can ensure that their children are those best equipped and developed to be competitive members of society. In contrast, other children are less likely to succeed as they are left with less guidance and adult supervision. As Tronto states, "individualized accounts of mothering make us inured to the social structures that contribute to the growing gaps among advantaged and less advantaged children."[72] Thus, the privatization of care reinforces inequalities of race, class, and citizenship among women—employers and employees—and, at the same time, it furthers the disparities in the prospects available to children.

Given the individual responsibility for care and denied the utmost benefits of a truly democratic regime, women in industrialized countries have been more able to take advantage of the economic resources that they have than women from developing countries: they do so by unloading their caregiving responsibilities on these other women. Those who receive less gender-sensitive welfare provisions from the state do so much more than others. And those who are able to negotiate with their male counterparts in the family for a more fairly gendered division of labor are equally less likely to do so. This indicates that greater state and male accountability for care would likely lead not so much to a decreased need for domestic workers as to a greater recognition of the worth of domestic labor.

Without a public family welfare system, women globally face cuts in public services. This shared predicament indicates that globalization has not boded too well for women. Women face compounded labor burdens, which Marianne Marchand and Anne Sisson Runyan have succinctly summarized: "many women must now simultaneously be in the workforce and at home to service the global economy, make up for the shortfalls in working-class men's declining wages and jobs in industrial sectors, earn money to pay for privatized social services, and provide the reproductive services for which the state is abandoning responsibility."[73] Though women universally share these conditions of inequality, their different locations distinguish the impacts of these shared inequities.

Some women have the option of living with their children, while others do not. A great number of Filipino women juggle the multiple burdens of family care brought on by the low salaries of men, the demand for their work, and the absence of benefits from the state through labor migration. In the process, their caring labor is diverted from their families to individuals in richer countries who pay for their services as domestic workers or nurses. The problem of diverted care confronts multiple generations of Filipina women. A new generation of adults—who have been raised in transnational households by their migrant domestic-worker mothers—now face the decision on whether or not to pursue migrant domestic work themselves, to secure the welfare of their families in the Philippines. One such woman is the earlier cited Josette Piedad. Some women resist because they remember their own childhood difficulties or traditional views of the family, but others like Josette, despite their struggles growing up in a transnational household, succumb to the more realistic view that migration is one of their most secure ways of enhancing their children's life chances.

## Conclusion

Women do not uniformly experience the gender inequities of globalization. Moreover, the shared injustices brought by the privatization of care have not become a convenient platform of alliance for women. Instead, women maintain relations of inequality based on these shared gender inequities. Without the benefit of a "public family" system, many overwhelmed working women in various Western countries have had few choices but to rely on the commodification and consequent economic devaluation of care work. Without government subsidies, low-paid care is what many families can afford. To lessen the burden of care work that they share with SAP-laden women in the global south, they pass their caregiving responsibilities on to these women. The restrictive migration laws that force migrants to form transnational families work to the benefit of these relieved women employers. In the long run, however, they hurt them, since they are only a surface solution to the deeper problems shared by women in globalization.

Care resource extraction enables richer countries to ignore the social inequalities of care caused by inadequate public services, low wages, and insufficient employee benefits. It also denies poorer countries the resources needed to solve these very same problems, which unfortunately they also call their own. More significantly, care resource extraction allows us to understand the formation of transnational families, specifically those of care workers, in the context of gender inequalities that shape welfare regimes across various states—both in poor and rich nations—in globalization.

# CHAPTER 2

# The Dismal View of
# Transnational Households

Transnational families are increasingly the norm in Philippine society. If people are not part of a transnational family, they are likely to know someone who is—a friend, co-worker, or neighbor. Yet, despite their ubiquity, the public still maintains quite a dismal view of these families, because transnational families, especially those of migrant women, contest the normative nuclear family with a nurturing (that is, physically nearby) mother and a breadwinning father and conflict with dominant cultural notions of the right kind of family. Despite the state's economic dependence on labor migration and its consequent reliance on the formation of transnational migrant households, the constitution of the Philippines still regards the nuclear family as the norm and denies public recognition of transnational migrant families.[1] Moreover, not only state organizations but schools and churches face public pressure to uphold the nuclear family and consequently enshrine this type of family at the cost of ignoring the different needs of other types of families.

This chapter situates transnational families in the public sphere and places them within the context of the normative set of cultural rules and symbols of the family in the Philippines. I draw from various supplementary data, including a survey of print media reports on migrant families, interviews and focus group discussions with guidance counselors, interviews with the clergy, and finally a survey of lesson plans that concern the family from both private and public schools in the area of my field research. This survey of the public integration of transnational families will demonstrate the limited extent of their moral acceptance in Philippine society.

The resistance against transnational families reflects a more general struggle against gender transformations in society. Moral boundaries of gender symbolize national identity, and cultural systems that transgress these boundaries—for instance, transnational households—threaten the identity of the nation. In her work on symbolic boundaries, Michele Lamont establishes that working-class men in the United States and France use moral standards to generate intergroup boundaries of race and class.[2] In other words, she establishes that moral criteria are symbolic markers of cultural compatibility, indicating one's inclusion in and exclusion from the categorization of rightful membership in the nation.[3] I would add to Lamont's discussion that while morally based cultural constructions determine boundaries across racial and class groups within a nation as well as across nations, moral criteria of gender also determine membership within the nation and determine the merits of citizenship, meaning the privileges accorded by membership in society.

We see this illustrated in the incorporation of transnational families in the Philippine public sphere. What I found is that the more that transnational families transgress gender norms, the more dismal are societal views of these families, and consequently the less likely they are to receive formal and informal support from public institutions. Thus, the transnational families of migrant mothers tend to receive far less support than do the families of migrant fathers.

## The Family

Transnational families question various conventions of the dominant family in the Philippines, including the daily routine of intimacy. In the Philippines, the dominant household pattern is that of the dual wage earning nuclear family.[4] Even so, most households still maintain a strong extended kinship base.[5] Rapid industrialization in the Philippines has led to an increase in women's labor market participation in the local economy from 34 percent in 1970 to 45 percent in 1996, not counting women's work in the informal economy.[6] Along with the increased participation of women in the workforce, the Philippines has also witnessed a nuclearization of households, with the percentage of nuclear households increasing from 72 percent in 1973 to 83.4 percent in 1986 and mean household size diminishing from 6.2 people in 1973 to 5.3 in 1990.[7] Statistical breakdowns of household composition in the Philippines do not account for the formation of transnational households, however. For instance, families of married overseas contract workers with children in the Philippines fall under the category of nuclear household, as they are only outside of the country temporarily. Still, the dominant household model is the nuclear family whose members spend a great deal of time together in the intimate space of the home. In contrast, transnational family members spend greater time apart than together as a complete family unit.

They are apart both temporally and spatially. Among my interviewees, the children in such families—who are now young adults—spent very little time in a complete household unit in the last decade. For the most part, migrant parents do not see their children grow up. Mothers of the children in my sample migrated on average 11.42 years ago and have returned 4.44 times, with an average length of stay of 5.39 weeks. Thus, in the last eleven years or so, mothers on average have spent a total of 23.9 weeks with their children, who are now mostly around twenty-one years of age. Likewise, children and their migrant fathers have not spent much time together. Among my interviewees, the standard length of separation was 13.79 years, with fathers returning 9.81 times for an average length of stay of 7.57 weeks in the Philippines. Thus, in more than a decade migrant fathers have spent approximately 74 weeks with their children, now young adults whose average age is 20.68 years old.

While lapses of time spent together occur almost every year in the families of migrant fathers, they occur more sporadically—once every two years—in the case of migrant-mother families. The shorter and more infrequent visits on the part of migrant mothers do not indicate any decrease in concern for their children. Occupational demands usually dictate the discrepancy between the rate of visitation among mothers and fathers. Most of the mothers of the children in my sample are employed as domestic workers, who are employed on contracts that usually extend to two years before they are allowed to return home to the Philippines for two weeks. In contrast, the fathers are mostly employed as seafarers and are allowed to visit the Philippines for at least two months every year.

Another factor influencing the greater length of separation for mothers is migrant status. In my sample, more mothers than fathers are undocumented workers, or have visa complications that make them legally unable to visit their children in the Philippines. (I address the latter question in Chapter 7.) Only a handful of the fathers fall in this category. Notably, most of the thirteen children who fall under the category of two parent abroad transnational families have undergone extended durations of separation from their parents. In addition to legal concerns, the fact that the mothers work in a diversity of destination countries also makes it less convenient for them to re-unite with their families. In contrast, the fathers—if not seafarers—tend to work in the Gulf region or in other Asian countries. The mothers are less likely to return because of the higher cost of travel, combined with the priority they must give to the immediate financial needs of the family.[8]

Generally, more mothers of the children in my sample are in countries where they aspire to someday acquire permanent residency status. These countries include Canada, the United States, and the United Kingdom. The undocumented status and visa complications faced by these mothers (and a few fathers) usually translate to at least a decade-long separation for their families. Only two migrant fathers of the children in my sample fall under this group, while nine children of migrant mothers and eight of two-migrant parents do. Among nine children of migrant mothers (excluding the one U.S.-born child living in the Philippines with her father) based in these countries, the average length of separation is 11.25 years. Most of these children were around the age of ten when their mother first left the Philippines. Due to the undocumented status of most mothers, most of these families have yet to be reunited, even temporarily. This is also the case for eight children of two migrant parents (excluding the one U.S.-born child attending school in the Philippines). On average, these families have withstood 11.57 years of separation. Most of the children were eight or nine years old at the time of separation.

The constructions of time and space of transnational families struggle contentiously against the norms of Philippine society. Families refer to the realities of both experience and institution.[9] In terms of experience, "family" refers to the daily lives of men, women, and children who share material resources and in cooperation and sometimes conflict provide one another with material, physical, and emotional care. In this view, the family is rooted in patterns of shared activities. If large doses of temporal and spatial proximity are necessary ingredients to a family, one could easily wonder how transnational families could possibly function as a family without the intimacy and familiarity gained only from the routine of daily interactions.

"Family" also refers to an institution, one embedded in particular social meanings constructed by ideological norms and power relations.[10] In any given society, people hold ideas about what families are supposed to be, what activities different members are supposed to do, how they are supposed to behave, and what immediate experiences members are supposed to gain from the routines and norms of family life. These ideas are shaped by systems of inequality and form the boundaries of the right kind of family. In Philippine contemporary society, the notion of conventional family mirrors that of most other modern societies. The modern nuclear family with a bread-winning father and a nurturing mother is the right kind of family. Women nurture and men discipline. Fathers earn income for the family and mothers can choose to supplement it. Mothers manage and budget households, yet they always manage to defer major decisions of the family to fathers.

Nevertheless, individuals do not always follow cultural prescriptions of gender. History shows that men and women cross borders and in doing so initiate ideological shifts.[11] Nevertheless, there is a limit to this process. Sociologist Cynthia Fuchs Epstein describes it:

We live in a world in which men and women violate conventional and historic role prescriptions that are defining what they should do in their work and family roles. . . . Women have moved into male-dominated spheres of work such as the legal profession and police work, and men are reconsidering their parental roles, and are performing more nurturing activities—mothering activities—as fathers—than they did before. Yet men and women face social controls that pressure and persuade them to conform to conventional roles and internalize norms that restrict them from exercising real choices.[12]

Building from Epstein, this chapter shows how everyday conventions limit the possibilities of gender border crossings in transnational families. I do so by looking closely at the integration or segregation of transnational families in the public sphere. According to Epstein, multiple mechanisms in society enforce cultural ideologies that curtail the border crossings demanded by our changing society. This process could not be truer in the case of the Philippines, which as a society has had to contend with the gender role breakdown stirred by migration in the family.

To Epstein's framework I would also add that mechanisms of social control do not prevent men and women from crossing borders uniformly or equally. Gender distinguishes the flexibility with which, and the extent to which, men and women can cross set boundaries of parenting. In terms of clothing, for instance, women can wear a business suit, but men, for the most part, cannot wear a skirt. In the same way, I have found that mothering expands and fathering narrows in transnational families. In the absence of their wives, men who transgress gender boundaries to redefine fathering—even if only temporarily—to include nurturing the family suffer from social disapproval. This disapproval strongly discourages men from taking on the role of nurturer. As I address in a later chapter, they are likely to engage in daily acts of nurturing only if their masculine identity is safeguarded against the threat posed by the greater income earned by migrant women. In contrast, women can incorporate multiple roles and act as both mother and father in the absence of migrant men but as I show not to the extent that they question the breadwinning identity of men.

## Public Perceptions of Transnational Families

Transnational families are not the right kind of family in the Philippines. This viewpoint is espoused by the law, media, and local community representatives, including religious figures whom people turn to for spiritual guidance, school counselors from whom students seek adult direction, officers of community-based organizations of migrant families, and finally teachers of government-mandated "values formation" courses. From the perspective of various community representatives, the more the transnational family diverges from the construction of the right kind of family—that is, the conventional dual wage earning nuclear family with a breadwinning father and a double day burdened mother—the more dysfunctional the family is considered to be. Mirroring the "family values" debate spurred by the foray of the TV sitcom character Murphy Brown into single motherhood during the early 1990s, the dominant perception of transnational families in the Philippines holds that children are much better off in traditional nuclear families with a mother and father both living at home.[13]

## The Law: The Constitution and the 1987 Family Code

The integrity of the family reflects the integrity of the nation.[14] This moral stance is still widely held in Philippine society. The law also upholds it. Judge Alicia Sempio-Diy, a drafter of the 1986 Constitution and the 1987 Family Code, states: "We must have strong marriages and strong families in order to have a strong nation."[15] Reflecting the dominant ideological views in contemporary Philippine society, these two legal documents were instituted soon after the dictator-president Ferdinand Marcos was ousted from office and forced to flee the country on February 25, 1986, by mass outcry and rallies throughout the nation. The newly elected government of President

Corazon Aquino instituted a new constitution to restore democracy and freedom in the Philippines. Ratified by an overwhelming majority of the people, the 1986 Constitution not only limited presidential power and reinstated the legislative branch of the Philippine government, it also unequivocally declared the "Filipino family" as the foundation of the nation: "The State recognizes the Filipino family as the foundation of the nation. Accordingly, it shall strengthen its solidarity and actively promote its total development."[16] If the family is the foundation of the nation, then what kind of family is to be strengthened? According to the 1987 Family Code or Executive Order 209, the "Filipino family" is a nuclear-based unit with a strong extended kinship base. Sustained by the abiding love of kin, the Filipino family is founded on the absolute marriage and mutual respect of a man and woman and follows the script of cohabitation, women's maternity, men's authority, and familism, including filial piety.[17] These characteristic features are the Filipino family's bases of solidarity and are accordingly to be protected, strengthened, and developed by the state.

Despite its call for the protection of women's maternity, the law does also recognize the right of women to enter the labor market freely. As section 14 of article II in the 1986 Constitution establishes, "The State recognizes the role of women in nation-building, and shall ensure the fundamental equality before the law of women and men."[18] However, as noted, the law also maintains women's role as the proper caregivers of the nation. The law does this by establishing that maternity, understood to include the care of the family, is one of women's primary duties to the state. For instance, women, as the mothers and wombs of the nation, are obligated to reproduce the population.[19] Women are thus subject to regulation, with proper womanhood defined by their role as biological mothers. Thus the stage is set for the construction of women's citizenship as defined by good or bad motherhood. Under the law, a child below the age of seven can be separated from the mother only if "the court finds compelling reasons to do otherwise."[20] Financial reasons do not fall within the range of what is compelling under the law. Instead, compelling reasons are solely determined by the moral values of the mother. Bad mothers are explicitly defined as those who maintain "a common law relationship with another man" or exhibit "moral laxity and the habit of flirting from one man to another."[21] In line with traditional Catholic ideological views on sex and reproduction, purity is a measure of women's good morals under the law.

Transnational families, particularly those headed by females, threaten women's civic duty of maternity. Geographic separation from the family, for instance, places women's purity at risk. Thus, we should not be surprised that one government-mandated training workshop for outgoing female overseas contract workers that was featured in the documentary *The Chain of Love* warned participants not to fall into the temptation of the "brother of homesickness . . . home-sex-ness" and the loneliness brought by their separation from their husbands.[22] Women who leave young children in the Philippines also technically fall under the definition of "bad mothers." By failing to fulfill women's civic duty of maternity, they not only fall short of meeting their moral obligations to the family but also fail to fulfill their duties to the nation.

Under the modernization-building project of the Philippines, a strong family begins with a solid marriage, which starts with the obligation of cohabitation.[23] As article 68 declares, "The husband and wife are obliged to live together, observe mutual love, respect, and fidelity, and render mutual help, and support."[24] Geographical distance in transnational families inherently prevents such households from fulfilling the categorical definition of a good "Filipino" marriage. Under the law, "a spouse who refuses to cohabit without a justifiable reason will be deprived of the right to be supported and may be compelled to pay moral damages."[25]

With marriage and cohabitation as its core, the "Filipino family" follows the script of the modern nuclear family.[26] By defining the Filipino family as nuclear, the code establishes this arrangement not only as the norm but also as the embodiment of the right kind of family. This kind of family does reflect the dominant household pattern in the Philippines, which as noted earlier is that of the dual wage earning nuclear family. However, the allocation of morals, whether negative or positive, through the construction of "a right kind of family" in the code fails to recognize the plausibility that other kinds of family arrangements—including single parent, transnational, and polygamous households in the Muslim region of the South—could represent "good morals."

If the nuclear family does indeed signify moral order, then these other kinds of families would represent moral decay. As for the transnational family, the Family Code does make special mention of this type of household, thus indicating its growing presence in contemporary Philippine society. One provision establishes that the transnational family could be considered an exemption to the obligation of cohabitation, as long as separation does not put undue stress on the "solidarity of the family." As article 69 reads: "The court may exempt one spouse from living with the other if the latter should live abroad or there are other valid and compelling reasons for the exemption. However, such exemption shall not apply if the same is not compatible with the solidarity of the family."[27] What conditions would threaten the "solidarity of the family"? If morals define the strength of the family, then only bad morals could justify the separation of the family.

In the Family Code, the few legal grounds for separation include immorality, such as perversion or the corruption of children; criminality, such as drug addiction or crimes worthy of six years of imprisonment; sexual deviancy as constructed by the law, which includes bigamy, homosexuality, and infidelity; domestic violence; and finally abandonment for longer than one year.[28] Abandonment as grounds for legal separation raises a red flag regarding transnational families. Abandonment is the central trope that signifies moral decay in transnational families.

Illustrating the ideological belief that women's migration risks abandonment of the family, headlines on May 26, 1995, from two of the largest-circulation newspapers in the Philippines read: "Overseas Employment a Threat to Filipino Families" and "Ramos Says Pinay OCWs [Overseas Contract Workers] Threaten Filipino Families."[29] In a speech delivered to the Department of Social Welfare on May 25, 1995, President Fidel Ramos had called for initiatives to keep migrant mothers at home. President Ramos stated: "We are not against overseas employment of Filipino women. We are against overseas employment at the cost of family solidarity."[30] By calling for the return migration of mothers, he does not necessarily disregard the increasing dependency of the Philippine economy on the foreign remittances of its mostly female migrant workers. However, he does make clear that it would be morally acceptable only for single and childless women to migrate. But why did President Ramos call for the return migration of mothers only, but not fathers, whose living abroad would also seem to constitute abandonment and thus threaten "the solidarity of the family?" He did so because under the code women still constitute the primary caretakers of children and other dependents in the family. Thus, in transnational and split-household units abandonment, particularly the abandonment of one's proper duties in the moral order of the nation, would only apply to women.[31]

A tension exists in which the national economy in the Philippines engenders the formation of transnational households—but at the same time the national identity upholds the nuclear family. This tension results in the disapproval of transnational families. The public pressure to uphold nuclear families leads to greater tensions in the transnational family life of migrant mothers as well as stronger disapproval of them by the public. The idealization of the nuclear family and the public conformity to such an ideal hurt women, since they hide the dysfunctions of the economy at the same time that they deny the nation's dependence on women's labor migration.[32]

## The Print Text: Media and Academic Reports

The negative perception of transnational families is not limited to the law. Public discourse in other regimes reinforces it. From the local media to academia, print reports without fail provide a gloomy depiction of the lives of children in transnational families. Mirroring the law's ideal construct of the family, print reports uphold this idealized construct as the right kind of family in the Philippines. Based on impressions rather than on scientific evidence, much academic and newspaper writing on transnational families asserts that children growing up in the Philippines without their parents, particularly their mothers, are prone to delinquency and declining moral values, particularly materialism.[33]

Quite a few studies on transnational families in the Philippines have been done, but most are value-laden. They are predisposed to promoting the unproven speculation that childrearing is best performed by two biological parents. For instance, the psychologist Francis Santamaria based on a limited sample of his patients concludes that children and spouses of migrant workers tend to suffer from heavy emotional and psychological tolls due to "separated anxiety."[34] Likewise, Marie Aganon argues that children growing up in transnational households suffer from "inadequate psychosocial development" and consequently the "likelihood of juvenile delinquency," because the "development of self-concept is likely to be impaired seriously when one of the parents is away."[35]

Notably, the most extensive study on the children of migrant workers, a survey of more than 700 children conducted by Graziano Battistella and Maria Cecilia Astardo-Conaco (1996), does not come to the same conclusion as these other studies.[36] Contradicting the dominant claim of emotional difficulties among children in transnational households, this more comprehensive study found that family separation does not necessarily lead to extreme cases of emotional disturbance and delinquency among children. The authors of this study pointed to the ability of children and other family members to adapt to household reorganization. However, they also observed that this flexibility is less applicable to the families of migrant mothers. The study reports: "children without their mothers seem to have more problems compared to the other children."[37] They pray less and "tend to be more angry, confused, apathetic and more afraid than other children," for instance.[38] The study does not offer explanations of why families of migrant mothers face greater difficulties than do other families. Readers are left to assume that their greater problems arise because biological mothers are more suitable caretakers of children than are fathers or the female relatives left responsible for their care.

With much more sensationalist flair than academic reports, the media also reinforce this view; their propensity is to present negative reports on the welfare of children in transnational families. Like many Philippine scholarly publications, media depictions of transnational families, especially those of migrant mothers, claim that children fare poorly and receive inadequate care.[39] For instance, media reports have associated the emigration of mothers with the sexual abuse of children. As one columnist boldly states, "Incest and rapes within blood relatives are alarmingly on the rise not only within Metro Manila but also in the provinces. There are some indications that the absence of mothers who have become OCWs has something to do with the situation."[40] Underlying this statement is the view that men cannot help but turn to their daughters to whet the sexual appetite denied by the migration of their overseas contract worker wives. Although incest is a social problem in the Philippines, its direct correlation to the emigration of mothers is an unproven speculation. For instance, studies have yet to show that there are higher rates of incest among children of migrant mothers than in other families.

Despite its questionable basis, the media's pathological depiction of transnational families, particularly those of migrant mothers, instills in the public's consciousness the view that migration facilitates a care crisis in transnational families. This crisis supposedly results in the instability of family life and consequently the use of "drugs, gambling, and drinking" among children of migrant workers.[41] Without doubt, sensationalist reports on the well-being of children in transnational families fuel the vilification of migrant mothers, whose migration is equated with the abandonment of children. This is the case because news media reports assume men are *naturally* incompetent care providers.

## Community Organizations

Community organizations are likewise not exempt from holding such dismal views of children in transnational families. During my field research, I met with members of various community support groups in the region of my study. I traveled to places far and near from the city center where I was based, often not in the most comfortable conditions. I rode on top of passenger jeepneys, hitchhiked in delivery trucks, and hired private vehicles to reach areas not easily accessible from the city center. I visited remote places in order to gather interviews with support groups of migrant workers and their families that the regional office of the Overseas Worker's Welfare Administration (OWWA) had identified to me.

Demonstrating the institutionalization of emigration, OWWA is an official government office assigned to provide social service support to migrant workers and their families. Through OWWA, migrant workers and their dependents could apply for housing and small-business loans from the government, qualify for college scholarships, gain eligibility for low-cost life insurance policies, and finally access emergency funds in case of the sudden deportation or death of a migrant worker. However, OWWA does not receive any funds from the government; rather, it funnels money from migrant workers and their families to the government. Membership in OWWA, which is required of overseas contract workers, costs migrants a nominal fee that covers the operational costs of the agency. However, OWWA does not reinvest its funds in programs that benefit its constituents. In fact, as one high-ranking OWWA official informed me, most of these funds "sit" in an emergency release fund reserved to cover the cost of the sudden mass deportation of Filipinos from high-risk destinations—for example, to evacuate Filipino contract workers from Israel if war were to break out there.

With most of its budget sitting in an emergency relief fund, OWWA does not have the fiscal means to provide hands-on support programs to its constituents. In destination countries such as Italy, for instance, programs are limited to legal counsel. In the Philippines, OWWA has not instituted wide-reaching programs but instead provides support on a case-by-case basis as problems arise individually for a migrant worker or family in the Philippines. OWWA actually functions on a patronage system; a migrant worker gets help for a "personal crisis," for instance a medical emergency, only after winning over the sympathy of an OWWA officer.

Operating on a minimal budget, the one community liaison officer of OWWA in the region where I conducted my study has few resources to institute programs providing welfare support for migrant workers and their families. For instance, the office lacks the funds to cover the cost of an after-school program for the children of migrant workers or a counseling program for their spouses. However, OWWA-sponsored organizations do exist throughout the region of my study. These associations have materialized in response to the grassroots efforts of the region's community liaison officer to reach out to OWWA constituents not located in the city center.

Due to the absence of official figures on the number of migrant workers per municipality (township) in the census, OWWA sought the assistance of mayors and *barangay* captains[42] to identify areas in the region with large concentrations of migrant workers. It then utilized networks to organize locally based associations in high migration-sending towns and cities across the region. By doing so, OWWA was able to effectively disseminate information that would otherwise have been inaccessible to the families of migrant workers in remote areas. Without having to travel to the city centers, constituents could now learn from local community members about the various services available from OWWA. These include scholarships for children, medical benefits, and guaranteed small business loans. From its efforts, OWWA successfully organized fourteen organizations, nine of which remained quite active during the time of my research. These nine organizations are scattered throughout the region of my study.

My research assistant and I met with members of these organizations.[43] Based on our discussions, it was clear that community groups, despite their economic dependence on labor migration, did not look favorably on the gender transformations it promotes. They disapprove of migration not only for limiting the time that families can spend together but also for threatening gender boundaries of mothering and fathering. In the opinion of most, if one parent does have to migrate, it should be the father. This view was made clear to me after the first focus-group discussion that I conducted, which left me stunned by the litany of depressing responses that participants gave to the question "What are the effects of overseas migration to the family?"

1. They are neglected.
2. Abandoned.
3. No one is there to watch over the children.
4. The attitudes of children change.

5. They swim in vices.
6. The values you like disappear.
7. They take on vices.
8. Men take on mistresses.
9. Like with the children, when you leave, they are still small, and when you come back, they are much older. But they do not recognize you as their real parents. And what they want, you have to follow. They get used to having a parent abroad and they are used to always having money.
10. That's true. That's true.

One by one, each participant gave a gloomy opinion of the transnational family. When I asked if they were speaking from personal experience, most had shaken their heads "no" and then referred to other families in their area. Neglected, abandoned, and deviant—those are the children of migrant mothers.

I should not have been surprised by this depiction of transnational families, which was shared by members of this community organization as well as others I visited, from remote fishing and farming towns to city neighborhood districts. Soon after conducting the community-based interviews and focus-group discussions, I realized that most participants in OWWA-sponsored organizations are members of households with migrant fathers. The families of migrant mothers are largely underrepresented in these groups. Rarely did I meet the husbands of migrant women or even the female kin of migrant women when I visited with organizations. Notably, men and women had been equally represented in our focus-group discussions, as they included returned male migrants and the wives of migrant men.

The relative absence of migrant-mother families indicates not only the lesser amount of support they receive from the government when compared to families of migrant fathers; it also confirms my observation of the greater social disapproval directed toward these families. A multitude of factors explain their absence in these organizations. First, more women than men are undocumented workers, and undocumented workers do not qualify for the services provided by OWWA. In sharp contrast, men's employers sometimes initiate formal support groups for their families in the Philippines; for instance, shipping lines often work with OWWA to organize formal support groups for the family members of seafarers. Second, the greater degree of social disapproval directed toward families of migrant mothers makes them less willing to participate in public activities such as get-togethers sponsored by community groups. A number of migrant women are single mothers, whose relatives would be discouraged by the stigma of single parenthood. The lack of representation of the families of migrant mothers in community groups exacerbates the adversities already confronting them. It perpetuates the government's tendency to underestimate their representation in the demographic composition of migrant families.[44] It also leaves their point of view largely absent from public discussions. Thus, their needs are less likely to be met. Finally, their absence sets into motion the greater invisibility of their families from the public sphere.

Not surprisingly, then, the opinions of community groups tend to reiterate mainstream views of families. They frequently attest to the lesser quality of family life for the relatives of migrant mothers, despite the fact that participants rarely if at all include the relatives of migrant mothers. This has been the case even in towns with large representations of migrant women. For instance, in one remote mountain community, the majority of families rely on the remittances of at least one overseas migrant worker. Households send women to work as domestic workers in richer countries in Asia and men to work as manual laborers for oil companies in Asia and the Gulf region. In this town, community members expressed a preference for sending fathers to work abroad.

Remarks one wife of a male migrant worker:

Well, I think it's much better if the fathers leave, because mothers can do it better, to play the role of both the mother and the father. But if the mother leaves, what's likely to happen is that the father cannot play the role of the mother, for the children. Not unless the father does not have any vice, does not smoke, does not drink or gamble. And men have this tendency to (pause), because in the marital relationship, if the mother is absent, the father might look for another one (Pause. Then laughs.). It's just natural, right? It's just natural, their natural needs, and if that happens, for sure the children will not be taken care of very well (Pause.). If the husband drinks, for sure, every afternoon, he will be found in a drinking session (Pause.). It's always better for children to come home in the afternoon with a parent in the home. What if the father who is left behind is not there and is spending his time drinking? It's an advantage if the father is the one to leave and work, (pause) because the mother can take the role of being the mother and the father, but the father, most likely he cannot play both roles. Men who do not have vices? You can only count them [and gestures with her hands, counting off on her fingers].

Other participants did not disagree.[45] Community opinions more than sub-scribe to gender boundaries of mothering and fathering. In the logic of com-munity members, the transgression of gender boundaries in the migration of women unavoidably leads to deviance. For instance, men who do not ful-fill expectations of fathering are considered more prone to succumb to vices than are other men. In other words, men in this high migration-sending town could only be prone to but at the same time could not be held account-able for the vices instigated by the departure of the women in their families.

While community representatives convey strict gender boundaries of mothering and fathering, they give greater flexibility to concepts of moth-ering than they do to concepts of fathering. For instance, they hold that mothers can both "mother and father," but fathers cannot take on mother-ing roles, such as nurturing and caring for children. One respondent, a wife of a seafarer, describes:

If the mother is not with them, especially that it is really the mother who takes care of the children, prepares for their need. Unlike with the father, he is only the breadwinner of the family. All he does is give his earning to the mother and it is really the mother who manages everything in the house. So most of the time the children really run to the mother. Even if the father is abroad, as long as the mother is in the home, it is better.

This conventional view of the family resonates in all of the interviews and group discussions that I conducted with community representatives. Often, concepts of fathering are limited to breadwinning, while mothering centers on domestic-sphere activities. Moreover, communities do not question the notion that men are incompetent care providers.

For instance, a male return migrant reinforces this view when he explains why children fare better if left under the care of a mother rather than a father:

Basically, the role of the mother is very different from the role of the father. Sometimes, when the mother is away, the father becomes misguided. So what happens is that it results to a bigger problem with the family. . . . It is seldom that you can see a harmonious behavior from a child when the father is left behind to take care of the children. There are a lot of pain and regrets that a child had, that he or she wishes a different situation so that things may be a lot different. . . . They are really neglected.

Narrow definitions of fatherhood deny to men the ability to nurture chil-dren. This means that men cannot cross gender boundaries. In contrast, con-structions of mothering encompass a wider range of responsibilities. Unlike

men, women can cross gender boundaries. Fathers cannot take on the traditional women's role of nurturing but mothers can extend their definition of
mothering to include the responsibility of disciplining. Not surprisingly,
mothers whom I interviewed frequently complained about the double burden of having to mother and father as a result of their husband's emigration.
In contrast, the few fathers who I had spoken to did not.

Most focus group discussion participants believe that the children of migrant fathers are far better off than the children of migrant mothers. Yet, in
the opinion of many, the double duty of mothering and fathering for the
wives of migrant fathers does not always bode well for children. In father-
away families, community members fear, the expansion of mothering to include traditional gender roles of men may lead to a troubling gender confusion among children. Explaining the difference between the families of
migrant fathers and those of migrant mothers in his remote agrarian town,
one male return migrant for instance states:

When a man leaves, he earns more. It is because when it is a woman who
leaves, she is most likely going to be a domestic worker, unless you are a
nurse or a medical practitioner. We have teachers here. She is a teacher before, but because domestic workers abroad earn more, she left her family.
Now she works as a domestic helper. But still, I compare the salary of a domestic helper with a technician, the technician earns more. That is why it
was men who left during the first wave.

It was only men who left, right? [Looks around the group for approval.]
Now, what is happening with families, mothers are left to act as a mother
and father. In disciplining, it is the mother who gives comfort. Isn't that
right? Mothers are comforting. Mothers today, in the absence of the father,
are finding it in themselves to become strict. That is what is happening to
families here in our town. So children are getting confused. Before the father
left, he was the disciplinarian and the mother was the pacifier. So when they
are disciplined, it is the mother explaining what is going on.

When I was gone, my wife was assuming the role of the disciplinarian. My
children were confused. They were wondering why their mother suddenly become the disciplinarian when she had been the pacifier. They did not understand why they were being punished and scolded. That is one effect. . . . Then
now it is my wife who is gone, in Manila. I am having a hard time. Because I
am a man and we are not nurturing to our children. We are a little bit stern.
Maybe it is because of the macho image expected of us? I don't know (Laughs).

Community representatives, when regarding transnational families, tend to subscribe to gender boundaries of mothering and fathering. They follow dominant sentiments: the more the family digresses from conventional gender boundaries, the higher the risk of children receiving inadequate care from the family.

However, as transnational households in themselves show us, gender boundaries are not fixed. Men and women can and do violate conventional gender prescriptions. At the same time, gender distinguishes the construction of boundaries for mothers and fathers. Society limits fatherhood to a very narrow definition that excludes the care of children. In contrast, society's view of motherhood expands to include the disciplining of children. But its expanded view of motherhood stops at the mother's role as breadwinner, especially if women's earnings threaten the breadwinner status of men. A breadwinning wife is seen to provoke the ill behavior of husbands, and this threat to the masculine identity may lead him to "vices."

The greater elasticity of mothering is not cause for celebration. The expansion of mothering duties in transnational families increases the work of women, in the same way that the narrow construction of fathering limits the responsibilities of men. I found that fathers left behind get away with having far fewer responsibilities than the mothers left behind. The logic of gender boundaries has made this discrepancy acceptable in Philippine society.

## PARISH PRIESTS

While conducting fieldwork, I regularly attended Mass in different churches throughout the city in hopes of learning about the views espoused by religious clergy on transnational migrant families.[46] Not once did I ever hear references to such families, however. On a regular basis, I did hear churchgoers pray for the safety and welfare of migrant workers. However, never did I hear references to their families. The absence of the issue of migrant families in the numerous churches I had visited in the medium-scale sending community where I did research did strike me as odd. It suggested to me that one of the largest support institutions in the country—the church—ignores the growing presence of these households.

In my region of study, the treatment of transnational families by the church was idiosyncratic at best. While some priests dedicate a significant portion of their work to the welfare of migrant workers and their families, other priests do not at all consider their issues as significant. Those who do consider the issues of migrant workers to be important tend to consider the problems of the family based on the standards of conventional nuclear households. This was the case for one priest whose parish had a 70 percent constituency of migrant households. He considered the families of most of his parishioners to be prone to delinquency. This was made clear in his response to the question of the effects of migration to the family. He states:

For instance, the worst effect would be of the children, because of the lack of parental love, even though most of them would be enjoying some kind of material prosperity, but it cannot substitute for the love or the concern of the parent, the presence of the parents. This is what usually happens, because the families are abroad, and the children are sent to good schools, private schools, but sad to say, they lack the parental guidance, the presence of parents, which is basically what they need more than anything else.

[Interviewer:] What do you mean?

[Priest:] Because of the problem that they have in school or in their homes, for instance, their substitute parents, their grandparents, their uncles and aunts, are saying that, you know, having money, the guidance of these substitute parents (Pause.). The children have money but when they go to school they have problems with their studies and the substitute parents could not really control these children because (pause) it's really different with the real parents.

In this priest's opinion, dominant notions of the family establish the innate inability of transnational family members to develop healthy lives. This attitude projects a despairingly unhealthy outcome for children growing up in transnational households.

Further reflecting the inconsistencies of the church, other parish priests portray transnational families as even more aberrant. This is the case with another priest, whose parish is located in a very poor neighborhood with a greater balance of migrant mothers and fathers among his parishioners. After enumerating the three "main problems" of transnational families as first "the lack of proper care of children," second, "marital infidelity," and third, "the spouses who are abroad, either the husband or the wife, they miss their family," he then named the ill effects of these problems. They include "poor academic performance," "a lot of vices," "very materialistic children," and "gamblers." Despite his persistently pessimistic views on transnational families, this priest admitted he very rarely acknowledges their issues in his sermons. By turning his back on these "problem-ridden" constituents, he inadvertently promotes the treatment of these families as an unacknowledged yet growing social reality in the Philippines.

Not all priests look at transnational families so pessimistically. Once again indicating the inconsistent ways that the church officially addresses the issues of transnational families, some priests in the area do not impose notions of the "right kind of family" on their constituents. Yet, I also noticed that this was the case among priests whose constituents are mostly families of migrant fathers. For instance, one such priest, when asked to address the issues faced by migrant families, spoke of the multiple burdens of parenting left to the wives of migrant men but remained silent about the families of migrant women. Members of migrant families, specifically wives of migrant men, frequently approach him for spiritual and moral guidance. He often gives them advice on how to maintain "good dialogue" and "good communication" with their husbands and how to downplay "the material things" and focus on "interior values of love, sacrifice, forgiveness, and understanding." In contrast, family members of migrant mothers hardly ever hear such compelling advice, because, as this priest admits, they rarely seek his advice. This is not surprising when one considers the greater social disapproval that confronts these families. However, it is surprising if one thinks about and agrees with the common public view that the families of migrant women face greater challenges than do the families of migrant men. Thus, despite their greater problems, the fathers, aunts, and grandmothers who care for the children of migrant women are less likely to seek the guidance of parish priests than the wives of migrant men are.

GUIDANCE COUNSELORS

In my visits to eight elementary schools in one district of the city, guidance counselors usually welcomed me to the campus, introduced me to teachers, and helped me identify students eligible to participate in a survey I conducted with children of migrant workers.[47] In one particular school, I had been touring the grounds with the counselor when we came across a group of young boys in the sixth grade plowing and planting seeds for an agriculture course. The counselor called my attention to three boys, who I thought to myself were not particularly distinguishable except for the fact that they worked together and were taller than the rest of their classmates. The counselor then proceeded to tell me how these three are the troublemakers of the school. She described them as rowdy, always ill prepared for class, and not very intelligent. She then blamed their deviance on their mothers' employment outside the country, as domestic workers in Hong Kong. Needless to say, I was struck by how strong her opinion of these boys had been and surprised by how much she blamed their mothers for their bad behavior.

In the course of conducting the survey of elementary schoolchildren, I had the opportunity to once again meet these three young boys. I soon realized that their behavior contradicted the comments of the counselor. During the course of our afternoon together, they acted only with respect and obedience. After I handed them the questionnaire, one of them inquired if he could proceed to complete it. I responded by explaining that we had to wait for all the other children participating in the survey to join us in the library, and he patiently waited for other students to make it to the library. After the arrival of every one of the ten students scheduled to complete the survey during that set period, we proceeded together as a group. It was soon clear that two of these boys outpaced the rest of the participants. Their cognitive skills seemed much higher. For instance, I did not have to explain the questions to them twice, as I did for most other students. After talking to teachers later, I learned that these boys were barely passing the sixth grade. They have been labeled to be underachieving students. Their case left an impression on me and made me wonder whether biases against children of migrant mothers adversely affect their school performance.[48]

However, my interviews with guidance counselors did not lead me to conclude that school officials uniformly hold a bias against children of migrant mothers or fathers. Some do and some do not. The inconsistencies in their judgments point to the absence of a standard to which they as counselors are held accountable by higher authorities. While some counselors in a school may think that children of migrant workers are disadvantaged, other counselors in another or even in the same school may beg to differ.

For the most part, counselors purport that children of migrant fathers fare better than those of migrant mothers, but often not on the grounds of a fair scientific assessment. In one high school where 65 percent of enrolled students are children of migrant parents, a guidance counselor informed me that the children of migrant workers, especially mothers, "lack attention, caring, love." When I asked her about the basis of her conclusion, she told me that they are "restless in the classroom. . . . They want to be given attention all of the time." I then asked her if this was the case for 65 percent of the students in the school. She responded "No," but then pensively frowned as if pondering the discrepancy between her judgment and the demographic composition of the school.

Though they constitute a preferred social arrangement, the families of migrant fathers are not always free from judgment by counselors. For instance, in one school, a counselor admitted, "[the children of migrants] are really not that different to other kids. . . . Their behavior, it's normal," but she added that children of migrant fathers are more prone to lesbianism. She continued, "Sometimes when the kids, especially the girls, when there is no father around, the role model is the mother. And that could develop into lesbianism, or homosexuality, because (pauses), well, there is no father figure (pauses) because all the images are feminine." The comments of this counselor surprised me, as they indicated once again the inconsistent ways that children are accepted, integrated, and treated in various school settings.

## THE CURRICULUM—VALUES FORMATION COURSES

In the Philippines, "values formation" is a core subject taught in high schools as well as in colleges. The family is frequently addressed in these courses. While I had not attended any of these classes, I collected syllabi and required reading materials assigned in six schools—both public and private—in the area. I did so to learn how the subject of transnational families is incorporated into these classes. Not surprisingly, they are not at all part of the formal curriculum of the schools in the area where I conducted my research. The teachers I had interviewed also admitted that they do not incorporate lessons on transnational family life in their syllabi.

I found that values formation courses uphold the definition of the family as presented in the Family Code. Even the curriculum of a school with a 65 percent student population of transnational family members ignores the existence of such families. Moreover, the course readings in this school hold that children of such families are prone to delinquency since their care falls outside the norm of the nuclear family. This attitude is clearly established in the following text, a standard reading assigned to students in values formation courses. The text is describing regular activities in the family:

If we trace back on [*sic*] our history, we are proud to say that we are a strong country. Each family goes to mass together, pray [*sic*] together, ate [*sic*] together, and happily shares stories before going to bed. The father works for the family. The mother takes care of the children. The parents help the children with their studies. They have enough time to talk to their children on their problems. In return the children showed their love by sharing, helping in the household chores. They love their parents so much that they give them their full respect. They never do things to hurt their parents. They consult their parents before doing anything. . . . Because of this, the children are not influenced by bad friends or peers.[49]

The text more than implies that non-nuclear households, such as those of single parents and transnational migrants, lack the resources to provide children with the experience required of them to gain the strength or knowledge to reject negative outside influences. For instance, it avers that children in transnational households are not able to go to Mass together and might not be able to "consult [with] their parents before doing anything."

The curricula of various schools do attempt to mirror other aspects of changing times. For instance, readings consistently reflect the increase in women's participation in the wage labor market. As one text that is required in at least two high schools states, "While the husband is still the breadwinner, he is no longer the sole provider; the wife can now work outside of home for a living."[50] Moreover, the readings attempt to expand constructions of mothering and fathering. For instance, the same text cited above also defines good fathers to have greater involvement with their children. It states: "Father is now expected to be not just a breadwinner; he is also expected to teach, discipline, to be a companion, a friend, a guide, a motivator, etc."[51] Yet, for the most part, readings in values formation classes still promote the conventional division of labor of nurturing mother and breadwinning father. This is despite the acceptance of women's "legitimate social progress."[52]

Various lessons recur in the values formation course readings; the most significant markers of a good family in these readings are time together, a conventional division of labor, the domestic role of women, family collectivity, and an awareness of the financial needs of the family. These characteristics epitomize the right kind of family in Philippine society. However, not all the children whom I interviewed used these traits to describe a family when asked to do so during the interviews.

For instance, interviewees from one school well-represented in my sample uniformly responded to the question "what is a family" with the statement: "the smallest unit in society." Needless to say, I was puzzled but also amused by their repeated, mechanical response to my inquiry.[53] When I asked interviewees to reconsider their answers and give a definition that applied more directly to their lives, many proceeded to define the family not on the basis of a household structure or with a social definition based on biological relations but instead gave definitions that referred to the fulfillment of particular emotions.[54] For these young adults who had grown up in transnational families, the family is composed of individuals whom they love, for whom they care, whom they trust, and with whom they feel comfortable and secure. Hence, they often consider their close friends as family. Needless to say, this flexible definition of family did not emerge from the course readings of values formation classes.

The family values of children do not necessarily mirror those espoused in schools, churches, and local communities. However, these views may influence them. For instance, they may make it difficult for children to imagine their migrant mothers as legitimate breadwinners. Moreover, the normative family values adopted in these institutions stigmatize transnational families. Finally, they depict the conventional nuclear family as the ideal, thereby underscoring the view that the transnational family is not the right kind of family.

One classroom exercise reinforces this with its vivid portrayal of the ideal family. It reads:

What activities did you enjoy doing when you were younger? An outing or a picnic with the family? Fishing together with Father? Baking a cake with Mother? Or watching a movie with Sister? You remember these activities because they have given you pleasant memories. And these memories you will always enjoy reminiscing until your old days. Now that you are older, would you want to have a similar activity?[55]

Without doubt, this passage would make children in transnational families—families where members spend greater time apart than together—feel different, or denied their rightful childhood activities. They are made to feel that only families who experience geographical proximity are the right kind of family. Educational psychologists Carola Suarez-Orosco and Marcelo Suarez-Orosco, in their longitudinal study on the children of immigrants in the United States, note that engaging students with cultural materials that provide a familiar mirror to their lives results in the reward of their greater enthusiasm for learning.[56] We can assume that unfamiliar cultural materials likewise curb their enthusiasm and increase their alienation. Although not present in the classroom while this passage was read, I wondered how the children of migrant workers felt when they read such passages in class. What type of feelings did they invoke and what kind of expectations did they raise?

## Conclusion

It should be no surprise that families in the Philippines would much prefer for a family member not to work outside the country. After all, time together allows intimacy while time apart breeds unfamiliarity. Thus, non-

governmental organizations tend to lobby for the reunification of transnational families. Such families are considered a symbolic metaphor for the
poverty of the Philippines. However, to uphold the nuclear household as an
ideal dangerously reinforces strict gender boundaries that limit the ways
women and men can care for their children. Idealizing the nuclear family, or
any kind of household structure, stigmatizes other kinds of families. Therefore, calls for family reunification should always come with the reminder
that nuclear families are not problem-free.

Families of migrant workers can seek support in various institutions, such
as churches, schools, and community organizations. These institutions enforce normative gender boundaries of mothering and fathering, however,
and discourage the participation of families that fall outside conventional
prescriptions of the right kind of family. Because families of migrant men
deviate less from conventional gender boundaries, they are more visible in
public institutions than the families of migrant mothers. The fact that conventional gender ideology discourages the participation of men in public institutions of support for the family further encourages the invisibility of
mother-away families. This invisibility indicates how the use of the moral
criteria of gender in determining membership within the nation leads to
lesser gains for individuals and families that transgress gender norms. Due
to pressures to conform to gender norms among fathers, who are not supposed to be nurturers, or mothers, who are not supposed to only be breadwinners, community and institutional support in the public sphere is far less
accessible to the families of migrant mothers.

Yet, the enforcement of gender boundaries against transnational migrant
families sets up a gender paradox in the Philippine public sphere. Due to the
greater acceptance of transnational families of migrant fathers in Philippine
society, as well as the gender elasticity allowed women, women in male migrant-based transnational families are more visible in the public sphere. This
select group of women is visibly present in public spaces such as church centers, schools, community town halls, city halls, and other government offices.
Notably, it is the class status that their families achieve via the breadwinning
contributions of men that helps empower them to visibility. In sharp contrast to the public visibility of these women is the striking absence in the
public sphere of the fathers in female migrant-based transnational families,
as well as other female members in these families. Their invisibility mirrors
the social disapproval attached to their families. For the men in these families, we can assume that their invisibility indicates that they as men tend to

comply with the narrow range of gender activities assigned to them, and that they cower against the challenge of increasing the services available to their families.[57] Hence, the operation of gender conventions works against the families of migrant mothers, but at the same time, in the context of the differences in gender elasticity between men and women, these same gender conventions, paradoxically, enable the empowerment of a particular group of women and promote the disempowerment of some men.

# CHAPTER 3

# Caring for the Family: Why Parents Leave the Philippines

We have noted that parents form transnational families in order to take advantage of the greater level of material security outside of the Philippines. In this chapter, I look beyond the macro-structural context of migration to consider also the micro-structural manifestations of this reality. I do so in order to take a closer look at how gender shapes the ways that children understand the individual decisions of migrant parents to relocate away from the Philippines. According to the young adult children with whom I had spoken, parents leave the Philippines purely for economic reasons. Either they leave to "provide for the family," to "escape poverty," or to "seek career advancements" and find "better labor market opportunities."[1] However, as I establish in this chapter, gender also shapes the ways that children make logical sense of these economic reasons.

In the previous chapter, I established that gender boundaries shape the integration of transnational families into the social-cultural landscape of Philippine society. I consider next how adult children try to make sense of parental migration in ways that fit and conform to these gender boundaries. I find that children of migrant fathers are more likely to say that their fathers left the Philippines "to provide for the family," whereas the children of migrant mothers more commonly claim that their mothers left "to escape poverty." Similarly, they say that men leave to "seek career advancements," while mothers leave only in the absence of labor market opportunities.

My interviewees recognized the economic incentives behind their mothers' migration, but they also insisted that these incentives were due to exceptional circumstances, for instance, single parenthood or poverty. In other words, they accept mothers as providers only in the absence of a male breadwinner in the family. The conditional status of transnational mothering reflects the continued struggle in society to accept women as rightful income earners in the family, despite the increase in women's labor market participation. The differences in the narrative construction regarding the causes of migration between men (who leave to provide) and women (who leave to escape) tell us that gender boundaries of breadwinning both determine the formation of transnational households and set the stage for intergenerational relations in transnational families.

## Gender Conventions in Filipino Families

The statement that biology-based gender attributes distinguish the parenting skills of men and women is reiterated by countless community representatives and used in indoctrinating students in values formation classes; it represents the dominant perception of the family in Philippine society. In turn, it shapes the ways children have come to understand parental migration. The "naturalness" of essential gender differences justifies the ideal of separate spheres and it distinguishes what women and men ought to be doing in the family. Men, perceived as physically superior, are relegated the heavy mechanical and outdoor tasks, while women, due to their biological function of childbearing, are seen as better-suited for child care and homemaking.[2]

In the Philippines, the division of labor between fathers and mothers is made crystal clear by metaphorical references to men as *haligi ng tahanan,* "the pillar of the home," and women as *ilaw ng tahanan,* "the light of the home."[3] My interviewees explained to me that the metaphorical reference to men as pillars establishes fathers as breadwinners, whose primary duty is to build a home for the family. As a pillar, it is he who makes the home stand and must metaphorically build a home for his family. Thus, the definition of fathering centers on the successful acquisition of a home for the family, whether it is a nipa hut for the working poor, a modest-sized cement structure for the struggling middle class, or a multilevel unit for upper-income families. Not surprisingly, I found that for men a common goal of migration is to acquire sufficient capital to build a home for their families.

In contrast, my interviewees told me that as the "light of the home," mothers do not face the cultural and social pressure to acquire material goods for the family; instead, they are the ones who must bring radiance to the home. In other words, a mother must care for the family. The metaphorical reference to mothers as the light of the home binds them to the domestic sphere. This metaphor limits the extent to which their labor force participation is accepted by society. Thus, it is commonly believed that the work of women outside the home should not interfere with their proper duties of nurturing and caring for children.[4] Not surprisingly, I found that only in dire situations do my interviewees excuse women from their role as *ilaw ng tahanan*.

Most Filipino families are composed of dual wage earning couples. For Filipino women, labor market participation in the local economy increased from 34 percent in 1970 to 45 percent in 1996.[5] But, although women participate in the formal labor force, their childrearing and other domestic responsibilities have not diminished. As the family sociologist Belen Medina observes, "There is still the double standard view that women have jobs and not careers due to the constraint of domestic responsibility."[6] Likewise, fathers are unlikely to take up the slack caused by women's greater labor force participation. They still spend more time resting and relaxing than they do lending a hand in household chores.[7]

A recent review of over 130 studies on child-rearing practices in the Philippines found an overwhelming pattern of gender binary split between men and women.[8] Women provide emotional comfort and support; men sustain the family financially. Conventional gender expectations of men and women's roles in the family lead to the prescription of certain gender characteristics. Thus, physical strength, brawniness, and a well-developed physical stature define masculinity, while modesty and a demure demeanor express femininity.[9]

The labor market participation of women may actually threaten men's identity to the point that they completely reject household chores. This is the case among some dual wage earning couples in the United States, where family sociologist Scott Coltrane among others has observed that "being dependent on a wife's earnings threatens some men's identity as the breadwinner, and can lead to more deferential behavior on the part of some wives and lower household contributions from husbands."[10] Like their counterparts in the United States, men in the Philippines have more leisure time than women. They do sometimes assist in household chores, but only under the same extreme conditions that force women to migrate as a means of escaping poverty. That is, they do so only if they have no other choice. For instance, a nationally based study of couples found men assisting in household chores only when their wives were sick or pregnant.[11]

In the Philippines, as we have seen, the commonly held view is that women can work but not to the extent that doing so would displace the breadwinning status of men. This threat is actually considered by some to be a health risk for men. Medina explains:

This discussion of the husband's traditional role is basically still true today at the level of norms and cultural expectations as well as that of actual behavior. In fact, it has been observed that premature deaths from heart diseases are 11 times more frequent among under-achieving husbands whose wives are over-achievers than otherwise. This shows the great psychological hurt on the husband's ego when his "masculinity" is undermined by his inadequacy as breadwinner.[12]

The accuracy of this claim, which is based on a media report on the state of the family in the Philippines, is irrelevant; in the context of its dissemination it seems true to the larger public, whose severe gender boundary constructs are only reinforced by such a statement.

GENDER BOUNDARIES IN THE FILIPINO FAMILY

According to Judith Gerson and Kathy Peiss, the term gender boundary refers to "the complex structures—physical, social, ideological, and psychological—which establish differences and commonalities between women and men, among women, and among men."[13] Jean Potuchek adds that gender, "defined by socially constructed relationships,"[14] is constructed via multiple interconnected and intersecting boundaries that mark and construct differences between "men" and "women," among women and among men, within a system of inequality.[15] Understanding the migration of their mothers as a way to escape poverty, but not so much as a means to provide for the family, is a strategy that children use to comprehend it in a way that does not contest the gender boundaries that are well in place in the Philippines, specifically the construction of fathers as the builders of the home and mothers as the light of the home.

In the Philippines, mothers can participate in the labor force, but not to the extent that this participation would dislodge the ideal of separate spheres. They can be breadwinners only if when doing so they do not undermine their role as the proper nurturers of the family, in other words. As the eighteen-year-old daughter of a domestic worker who has worked in Hong Kong since 1984, Theresa Bascara states:

You cannot say it is a family if your mother and father are not there with you.

It's like it's not a whole family if your father and mother are not here, if they are far. A family, I can say, is only whole if your father is the one working and your mother is only staying at home. (Pauses.) It is OK if your mother is working too, but somewhere close to you, not somewhere far away.[16]

Moreover, the migration of married women cannot destabilize the position of men as breadwinners of the family. Hence, at most, as my discussion shows, migrant women who leave spouses are often perceived by children as co-breadwinners or just supplementary breadwinners. Additionally, I repeatedly found that children view married migrant mothers as reluctant breadwinners or breadwinners by default. According to Potuchek, reluctant breadwinners or reluctant providers are women who view their economic provisions to be essential to the well-being of the family but at the same time hold the perception that men are the rightful breadwinners.[17] The construction of women as reluctant breadwinners is significant to our understanding of the division of labor in transnational families, showing that children still do not free their mothers of the traditional care responsibility of nurturing the family. It suggests that migrant women face dual responsibilities in the transnational family, as their economic provisions do not ease the care expectations that children have for them.

The gender boundary of the family resonates throughout the narratives that children provided about why their parents leave the Philippines. Migration enables fathers to be breadwinners as it allows women to do it only by default. For instance, of the sixty-nine children I interviewed, fifteen consider *providing for the family* to be the primary motive behind their parent's decision to migrate.[18] Most of these were the children of migrant fathers. Interestingly, the three children with migrant mothers who fall into this group premised the economic motives behind their mother's migration under the guise of needing to afford adequate health care, which is a gendered female responsibility. Moreover, they were all middle class. Their families all owned land and cement houses, even if only partially built, prior to the migration of their mothers. Thus, for them the wages that their mothers could earn, even if a significant economic source that secures the reproduction of the family, only supplement what the father had already provided prior to the mother's migration—that is, homeownership, a home being the major purchase symbolizing stability among middle-class families in the Philippines.

Illustrating the female gendered conditions placed on the economic provisions of migrant mothers to the family are the views of Trina Jara, a twenty-year-old college student. Her father had worked as a seafarer for seven years and more recently her mother had been working in Saudi Arabia as a nurse for the past twelve years. Trina describes her mother as a reluctant breadwinner, whose primary reason for migration had been to subsidize the earnings of her much older father. Explains Trina:

My dad had come back then my mother left. I told her "Mom, don't go." Then, she told me that she was leaving for my sake. We needed to finish building our house because we were only renting before. Then, we needed to cover the medical needs of my grandmother. She is sick. And she has all these complications, like with her diabetes, high blood pressure, and all these other ailments. So that is expensive.

In Trina's family, her mother took over the task of "building the house" and the costs of Trina's education after her father had retired from his position as a seafarer. Doing so technically makes Trina's mother an economic provider, who as such is able to contest the gender order of the family; however, I found that the actions of the mother still were not seen to subvert the gender order in the family. According to Trina, her mother often reminds her that her breadwinning provision includes the female responsibility of caring for her ailing mother.

Moreover, Trina's mother only supplements the breadwinning contributions of the retired father, whose prior earnings had enabled them to build a house. The father's earnings already financed the major expenses of the house, including the land and basic infrastructure. At most, the mother's earnings cover various fixtures that beautify the house such as the lighting, flooring, windows, and draperies. Clearly, gender dictates how the foreign earnings of Trina's parents cover the costs of building a home, as the split mirrors the traditional division of household work in the family. This too indicates that even after migration, the mother usually views her new role as breadwinner in the context of performing the traditional duty ascribed to women in the family.

Unlike women, men do not have to negotiate or downplay their role as breadwinners. Expected to be a "good provider," men migrate in order to fulfill their masculine role of extending material provisions to the family.[19] The counterpart to the "good provider" would be the housewife. The employment of wives and mothers is equated with the failure of men to be "good providers." As I noted, men often leave so as to earn sufficient wages to build homes or to send their children to good schools. Moreover, they also leave to earn a salary sufficient to support a stay-at-home mother.

Caridad Candado,[20] an eighteen-year-old student whose father has worked as an auto mechanic in Brunei for more than six years, sees her father as a "good provider"; but, unlike Trina, she does not feel compelled to justify his geographical distance from the family. As Caridad describes, "We did not have enough money. Because we were enrolled in private schools and the money was not enough for my mother's household budget. . . . So when he first left, my mother sat me down and explained to me why. She explained that he left for the family. He left so that we can acquire a house, even if we still do not have one yet." For Caridad's family, the father had to seek employment outside of the country to fulfill his duties as the breadwinner of the family. For her father, the achievement of masculinity, as symbolized by acquiring a house with the added prize of a stay-at-home mother, could be secured only with the higher wages available outside of the Philippines.

In addition to providing for their families, migrant fathers also leave to pursue their careers. This is rarely true in the case of migrant mothers. I interviewed eleven children who recounted that their fathers left primarily to seek better career options available outside the Philippines. Notably, not one child of a migrant mother gave this reason for their mother's migration. Most children whose fathers had migrated as a career choice were born after their fathers had already started working outside of the Philippines. This means that the transnational family is quite the norm for these children, since it is the only type of household arrangement in which these children had been raised.

The fulfillment of the father's dreams of economic and career success is usually considered beneficial for the entire family. For instance, Gregoria Tremania,[21] a twenty-three-year-old student whose father has worked as a seafarer for more than twenty-eight years, states:

It is because since I was young, I already tried to understand that if he did not work, we would not have money. We would not have money to spend for the household. So, I thought, I said, the sacrifice on his part, up to now, is that while he wants to stay in the Philippines, he cannot because he got used to depending on his work outside the country and then he will probably miss his work if he just stayed here in the Philippines.

Like other children of migrant fathers, Gregoria recognizes the satisfaction that her father gains from his work, accepts his need for the personal fulfillment that only work could bring, and does not see this fulfillment as oppositional to the family, which he sustains as a breadwinner. Thus, when children such as Gregoria describe their father's motive for migration to be a career choice, they usually leave it unsaid that it is a choice made for the benefit of the entire family. In other words, they believe that their fathers migrated to provide for the family.

Mothers are not as fortunate as fathers, as their children do not give them the same flexibility in their choice of viable employment. This is the case among the eleven children who said that their parents left because of labor market difficulties in the Philippines. Two of the eleven have migrant fathers, another has two migrant parents, and the rest have migrant mothers. Once again conforming to gender boundaries, children do not give mothers the luxury of migrating as a career choice. Instead, mothers can only do so *by default;* that is, they only leave the Philippines because they have few opportunities in the domestic labor market.

A nineteen-year-old college student, Rodney Palanca,[22] explains why his mother sought employment as a nurse in Saudi Arabia by stressing the instability of employment for his mother in the Philippines. As he states,

*She did not have a choice.* It's because her salary was not enough to support us. We also thought about it. We knew that her salary at the hospital was not enough to raise us. At that time, we were having a very hard time financially. It's because our farm was not generating any income. Even if we had stocked up on our products, we still lost [*sic*]. Prices were so cheap. . . . So my mother needed to go abroad. She said that it was expensive to send us children [himself, his twelve-year-old brother, and his fourteen-year-old sister] to private schools supposedly. Our tuitions were high. And then of course there is the food we eat every day. Then there are other daily expenses such as the wages of the household help. We couldn't afford the daily costs of living. [Emphasis my own.]

Market demands do dictate the division of labor in the family and can push the envelope toward the reversal of material inequities between men and women. In the case of Rodney's family, the mother opted for labor migration while the father decided it would be best for him to stay in the Philippines to run the family farm. This division makes sense, because her salary as a nurse could generate more income than his business degree skills could. Likewise, the father's business acumen makes him better equipped to run the family farm than the mother, with her nursing skills.

Women such as Rodney's mother are now earning more than their spouses, yet this does not necessarily make them primary breadwinners, if understood in the context of the life history of the family. Seven women who left for the greater rewards offered in other countries for their skills as nurses or nutritionists were all older women, more specifically middle-class homeowners, at the time of departure. Like the other group of female economic providers in my study, those with male partners are leaving behind men whose masculinity has been made secure already by their own acquisition of property. At most, these women are leaving the country as supplementary breadwinners, despite the fact that by going outside the Philippines they will earn more than their husbands.

Even among those departing for the better labor market opportunities outside the country, rarely do mothers leave unless compelled by dire necessity. If they do not leave out of necessity, their children are more likely to question their motives. The comments of the few children whose mothers' migration they see not as an economic necessity but only as an economic advancement all reflect this. One such child is Fidela Lacsamana, an eighteen-year-old student whose father works as a prison guard and whose mother, formerly an office worker in the Philippines, has been a domestic worker in Taiwan since 1996. Fidela expresses doubt about the necessity of her mother's migration when she states:

I think that if Mom was not able to go to Taiwan, we probably would have been able to afford to go to school at [an expensive private school]. It's because my grandfather is there and my family is there in case we are short. They are there to help us. But my mother is the type that once an idea is in her head, then she has to just do it. And she was set in planning for our future. So she really went out of her way to get a job outside the country. She really goes out of her way to make sure that we get good schooling.

While Fidela recognizes the financial gains for her family that come from her mother's migration, she does not see her labor migration as a necessity, not even for her schooling, despite the family's working-class status. Fidela uses romantic notions of the help available from extended kin to place doubt on the significance of her mother's contributions to the collective mobility of the family. By doing so, Fidela inadvertently suggests that her mother gives greater priority to herself than to her family.

In contrast, the children of migrant fathers are not as likely to doubt the motives for parental migration as the children of migrant mothers are. They are more likely to see their fathers' economic contributions as, if not a necessity, done for the collective good of the family. For instance, the accepting attitude of the earlier cited Gregoria toward her father's occupation as a seafarer is in strong contrast to the doubt held by Fidela. This is so despite the greater economic security long achieved by Gregoria's family.

Further emphasizing that migrant mothers indeed are breadwinners only by default, most of their children cite *escaping poverty* as the reason why their mothers had left them in the Philippines. Twenty-five children explicitly cited poverty as the cause of parental migration in their family, with thirteen of these children further explaining that it had been the difficulties that their mothers had faced as single mothers that initiated migration in their family. Of the twenty-five children in this category, five have two migrant parents, three have widowed mothers, and only two are the children of migrant fathers. That escaping poverty is the primary cause for the migration of mothers strongly suggests that it is less acceptable for mothers to leave their children in the Philippines than for fathers. Mothers only leave out of desperation. Notably, many of the women who migrate for this reason had married irresponsible men, for instance jobless alcoholics or womanizers. This suggests that it is usually the absence of a male breadwinner that makes the migration of mothers acceptable to children. In other words, mothers can only justifiably cross gender boundaries in desperate circumstances.

This had been the case for the transnational family of Marinel Caligdong, a seventeen-year-old college student, whose father left her family when she was still an infant. When she was to begin elementary school, her mother decided to leave the country and work as a nurse in Libya. Explains Marinel, "She left because of our needs. Our needs. Aghh, it's because she is a single parent. Then we needed to study and then it was good for us not to rely on my grandfather and grandmother to work. It was important that my mother earned enough money so that we could go to school." Although Marinel's mother could have stayed in the Philippines and relied on the financial support of her aging parents, she decided that a transnational household would be a more stable option for her family. It secures the access of her family to the higher wages available in other countries.

The conditions of departure that children impose on their mothers are striking. Responding to the effects of care resource extraction, both men and women take on the role of economic provider, yet children face greater difficulty accepting their mothers as the income earners of the family. Existing gender boundaries of mothering and fathering often mean that women receive less credit for the same work than men do. Moreover, fathers have greater flexibility in choosing jobs, as children accept their right to work for personal fulfillment. Mothers are not given this flexibility, however, if it puts at risk their primary duty of nurturing the family. While children such as the earlier cited Gregoria can consider the personal satisfaction gained by their fathers from working outside the country as not oppositional to their responsibilities to the family, children such as Fidela cannot do the same for their mothers. Instead, the work of their mother abroad is seen as oppositional to the interest of the family and acceptable only if done in desperation. This difference exists because fathers subscribe to gender boundaries and mothers break them when they migrate.

## Conclusion

In multiple terrains, gender controls the formation of transnational households. On a macro-structural level, transnational households occur in the context of care resource extraction, a macro-process that speaks of the gender inequities embedded in global restructuring. On the level of social relations, gender also influences the ways that children understand the migration of their parents. Thus, labor migration is a process of negotiating gender for mothers and fathers in the Philippines. Fathers leave so as to fulfill their gender-ascribed role as breadwinners of the family, while mothers are only justified in leaving when they have been denied their right to a breadwinner.

This chapter begins to show us that gender contestations occur in the households of migrant mothers, but not so much in those of migrant fathers. Men's migration abides by gender norms, but women's migration does not. The narratives of children suggest that much greater challenges face mothers toward creating healthy intergenerational relations with their children. Unlike fathers, mothers are not automatically assumed to migrate for the sake of the collective mobility of the family. Therefore, mothers must perform greater work to show their children that despite the distance they do really still care for the family. This burden raises the bar in the transnational family work of migrant mothers, who find themselves responsible for both the emotional and the material well-being of their children in the Philippines.

CHAPTER 4

# The Gap Between Migrant Fathers and Their Children

Growing up in a transnational family presents a wide range of challenges for a child. For one, the distance in time and space between migrant parents and their children threatens to weaken intergenerational relations. As Erlinda Gaylan,[1] a nineteen-year-old college student whose father began working outside the country fourteen years earlier, astutely points out: "Well, you do not know what is happening with your family, especially when you only keep in touch every month. You do not know what happens to them every day." Both temporal and geographical separation breeds unfamiliarity, which in turn may lead to variegated feelings of insecurity and loss for children.

This chapter focuses on the transnational family life of the young adult children of migrant fathers. This group of children frequently voiced their feeling of a *gap*, or in other words a sense of social discomfort and emotional distance, toward their father. This alienation stems from unfamiliarity in these families. In most father-away families, I noticed that the children prefer to minimize the time they spend with their fathers—that is, they wish to reduce their ties to monthly remittances and would rather fathers prolong their stay outside the country. This is not to say that children consider the gap to be irreparable. In fact, they believe that greater time together would eventually mend this gap. However, they would rather mend it later and not sooner.

This chapter begins my close interrogation of the transnational family life of young adult children. I found that problems plaguing children vastly differ in mother-away versus father-away families. For instance, in mother-away families children rarely ever spoke of the existence of a gap. Instead, they more frequently complained about feelings of abandonment, which is a topic that the children of migrant fathers rarely mentioned in our interviews. Due to this stark difference, I will discuss the experiences of children in transnational households according to the gender of the migrant parent.

This chapter focuses solely on the transnational family life of the children of migrant fathers, thus focusing on the issue of "the gap." My discussion presents the factors that aggravate and ease this gap. I argue that subscribing to gender norms aggravates this gap, while questioning gender boundaries, for instance via the inclusion of maternal acts in the performance of fathering, eases it.[2] In other words, I show that gender transgressions in fathering and mothering relieve intergenerational tensions in the families of migrant men, whereas the maintenance of gender norms further strains them.

## Father-Away Families

Father-away migrant families usually mirror modern nuclear households. For instance, in contrast to mother-away migrant families, these families are hardly ever based on single parents who have to rely on extended kin for the care of their children.[3] Instead, the families resemble conventional nuclear families. The only difference is the temporal and spatial rearrangement brought on by the father's work: instead of the father routinely returning home to his family at suppertime, he comes back home from work every ten months. Migrant men usually leave their children behind under the sole custody of their wives, whom they often do not allow to enter the formal labor market. First, as the children and their mothers explained to me, the high earnings of migrant men allow them to be the sole provider of the family. Second, migrant men prefer to limit the regular interaction of their wives with other men during their absence from the country. Third, if fathers are fulfilling their breadwinning responsibilities, then wives should ultimately fulfill their traditional roles as mothers and put not just part but most of their energy into meeting the daily needs of their children.

The mothers I spoke to constructed their husbands as ultimate breadwinners of the family, and in return they wanted to fulfill the corresponding gender role of "intensive mothers."[4] Sharon Hays defines "intensive mothering" as the work of expending a "tremendous amount of time, energy and money in raising [one's] children."[5] In these families, men are "good providers." As such, masculinity is based on men's material contributions to the family.[6] Thus, the fulfillment of the "good provider" role frees men of other obligations, for instance the emotional work required in a family. This typical construction of fatherhood fits the earlier observations of Jesse

Bernard, who notes that "good providers" usually become "emotional parasites," as they are likely to expect women to do all of the work required to secure the emotional stability of the children in the family.[7]

Perhaps because no social expectation to do so is imposed on them, migrant fathers rarely communicate with their children. Moreover, they usually enforce discipline during the few times that they do so. To remind children of their authority in the household, migrant fathers typically take on the habit of reprimanding their children from a distance for having low grades, selecting the "wrong" major, or not performing adequately in other school activities. In fact, many children noted that "distance disciplining" is a central part of transnational family childhood. However, for children the tendency of migrant fathers to discipline them from a distance usually leaves a sore spot, and consequently reinforces the emotional gap in their families.

In the transnational families of migrant fathers, intensive mothering usually does not make "parasites" out of financially dependent women. Intensive mothering includes the responsibility of capitalizing on the income earned by the migrant spouse. These mothers tend to partake in petty business dealings and acquire property using their husbands' earnings. Women's participation in petty business is well documented in history.[8] Women, even if not in the formal labor force, participate in small business ventures to augment the family income.[9] Therefore we should not view the spouses of migrant men as disempowered women locked up by their husbands in their homes. Though most of the children in my sample grew up under the care of a stay-at-home mother, these mothers ran various enterprises including managing fishponds, poultry farms, and fruit farms. Some of these mothers did seek wage employment, often for the reason of personal fulfillment and not out of financial necessity. In my sample, most of the working mothers were public school teachers.

The father-away families in my sample also represent the average middle-class household in the Philippines. Studies show a higher concentration of migrant men than migrant women in professional and technical positions. A 1996 survey of overseas Filipinos reports that 82.8 percent of service workers but only 39.8 percent of professional and technical workers are women.[10] Most of the migrant fathers in my study are skilled workers. Twelve are officers and four are crew members of shipping lines. Of land-based workers, three are professionals, mostly engineers, and seven are manual laborers or low-wage service workers. Most of the twenty-six young adult children whom I interviewed grew up in comfortable middle-class households. In the Philippines, "middle class" means that their family owns a motor vehicle, resides in a cement-structure house, and can afford private education for the children.

In my sample, most families slowly acquired these material comforts, including, for instance, the ownership of a cement-structure house. Families would purchase the land in the first few years of migration, then set up the foundation of the house, after which they would slowly build the house to completion. These projects take years to complete, I noticed, as some of the homes of my interviewees were still "under construction." One home that I visited consisted of partially built cement walls that only reached the level of my knees. To make do while they saved money for the construction of their home, this family had utilized bamboo, a more affordable material, to stand as temporary walls for their house.

Interestingly, the project of building a house never seems to end. Some families will even add an entirely new floor to their homes, even if they do not seem to need to expand, just because the resources are available for them to do so. We can speculate that the home measures the masculinity of men in the Philippines, with its size considered to be one determining criterion of the successful fulfillment of one's role as *haligi ng tahanan*, the "builder of the home." The process of building the home allows children to witness the mobility that migration affords their families. The visible material improvements brought by the slow building of the house reinforce the breadwinner status of men and in turn reinforce the conventional gender division of labor in the family. In contrast, the subject of building a home was rarely mentioned in my interviews with the children of migrant mothers and their guardians.

As noted earlier, the families of migrant men rarely depend on extended kin; instead, they more often help extended kin. Of the twenty-six now young adult children whom I interviewed, all but one resides in a nuclear-based household. Many did identify the presence of at least one extended kin in their household, usually a grandmother or a cousin from a poorer family. However, these families do not reside in their ancestral homes, nor do they share the ownership of a residence with extended kin. As nuclear-based units, father-away families tend to be self-reliant and have a less dense social network, depending less on grandparents and other kin. This gives them autonomy in household decision-making. While customary respect makes them defer to the opinion of elders, financial independence gives them the flexibility not to abide by their views.

The relatively weak dependence of father-away families upon extended kin gives families greater flexibility to incorporate a less traditional distribution of housework. In his study of couples that share family work in the United States, Scott Coltrane found that dense local kin networks deter husbands and wives from sharing childcare and housework.[11] These relationships with kin, especially the elderly, impose pressure for families to conform to convention. This is true as well in the Philippines. Since various social forces in the public sphere impose conventional gender norms on families, I found that the private sphere of transnational families, especially those with minimal kin pressure, becomes a haven from the heartless bombardment of traditional views.

In father-away families, migrant men take over some of the family work of women whenever they are at home in the Philippines. While the migration of fathers reinforces the modern nuclear family, the practices that constitute their transnational households can also involve a great deal of gender boundary crossing in housework. More often than not, fathers cook, clean, and change the diapers of their children whenever they are at home. In fact, they tend to do more housework than fathers in mother-away families do. Perhaps they do so because their masculinity is more intact and made secure by their financial contributions to the family. As Jesse Bernard notes, the role of the "good provider" usually overrides other aspects of fathering and singularly determines the masculinity of men.[12] Still, rather than performing child-centered caring practices, fathers instead do the more emotionally distant labor of cooking and cleaning. This is most likely due not so much to their lack of desire to spend time with their children, but perhaps more to the awkwardness imposed by the effects of geographical distance and minimal communication between them.

## The Gap

What did children mean when they referred to a gap? I repeatedly heard them complain about a gap and I accordingly asked them to describe this gap. As noted earlier, the gap refers to this sense of discomfort, unease, and awkwardness that children feel toward migrant fathers. Additionally, it refers to the inability of young adult children to communicate more openly with their fathers. Finally, it also captures the ambivalence they feel over the unfamiliarity that has developed in their family.

The children themselves perhaps best described this gap. "Embarrassed" is one word they frequently used to describe their feelings when it comes to their fathers. For instance, Danica Lavilla,[13] a twenty-year-old college student preparing for law school, states: "I am very grateful that my father has worked hard for us but then it's like something is really lacking. Look at our situation. We are already so grown up but yet we are still embarrassed around our father." Danica's father has worked as a seafarer for more than twenty years.[14] This extended length of separation explains why his twenty-four-year-old son and younger daughters including Danica still feel quite embarrassed around him. Similarly, Claudio Regala,[15] cannot open up to his father. He explains: "I tell my mother all of my problems, for instance with my girlfriends, grades, everything." "How about your father?" I asked him. "Oh, I am embarrassed." When asked the reason why, he added: "I am not as close to him as I am to my mother. It's because, well, it's because we never get to be together. So we have this gap. We get embarrassed around him."

Like Danica's father, Claudio's worked as a seafarer for more than twenty years. Children whose fathers have worked outside the country for most of their lives feel a greater sense of emotional distance in the family than those children whose fathers did not leave the Philippines until their early teenage years. This is understandable, as a certain level of familiarity gained from the intimacy and routine of daily life would have already developed prior to migration in the family life of this latter group of children.

Another interviewee, Kiara Billones,[16] visibly recoiled and grimaced when I asked her to describe her relationship with her father. She then laughed in discomfort before proceeding to explain the distance between her and her father:

The first time my father went home, it was as if I was really afraid of him. (Laughs.) It is because I was not used to having him around. See every night, I would kiss my mother good night. But when he is around, I am so embarrassed. So when he and my mother are together when I am about to go to sleep, I do not kiss my mother. I get so embarrassed when he is around. My mother of course noticed this. She asked me about it and I told her that I am embarrassed around him. She told me not to be because he is my father. She told me that I should try to be close to my father. So I agreed and I tried, but it is still the same. I am still embarrassed around him. Up to now, I am still very uncomfortable around him.

Kiara's father left the Philippines to work as a seafarer eleven years earlier, when Kiara was only seven years old. She has few memories of her father and believes the "gap" in her family is due to the lack of shared experiences between them. I should note that even the most confident of children feel embarrassed around their fathers. This suggests that we cannot simply attribute the awkwardness that has developed in these families on personality traits (e.g., shyness) of children. For instance, Kenneth Matugas,[17] the student body president of his university, cringed when I asked why he did not ask his father for advice and responded by saying "Oh, I get embarrassed."

Distance breeds unfamiliarity and this unfamiliarity leads to discomfort. As Leonardo Monfort,[18] also the son of a seafarer, explains,

Love. You can secure it from far away but not that strongly. It is better if your family is physically close. Sometimes, if you are far away and even if you are sincere in your love, your children will feel that it is only money that you can give. If you are there, then you can give more than money. You can give emotional support. You can be there for the emotional problems of your children. You can be there on the phone, but that is not very practical. That is why a gap forms. You develop a tendency to be inhibited. It's because you have not seen each other for years. They become inhibited because they are not used to having them there every day.

Because distance combined with unfamiliarity imposes a gap of inhibition, children are less likely to share their problems with their fathers.

Unfamiliarity also breeds ambivalence. For instance, Ton-ton Ilano,[19] an eighteen-year-old college student raised by paternal extended kin who financially depend on the remittances of his seafarer father, describes the distance between him and his father: "Emotional. I do not think I have an emotional connection with my father. It's probably because we are so far away from each other. We are so far apart that I cannot relate myself to him. He also cannot understand me. He also never listens to me. It always has to be his way. He does not even want you to make a comment." I asked him if he would ever be close to his father, and he replied: "Never. Maybe, I do not know. Sometimes, it enters my mind to think what will happen when he dies. Would I shed a tear? That enters my mind. With my mother, my grandmother, I would probably cry, but with my father, I do not know if I would or I would not cry at all. Most likely, I will not."

Most children do not believe that the gap is irreparable, but some like Ton-ton do think that the possibility of a closer relationship developing between him and his father is quite bleak. In the case of Ton-ton's family, the tendency of his father to aggressively discipline them aggravates their feelings of emotional distance. Not unlike other migrant fathers, Ton-ton's tends to act like a military commander when at home and orders his children around as if he were still the chief engineer on board a shipping vessel. Not surprisingly, this tendency to constantly discipline children aggravates the emotional rift that already exists in these families. In the next section, I build from this example and enumerate the factors that aggravate the emotional gap between migrant fathers and their children. In the process, I show how abiding by conventional gender scripts in the family furthers the gap in transnational families.

## Aggravating the Gap

In the Philippines, the gender script of the family relegates the task of implementing order and discipline to fathers. Similarly, the final authority in the family is legally designated to men, thus, whether unintentionally or not, upholding their "macho" image.[20] Though the flexibility of gender practices allows men to expand ritual performances of fathering to include traditional women's roles, I found that they still prefer to cling tightly to authoritarian measures of discipline. Unfortunately, as was shown by the case of Ton-ton Ilano, the practice of doing so only aggravates the strained ties between migrant men and their children in the Philippines.

As noted earlier, child-centered activities of caring are not usually performed by men. Their intimate involvement with children remains minimal at best, as they usually limit the extent of their nurturing to token bonding rituals between fathers and sons—for instance circumcision in the pre-pubescent stage of life—and other initiations to adulthood. Not surprisingly, fathers rarely communicate with their children. Suzette Doligosa,[21] a nineteen-year-old college student who lives with her mother in the Philippines, complains:

It's hard to explain. Honestly, I do not have an easy time approaching him. It's because I am like afraid of him. It's just like that. And I am embarrassed around him. . . . My father calls home two times a month. Sometimes we do not talk on the phone. He only talks to my mother. We only get to talk when I happen to be the one to answer the phone and my mom happens not to be there. Sometimes I get so mad. It's because I can't help but wonder why it's like that. Why is that it is just my mom and dad who talk to each other? He should also talk to us. He should ask us how we are doing. Of course it's because that will show you that he really cares.

I asked her, "Does he ever show you that he cares?" She answered: "Maybe, when, when he gives me what I want. He will ask me what I want. But my brother and I are the type of children who would not openly tell him what we really want when he asks us. We are embarrassed. We are too embarrassed to ask him to buy things for us."

Suzette's father conforms to the most traditional of gender scripts. Not unlike other male migrants, he reduces fathering to the role of the good provider. Thus he completely depends on his stay-at-home wife to take care of the emotional needs of his children. This clear-cut division of labor surely strains intergenerational ties in his family, since his children cannot help but feel emotionally distant toward him. This is not to say that Suzette's father is a bad father, but only that his relegation of the nurturing tasks to his wife aggravates the emotional strains in his family. Other children share Suzette's problems, and they often complain about the tendency of migrant fathers to reduce expressions of love to the provision of material goods. Claudio Regala, for instance, said in a resigned and disappointed tone: "My dad. He supplies us with our financial needs, but he does not give us anything else."

However, children crave more emotional guidance from their fathers. Unfortunately, the gap usually prevents them from expressing this desire. Kiara Billones is one pent-up child who longs to talk openly to her father. Kiara took me by surprise during our interview when she began to cry immediately after she sat down in front of me. According to Kiara, it is her inability to communicate with her father that leaves her quite frustrated about her family life. She explains:

[My father and I] write frequently. But the letters are always about my studies. It's like there is nothing in there about problems. I never write about problems. Not at all. We also don't get to talk too well on the phone. We don't get to talk. He'll just ask me how I am doing. I say, OK. Then, that's it. Our conversations are never that intimate. . . . I would like to have a deeper relationship, one that I can tell my parents what my problems are, what's inside my head, if I am not feeling good. It's like, you want to be able to approach them. It's not like just coming up to them and asking for the material things that you might need.

From her wish to convert to another religion to her desire to change her major, Kiara has quite a number of concerns that she would like to address openly with her father. However, she feels that the gap between them prevents her from doing so.

Perhaps because they consider being a "good provider" to be their primary familial duty, fathers rarely communicate with their children and when they do it is not to allay their fears and insecurities. Instead, fathers often communicate to discipline their children. As noted earlier, fathering from a distance often also means abiding by the traditional gender script of disciplining. As Ton-ton Ilano complains, "My father only writes letters to my mother. There he would ask about us and our school grades. Then he asks that my mother photocopy our report cards and send them to him. Then if we have a low grade, he will call immediately and reprimand us. He will spend everything, his entire phone card, on scolding you." I ask him how he feels about this, and he replies: "Nothing. He always says the same thing again and again and again." Ton-ton long ago gave up the hope of ever achieving close ties with his father, despite his recognition of his father's economic contributions to the family. For Ton-ton, these contributions do not override the strains imposed by the gap, as well as the fact that Ton-ton's father is a somewhat extreme disciplinarian. He disciplines not only from afar but also from up close. Whenever he is home, for instance, he makes a concerted effort to instill a work ethic in his children. Complains Ton-ton:

First, everyone has to work when he is at home. Every single person in the house must work. No one can just sit around in the living room, watching TV, nothing. Everyone has to work. He wakes up and eats breakfast then he starts working. He just works and works. I keep on thinking, doesn't he ever get tired? When he is outside the country, he works. And when he is here, he also works.

"What does he do?" I ask, and Ton-ton replies: "He takes care of his poultry. He cleans everything. He cleans the house, everything. When he is not home, we do not do much. We watch TV. We do not have to cook. We do not clean everything. So I do not like it when he is around. It is very peaceful and quiet when he is not around, quiet for sure." During our interview, Ton-ton kept on stressing that he would much prefer for his authoritarian father to work permanently outside the country and never come home. He appreciates the monthly remittances that his father sends his family, but he would rather not interact with his father at all.

It is not only Ton-ton's father who feels compelled to impose authority in the household when at home in the Philippines. Most other fathers do likewise, as they tend to superimpose themselves as an authority figure over their children. Clara Maria Tantoco,[22] whose father emigrated from the Philippines six years ago to better provide for his stay-at-home wife and three children, gives us another example: "We get reprimanded more when he is home. See, I am used to walking around the house barefooted and my father does not like that. So he gets mad. He does not like it when I do not wear slippers around the house. He gets very mad. And so he scolds me."

Why do fathers superimpose their authority as the head of the household? We can speculate that, coupled with the awkwardness of not knowing how to act around their children, fathers may also feel pressure to act with authority, since they think they ought to be doing so to be good fathers. In other words, they assume that they must discipline their children to fulfill their parental duties. Yet, when they discipline, they do not seem to consider that their children have developed set behaviors in their absence. Instead, during their annual visits to the Philippines, they impose disciplinary standards that do not take into consideration the habits already formed by their children. This is illustrated by the case of Clara, who developed the habit of walking barefoot while her father worked outside the country.

It is not that the children don't want to be disciplined; instead, it is the way that it is done that they frequently complain about. Children dread the return of fathers because they equate their homecoming with the arrival of an unrelenting figure looming over the household. Mothers do not overlook the anxiety and trepidation with which their children frequently greet the arrival of their fathers, and they often push their husbands to incorporate maternal acts in their performance of fathering. Cautious of her husband's authoritarian demeanor toward his children, Adelaida Quilaton,[23] a mother of two teenage daughters whose husband has worked as a seafarer for most of their married life, criticizes her husband for literally taking the regimented culture of his work home with him.

The way he treats the children. The way he treats them is like the way he treats the people at his work. He is the head chief mate. So he takes that identity with him at home. When he is here, everything has to always be spic and span. He is very strict about it and then he does not communicate well. He orders his command then he goes back to the room. He does not communicate fully, like he is imposing this gap, as if his children are his crew who are lower ranked and he is the head.

Adelaida often finds herself acting as a go-between between her children and husband. While she urges her children to extend greater compassion and understanding toward their father, she likewise presses her husband to be softer, more patient, and more encouraging toward his children. In other words, she urges him to be more nurturing.

Fathers do not abandon their familial duties upon migration. From a distance as well as up close, they try to do what they think they ought to be doing to be good fathers. Accordingly, they provide material security, impose discipline, show authority, and finally enforce order. In short, they are "good providers," as they materially but not emotionally provide for the family and at the same time act as strict disciplinarians. Although children know that their fathers do care, they want fathers to change the *way* that they care. They would like fathers to not abide so completely by the gender boundaries of fathering, but instead extend fathering to include acts of nurturing. While appreciative of the material security afforded by migration, children would like their fathers to make a more concerted effort to achieve intimacy in the family. In the children's opinion, doing so would ameliorate the gap that plagues their relationships.

## Easing the Gap

Almost every child whom I interviewed considers the gap in his or her family to be reparable. Time together, mutual efforts for more open communication, and greater understanding could alleviate the gap in father-away families. To illustrate the process of easing the gap, I describe the experiences of one family that successfully did so, the family of Efren Papelera, a nineteen-year-old college student. He lives with his recently retired seafarer father, his schoolteacher mother, and three younger brothers, who are seventeen, fifteen, and thirteen years of age.

From the start, Efren and his siblings understood why their father had no choice but to migrate and seek employment as a radio operator in a shipping vessel. Only through migration could their father provide for the basic material needs of their family. Prior to his migration, the father held a job as a manager of a local radio station in a remote town. He earned a monthly wage of only 350 pesos, which at the time was roughly equivalent to $17. Their family lived in a nipa hut on a parcel of land no bigger than 300 square feet. According to Efren's mother, the father's salary was just enough to lead "a very simple life," eating daily staples of "vegetables and fish." Even with the mother's supplemental earnings as a teacher, the family income could not provide them with the money needed to "spend outside, even for clothing and schooling of children."

By the time I met Efren, his father had worked outside the Philippines for more than ten years. Unlike other families, they had managed to maintain a fairly strong relationship defined by openness and familiarity. Achieving familiarity had not come easily for the Papelera family, but it developed after they had struggled to recognize the efforts of each one to achieve the collective mobility of their family.

First, the recognition and understanding of migration as a decision made for the collective good of the family had pushed children to overcome the gap. In the case of Efren's family, the entire family's mobility had been made visible by the vast improvement in their home. Efren's family currently lives in a modest-sized three-bedroom bungalow, which is a far cry from the nipa hut they inhabited eight years ago. Through migration, the father successfully fulfilled his role as the *haligi ng tahanan* and accordingly had a house built for his family.

The process of building the house started immediately after Efren's father began working as a seaman. The mother and father explain:

Mother: We started to have the house built in 1990, during the first year abroad. We started with only 100,000 pesos and tried to minimize our expenses.

Father: This was the money which I saved while on board. This was my living savings. So we budgeted to only build the roof and then with walls. We could not afford windows.

M: So when he returned after the second year, we bought the door.

F: That was another year, after one more year.

M: While on board monthly, I would receive a monthly allotment. I would use the money for a little improvement each month. But the bigger projects we wait until he goes down the boat.

Interviewer: Can I ask why?

M: It's because he would have saved his share of his allotments. So we have a larger budget.[24]

F: So this last time, our project was for painting.

Efren's mother and father still have many home improvement projects in mind. The roof is quite visible from the interior of the house as there is no finished ceiling. Additionally, the windows have no screens to keep away mosquitoes. Bathroom fixtures, such as a flush toilet, have yet to be installed. However, these are all just aesthetic improvements and can wait, as far as the Papelera family is concerned. What is important to them is that the roof does not leak and that they can lock the doors at night.

Second, the efforts of mothers to broker the communication between children and their fathers also help ease the gap. Mothers use their position as intergenerational brokers to prevent possible misunderstandings between migrant fathers and children, as well as to calm the insecurities that might brew due to the spatial distance in the family. This was the case in Effren's and other families. For instance, the mother of the earlier cited Claudio Regala saw to it that her children fully understood why their father had to work thousands of miles away from home. As Claudio told me, "I am very excited when my father comes home. My mother explained my father's work to us since we were kids. She would make us do the boat ride to [a neighboring island], the mini boat. Then she would tell us that our father works on a boat and we will understand it more when we get older." Claudio recognizes the efforts of his mother to bridge closer ties in their family and he accordingly reciprocates by making efforts to reach out to his father. Claudio does not harbor any resentment over the minimal time he has spent with his father but sees this as reason to make the most of the time they do spend together.

Third, children do not fail to notice their fathers' attempts to involve themselves in their lives whenever they are back in the Philippines. Children often wish to reciprocate for these efforts and are more likely to do so when fathers are less authoritarian and instead demonstrate softer qualities that speak of nurturance and emotional care. Efren notices these efforts from his father.

When my father returns, he asks us how we are doing. He asks about our studies. Studies, that is what is most important to him. Then, he sometimes jokes around about our love lives. Whenever he is home, he tries to make up for all the time that he lost away from us. He wants to make up for what he was not able to show us. So he wants to do everything that needs to be done in the house. He wants to do everything. For instance, he wants to be the one to cook. He wants to clean. Everything. He wants my mother to be a queen whenever he is home. Then he is there to serve, to serve my mother and to serve us. That is what he does whenever he is home.

Children like Efren welcome the efforts of fathers to take on family-centered nurturing tasks. Doing so actually allays the fears and insecurities imposed on them by the spatial and temporal distance in the family.

Finally, migrant men who perform distance fathering and do so by incorporating maternal acts of caring and nurturing are more able to ease the gap in transnational families. For instance, Efren's father frequently relays guidance and advice to his children while abroad. His mother explains:

In the school, my co-teachers used to ask me how I could possibly discipline my children in the absence of their fathers. I explained to them that even though their father is working in a vessel, he writes them and sends them advices [sic] all the time. They see how much their father cares about them. For example, there was a student council election and their father, from the boat, sent pages and pages of letters with the speeches for his son. There was [sic] so many. Then my husband would tell me not to hesitate to spend for whatever they need, for instance streamers, billboards. He wants it all to be done regardless of the cost.

Efren's father then proudly interjected that one of his sons served as president of the student council for two years in a row. I noticed that he demonstrated a great deal of knowledge about his children's lives. He can do so because he has expanded his definition of fathering to go beyond the role of breadwinner or stern disciplinarian to include acts of nurturing.

His sons are well aware of his efforts to expand the gender boundary of fathering. They recognize that he tries to keep abreast of their activities and be there as a father through advice and encouragement. To stay familiar with the trials and tribulations of his family, he actually called them at least twenty times a month while working outside the country. Describes Efren:

He would call about 20 times in one month. It's because he said that he did not want to write anymore. We did not have a phone before, but now that we do, he just calls all the time. He reasoned that instead of just spending his money on material things, he would just use the money to call us. Whenever he calls, he just asks us how we are doing and has us tell him what is going on in our lives. Then, that is it. . . . He would call us from the port or sometimes from the boat. He would use the radio. He told us that his bills sometimes reach 50,000 pesos [approximately $1,000].

Efren and his brothers cannot ignore the concerted efforts of their father to stay involved in their lives. Consequently, they go to great pains to reciprocate for his efforts.

The efforts of Efren's father to reach out to his children are quite a foreign experience to most. As I noted earlier, other families usually subscribe to the ideal of separate spheres and migrant fathers accordingly relegate all acts of nurturing to mothers. However, children in father-away families that do not conform to the ideal of separate spheres tend to achieve closer ties, suggesting that families that cross gender boundaries are more likely to form a cohesive sense of family collectivity than those who abide by strict gender conventions. This phenomenon is illustrated in Efren's motivation to study harder for the sake of his father. He describes:

We work very hard for the sacrifices that our dad has given us. I do not want to brag but we are all honors students, ever since when we were in elementary school. It is our little way of paying back our father for the sacrifices that he makes for us abroad. We make up for it with our school awards. He can feel that whatever he is experiencing abroad is worth it. So it is like that. Since we were children, our mother told us that that is the most concrete way we can give back for our father's efforts. We tell him about our achievements in letters.

The most tangible way that children can reciprocate for their fathers' struggles is to excel in school. I found that children whose fathers are greatly involved in their lives tend to find greater satisfaction in school than those who feel distant from their migrant fathers.

However, the high expectations of migrant fathers toward their children can impose undue pressures on them. These expectations have also become a measure of competition among migrant fathers. For instance, seafarers often compare the quality of their children's schooling and boast about their children's performance at school. Efren describes the process: "Whenever my father receives a letter when he is in the vessel, he shares the letters with others. He lets others know about his son's accomplishments. So he is very proud of us. So it is important for us to make him happy. So even though we do not see his personal reaction, we can at least imagine it." This culture of competition filters down to amplify the pressure that fathers impose on their children. It not only poses the danger of raising feelings of inadequacy among those who do not perform well in school, but it also pushes fathers to go overboard with their demands on children. Thus it can lead to the even greater alienation of children in transnational families.

An example of an alienated child is the earlier cited Kiara Billones, who lost all motivation to do well in school because of her father's unreasonable standards of success. Explaining why she feels that migration has not brought her many gains, she states:

I think I lost out in this family situation. In my relationship with my father, he doesn't know and understand what is going on in the house. He doesn't know what you want to pursue in life. So when I think about it, I lost being in this situation. I don't think I gained at all. You first lose by being far away from him. So he can't understand you. Plus, he expects you to major in what he wants. So you don't care about the subject and your grades start to go down. You lose any motivation to study because you are studying what he wants you to study.

Untended emotional distance in transnational families results in mutual disappointments between migrant parents and their children. Neither Kiara nor her father meets the expectations of one for the other. However, they would be more likely to do so if her father would follow the lead of Efren's dad and become more familiar with his children by integrating maternal acts of greater intimacy into his performance of fathering.

Although I provide quite a positive description of the Papelera family, I do not mean to imply that this family is without their set of problems; a gap still does strain Efren's feelings toward his father. Efren explains: "I am often inhibited around my father. Our mother would ask us, 'why are you uncomfortable around your father?' I really do not know why. I just feel like that. I am comfortable talking to him on the phone, but everything changes once we are in front of each other, in person." This indicates that even the closest of families cannot completely eliminate the emotional gap stirred by unfamiliarity. Extended amounts of temporal and spatial distance deny families the intimacy only achieved by the routine tedium of daily life.

Keen on mending the gap that still threatens his family, Efren's father decided to retire from seafaring and to forgo the material security that labor migration has provided his family for many years. Although he has been back in the Philippines for more than a year at the time of our interview, he still notices that his sons are quite inhibited around him. He and his wife express their concern over this rift:

Father: I feel that my sons are inhibited around me. They are shy when it comes to me.

Mother: It's because he does not know them very well. And then his sons do not know him very well. Even now, because for instance, our eldest son leaves at 5:30 in the morning and does not come home until 7 at night. How can they get to know each other then? Then, when he was working overseas, he would only come home for two months at a time. How can he get to know his sons for such a short time?

F: You do not get to know their character very well.

I asked them, "How does that make you feel?" The father answered: "In my mind, I keep on thinking that I would like the opportunity to be close to them, but then you see that they have this fear of you. Then sometimes, you can really see their fear of you. Then when you come close to them, the fear wanes. . . . I am still trying to get to know them." Technically, Efren's father has yet to completely fulfill his duty as *haligi ng tahanan* (pillar and builder of the home). From window screens to flush toilet, their house is still in need of improvement. However, he made a conscious decision to return to the Philippines permanently despite the threat it posed to the fulfillment of his role as the *haligi ng tahanan*. Not only did he forgo his access to the higher wages of seafaring, he now must rely on his wife for their primary income. Her modest salary as a public schoolteacher does not afford them more than the basic necessities of food and clothing. There is little money for leisure for the Papelera family. The drastic material loss brought by return migration is well worth it, though, for Efren's father, who reasons that a solid relationship with his sons is more important than the achievement of greater material security.

Clearly, Efren's father has redefined fatherhood to be based less on the role of provider and be more inclusive of maternal functions. As pillar of the home, he stands as not only a pillar of material security but also a pillar of emotional and moral support. He measures being a "good provider" to include the provision of emotional care and moral guidance. Efren's father can take this step forward only because he is quite secure about his fulfillment of the conventional duties of fathering. During his tenure outside the country, he accumulated enough capital to purchase 1,800 square meters of land. He plans to divide this property equally to accommodate future houses for each of his sons. Thus, it seems it is only the accomplishment of the conventional definitions of fathering that allows Efren's father to challenge them.

*Other Measures of Easing the Gap*

As we see from the family of Efren Papelera, various factors help ease the gap in transnational families. They include the recognition of material provisions, hence the recognition of the fulfillment of the father's conventional gender role; mutual efforts at constant communication; the intergenerational brokering of mothers; the expansion of gender boundaries of fathering to include maternal acts of care; and finally the intimacy gained only by extensive amounts of quality family time spent together.

In this section, I address the work required of women in the process of easing the gap between migrant fathers and their children. The amelioration of the gap is not a one-way street but requires a process of reconciliation that often relies on the arbitration of the mother. Credit the intensive work of mothers to bridge ties between fathers and their children for easing strained relations in father-away transnational families. From this I would argue that the position of mothers as brokers of the family allows them to wield power, as it lends a hand in countering the strains imposed by temporal and spatial distance in father-away transnational families.

The work of intensive mothering pushes both fathers and children to make mutual concessions toward the achievement of closer relationships in transnational families. This labor often begins with the extraordinary efforts made by mothers to ensure that children and fathers stay equally abreast of each other's activities. This work is not easy and requires the patient and meticulous reporting of the most mundane activities that the ordinary person tends to overlook. Ilonah Monticello,[25] the wife of a seafarer and mother of five daughters, illustrates the tediousness of bearing this responsibility when she describes the daily log of activities that she uses to keep her husband informed of the activities of his family:

When my husband is away from home, I am his secretary. I write everything down. I write everything that is happening with the children. I write it in 10 pages, per week. I do this every week. I never miss a week because he might forget that he has a home, a wife, and children here in the Philippines. So I have to remind him always. I tell him how I spend my time. I tell him whenever a child gets sick. He is always well informed. So he is up to date whenever he comes home. So my life is very difficult, but it is worth it.

To retain a high level of intimacy in her family, Ilonah must add to her work of mothering the role of transnational informant. She likewise must keep her children familiar with their father. She does this by regularly telling them stories of his challenges, ordeals, and novel encounters at work outside the country.

Wives left behind often maintain an extraordinarily high, intensive, in my view even extreme, standard of mothering. Adelaida Quilaton, for instance, reminds me of one of those ideal mythical mother figures when she describes her proactive involvement in her children's lives. She describes her daily ritual, one that she regularly reports to her husband, a seafarer for more than seventeen years.

I take lunch to my children every day. The reason is the food. I do not like them to eat food outside. I do not like the risk of them getting Hepatitis B. . . . I take very good care of my children. We are very close to each other. I cannot live without seeing my children every day during lunchtime. I wake them up early in the morning. I cook their food. I am awake by 4 o'clock dawn. We eat breakfast and I have them drink Sustagen[26] and their vitamins. And then I really check their appearance. Some parents, they do not do that, but I do, because I want to raise good children.

The only way Adelaida feels that she can justly reciprocate for the sacrifices that her husband makes working in the isolated setting of a shipping vessel is to act like a super mom. Adelaida reports her intensive mothering activities to her spouse regularly. In so doing, she hopes that he comes to feel that the sacrifices he makes to maximize his earnings are made well worth it by her fulfillment of her own set of conventional duties in the family.

Ironically, it is the efforts of Adelaida to retain the ideal of separate spheres that facilitate the constant communication in her family. Her acts of mothering maintain the high level of familiarity between her husband and children. This mutual knowledge helps ease the gap in her family. As Adelaida explains,

The relationship of my husband and our children is OK. It is because when they were still small, I would show them the picture of their father. They would see it when they were still small. While they were growing up, I would introduce them to their dad through the picture. I would tell them that the man in the picture is their father. Then I explain to them what their father does to support them. I would tell them that their father is a good man. That is the best thing that I could do for my husband. I help my children adjust to their situation. So they can understand what their father is doing. I tell them their father is a good man. I tell them he does laundry. I would tell them that he bathed them when they were younger. I inject in the minds of my children a certain picture of their father. . . .

Then once a week we send voice tapes. The three of us do this together. He writes and we write. It is important that we send a tape every week because for a seaman it is important to have constant communication. It is necessary because they are lonely. I do not send letters but instead voice tapes. We do this at least four times a month, all of us three. It is fun because we turn on the tape when we are eating. It is like my husband is just there with us. So he hears us wash dishes as someone else is talking. We talk to each other on the voice tape and then we pray together on the tape.

By facilitating the close communication of their family, mothers like Adelaida more than compensate for the geographical distance of fathers. One can thus imagine father-away transnational families as a perfect split with the two parties fulfilling each of their gender roles in the ideal of separate spheres, but in a transnational setting.

However, this can also only work if women reconstitute mothering to include conventional male-gendered responsibilities. When it comes to disciplining, mothers for instance cannot follow the old adage of "wait 'til your father gets home," because doing so would delay the disciplining of their children for at least a year or two. Thus, women have no choice but to expand mothering to include this responsibility. They usually do not hesitate to do so. For instance, Generosa Matugas, the mother of the earlier cited Kenneth, describes how she instilled a strong work ethic in her children by making them do housework. As she states,

I told them that I am having a hard time so it is important that we help each other out. I told them that they really needed to learn how to do household work in case their wives do not know how. So it is important that they also learn household skills. I told them that it is not just enough to be able to buy your way out of things. It is also important that they know how to cook their own food. So I started training them when they were still young. I would order one to do work in the garden, another in the front yard, another to the left of the house, and another to the right. Then, they would rotate cooking and washing dishes.

Generosa did not wait for her husband to instill this disciplined routine into her household. Her children also could not protest, as they feared the wrath of their mother.

Similarly, Ida Monticello does not question the ability of her mother to discipline her and her sisters in the absence of their father. She describes:

Our mother is very disciplinarian [*sic*]. When we go to church, when I was three years old, I would like to go around like the other children, but my mother did not allow it. If they sit, we sit, say kneel, we kneel, and pray, we pray. We never talked because if we did, she would pinch us. She is a disciplinarian when it comes to food too. We have to finish everything.

Although mothering expands to include the fulfillment of traditional male gender roles such as disciplining in father-away families, I did also find that fathers hesitate to let go of this designated parental duty completely. As I described earlier, most have a tendency to impose authority and discipline on the members of their households whenever they are at home. To give fathers the benefit of the doubt, I do not assume that they doubt the ability of women to discipline children. We can speculate that enforcing discipline from near or far is one way they can tangibly feel the performance of fathering and, by fulfilling what they think they ought to be doing, accordingly still feel part of the family.

Even so, fathers who successfully let go of disciplining and who are able to entrust mothers with the ability to do so are more likely to achieve stronger ties with their children. Ereno Monticello, the husband of Ilonah, is one such migrant father; he has relegated almost all of the disciplining done in his family to his spouse. His children including Ida recognize and appreciate this gender boundary crossing and value the child-centered quality time they get to spend with him during the little time he has in the Philippines. Describes Ida:

Well, my father only comes home twice in a year. So every time he is around, he never punished us. (Laughs.) Cause, he said that if he would punish us, then how would we look to him? He is never there. So when he comes home, we do a lot of things. He taught me a lot of things. He taught me how to use a gun, go fishing. We do not have a brother and I have interest in technical things. When he comes home, we have a concert at home every night. (Laughs.) He talks to us and he tells us that he loves us. But it is hard to open up to him. We are not that close but he shows you that he loves you. He tells us. . . . So we are always happy. There is a festive mood in our house. Whenever he is coming, mother is cleaning the room, working on our room, and then we are fixing the car. So we are very excited when he comes home. And then when he leaves it is like a silent mood in the house. Like there is a dark cloud. He is leaving.

Having worked outside the country for most of his children's lives, Ereno devotes a great deal of his time to his wife and children whenever he is in the Philippines. This is his conscious way of easing the gap that is unavoidably engendered by the temporal and spatial distance in their family. It is an effort appreciated by his children including Ida.

Without doubt, time spent with a non-authoritarian father enables children to open up more. In contrast to those with authoritarian fathers, children whose fathers incorporate maternal acts in the fulfillment of their parental role look forward to the homecoming of their fathers. They welcome the opportunity to spend greater time with them. For instance, Caridad Candado[27]—like Ida Monticello—spends a great deal of time with her father whenever he is home. She states:

I see the sense of responsibility that my father has despite the fact that he works so far away. He cares a lot for us. Every day, he cooks our breakfast. He wakes us up. Then, he is the one who supports us with our financial needs even though he is only a high school graduate. Then, he is fond of teaching me how to cook. He is the one teaching me how to cook our dinners and breakfast.

By letting go of certain conventional gender roles, fathers do not put at risk their children's recognition of their masculinity. The expansion of gender boundaries does not necessarily make them less of a father but allows them to redefine fathering—perhaps because their masculinity is guaranteed by their economic provisions to the family.

Fathers should cross gender boundaries if only to lessen the gap that strains the ties in their families. Easing the gap is actually the most effective way for fathers to see positive results emerge from their struggle to provide for their children's future mobility via migration. Children who do not feel so much of a gap with their fathers are more likely to be willing to reciprocate for their struggles. For instance, Bethamay Roncesvalles,[28] a twenty-year-old college student whose father has worked as a seafarer for more than twenty years, cannot wait to graduate from college so that she could be in a position to help her family financially. Bethamay adds: "I would really like for my father to stop working outside the country. I just feel like he has been doing it long enough. He has been sacrificing for us for a very long time. So I think that it is about time that it be me who is taking care of him, who is feeding him, and providing for him." Without direct pressure from either her mother or her father, Bethamay aspires to secure a job that will pay enough so that she can not only support her family but also enable her father to retire comfortably in the Philippines. However, she only hopes that supporting her family in the future will not mean that she will also have to make the same sacrifice as her father did and work outside the country.

## Conclusion

Some children are like Bethamay, as they aspire to spend more quality time with their fathers in the future as well as find the means to someday reciprocate for their father's material contribution to the family. Regardless of their gender, these children aspire to achieve a high level of educational attainment in order to secure well-paying jobs that would bring in enough to support not only themselves but also their natal families in the future. It is those who have reconstituted fathering to limit disciplining and include a tempered authoritarianism that see their children aspire to do so. Most children are not like Bethamay, however, but are more like the earlier cited Tonton Ilano, and would rather not spend time with their fathers.

Most children feel the strains of the gap, a gap aggravated by the shortness of their family's time together as well as by the authoritarianism of fathers. Yet despite the gap and despite the heavy disappointments that children feel growing up in father-away transnational families, most do not believe that their families have irreparably broken familial ties, as typical media depictions of their families purport. Acknowledging their own resilience in adjusting to their household, they are the first to defend transnational families. As one child states, "In spite of the distance in miles, we are not broken, because we are bound with love." Another explains, "We are not broken. We still have opportunities to spend time together. Also, there is love for each other. You still have moments shared when you are all there. So you cannot say that we are broken."

Having the experience of living in a transnational family does expand a child's definition of the right kind of family, moving beyond the narrow conventional views espoused in the public sphere. Ida Monticello illustrates this flexibility when she states,

We are entering an age when people go anywhere they want. To say a family is only a nuclear family is very naive. You have to stick together no matter what. Because for practical reasons, you have to go outside and go to another place to find work and support everybody. So because we are not together does not mean that we cannot function as a family. Other people stick together but then they are not good to each other. How can you call them a family then? I think a definition of a family is not whether you are physically close to each other, but it rather should be based on the emotional level of support. You may be in the same house but you hate each other. I would rather be in a different house as long as my family loves each other. Emotional support.

As shown by this defense of transnational families, the ways children understand the family could go beyond the conventional textbook definitions that are inculcated in schools. As described by Ida Monticello, the emotional quality of the family bears greater significance than the physical makeup in children's perceptions of the right kind of family.

In the transnational families of migrant fathers there is a mixed bag of conformity to and dissension against gender boundaries. The easing of the gap requires dissension, for instance forgoing some responsibilities of fathering and passing them on to the mother. Thus we see that the ideal of separate spheres is not and should not be considered set in stone. However, gender boundary crossings in father-away families are limited at best, because the authority of migrant fathers is made indisputable by their role as "good provider." However, mothers do wield a tremendous amount of power in these families, since fathers must rely on the mothers' intensive brokering to ease the gap formed by the families' temporal and spatial distance.

Whether a gap exists or not does not say much about children's attitudes toward transnational families, that is, about whether or not they feel that it is an acceptable household model for raising children. Children with distant fathers, such as Ton-ton, would never leave their children in the Philippines. As he states, "I do not want my children to experience what I had experienced. Like with my father, he does not know how to try to understand me. . . . It is hard." However, children who pride themselves for having attained close ties with their fathers also hold the same sentiments as Ton-ton. One of these children is Erlinda Gaylan, the nineteen-year-old daughter of a migrant worker who first began working outside the Philippines when she was five years old. She states:

I do not want to be separated with my children [sic]. Maybe I can be if they are older but not when they are younger. I really do not want it. I will take them with me wherever I go. Me, I do not want to marry a seaman. See, I experienced what it is like to have a father abroad and it is really different if your father is close to you, next to you.

Most children claim that their families are not broken. They point out that their families are not without close ties and that they can make do with their situation. However, as the sentiments of Ton-ton and Erlinda indicate, making do does not mean that transnational families are the most ideal situation for children. The negative sentiments of children tell us that if given the choice, they still would rather not grow up in transnational household arrangements, but prefer households that allow for greater proximity, time together, intimacy, and familiarity.

# CHAPTER 5

# The Gender Paradox: Recreating "the Family" in Women's Migration

The transnational families of migrant women hold tremendous promise for the transgression of gender boundaries. Women's migration not only increases the economic power of women vis-à-vis men, it also places biological mothers outside the domestic sphere. In this chapter, I interrogate whether such structural rearrangements engender ideological shifts in the family. I do so by examining the gender division of labor in transnational families of migrant women. From the perspective of children and other family members left behind in the Philippines, I look at the work of migrant mothers, fathers, children, and extended kin. In my discussion, I show that the maintenance of transnational families simultaneously questions and retains the ideology of separate spheres. It does so not only due to the occupational segregation of migrant women into care work, but as I establish in this chapter also because the ways that migrant families adapt to transnational households enforce gender boundaries.

This enforcement happens in various ways: fathers minimize their household work; migrant mothers maintain responsibility for nurturing their children; eldest daughters and female extended kin bear the brunt of household work left behind by migrant mothers; and finally extended kin impose social pressure on families to follow gender conventions. This process of gender reinforcement contradicts the gender reconstitution initiated by women's migration. This contradiction sets up a gender paradox: the reorganization of households into transnational structures questions the ideology of women's domesticity but the caring practices in these families maintain this view. Significantly, this paradox mars children's acceptance of the reconstitution of mothering and consequently hampers their acceptance of growing up in households split apart from their mothers.

My discussion begins with an overview of transnational mothering and then moves to the general characteristics of the mother-away transnational households in my study. Then, I examine the constitution of gender in the transnational families of migrant mothers via a discussion of the care practices in these households. I argue that the care received by the children of migrant mothers from afar as well as from up close upholds the gender division of labor, that is, of mothers as "the light of the home" and fathers as "the pillar of the home." The reinforcement of this division of labor inadvertently downplays the non-traditional forms of care that children do receive from either their surrogate parents or from their migrant mothers who must provide a reconstituted form of care from a distance. I found that children themselves sometimes do not acknowledge the care that they receive in the transnational family.

## Transnational Mothering

Numerous studies have identified the increasing phenomenon of "transnational mothering" among migrant domestic workers from various poor countries including El Salvador, Peru, Poland, Sri Lanka, and the Philippines.[1] Pierrette Hondagneu-Sotelo and Ernestine Avila define the process of transnational mothering as the organizational reconstitution and rearrangement of motherhood to accommodate the temporal and spatial separations forced by migration.[2] They found that this arrangement forms new meanings of motherhood; specifically it expands mothering to encompass breadwinning. This process must not be seen outside the context of the inequality of "stratified reproduction," an idea developed by anthropologist Shellee Colen to refer to the power relations between those able to reproduce their families and those who are unable to do so.[3] In globalization, migrant women from the Philippines are subject to inequalities of reproduction, because they often face legal restrictions that exclude the members of their families from host societies whose next generation they are reproducing via their care work.[4] Thus family reunification is not always a choice, and transnational mothering becomes an inevitable outcome of migration.

While the issue of transnational mothering has generated a great deal of attention from scholars of the family and migration, still sorely missing from this burgeoning literature is the experience of children. Families are not homogeneous units; instead, "women, men, and children of different sexes do not experience their families in the same way."[5] However, variations in perspectives on transnational family life remain missing in the literature, as studies continue to focus mainly on the perspective of migrant mothers, but not family members in the country of origin.[6]

Helping amend this gap, anthropologist Michelle Gamburd looks at the cultural transformations engendered by women's migration on family and community life in one Sri Lankan village. More specifically, she asserts that migration forces the rearrangement of household labor in transnational families as it "distribute[s] a portion of women's household chores [including childcare] to men."[7] However, her observation that transnational households still largely depend on the work of female kin suggests that transnational households do not completely transform gender relations. Moreover, she also found that men conveniently avoid housework by drinking or relocating to another area for employment. This finding suggests that a more nuanced process of gender is at work in these families, one that involves a struggle between change and tradition.

Scholars in the Philippines likewise address the cultural transformations engendered by women's migration in the family. Migration scholar Maruja Asis notes that migration poses the risk of endangering the institution of the family, because separation may lead to higher rates of infidelity, strained kin relations, and "wayward" children.[8] However, she is careful to add that the negative consequences of migration to the family are not as extensive as generally assumed by either the media or other scholars.[9] Indeed, the extensive survey conducted for the Scalabrini Migration Center by Graziano Battistella and Maria Cecilia Astrado-Conaco with more than 700 schoolchildren indicates that transnational households do not necessarily result in "severe cases of emotional disturbance nor does it translate into disruptive behavior."[10] Even so, they acknowledge that the "single most important finding in the survey is that the absence of the mother has the most disruptive effect in the life of the children."[11]

This finding does not necessarily suggest that the children of migrant mothers are without care. As Battistella and Astrado-Conaco acknowledge, fathers provide care and extended kin do as well, even if only to a somewhat limited degree. Our survey of 228 schoolchildren in transnational migrant families supports their conclusion. For instance, 61 of 94 children of migrant mothers who participated in our survey claim that they "never" feel unloved while only two "always" do. The rest categorize feeling unloved either "sometimes" or "seldomly." Likewise, 61 children of migrant mothers "never" feel neglected and only three "always" do. Even though fathers and kin left behind in the Philippines do not neglect children, we should acknowledge that their efforts rarely reach the extent to which the wives of migrant men compensate for the geographical distance of their husbands from their families. The efforts of these mothers, which I described extensively in the previous chapter, seem to pay off. Of the students participating in the school survey, 43 of 124 children of migrant fathers are in the top ten of their class, while only 16 of 94 children of migrant mothers are in the same position.

## Gender and Care

My discussion of care practices in the families of migrant mothers continues the discussion in previous chapters of gender boundary work in the institutionalization of transnational families in the Philippines. I looked earlier at gender constructions in the public sphere, but I now focus specifically on caring acts in the family. This discussion of caring practices in the family builds from sociologists Sarah Fenstermaker and Candace West's discussion of "doing gender" as well as Judith Butler's on gender as performance.[12] According to them, gender is a construction, produced in repeated actions that constitute concealed rules and norms. If so, the possibilities for gender transformation, as Butler notes, are to occur in action as well, specifically in the deformity of the repetition, or in the failure to repeat what one ought to be doing.[13]

Institutional rearrangements make this all the more possible, as Barbara Risman establishes in her study of American families, Gender Vertigo.[14] According to Risman, gender is a structure and is not only constituted in practices but created in individual, interactional, and institutional levels and must be tackled on all three levels to generate genuine transformations in society. Looking to "unpack" the social process by which gender transforms in the family, Risman argues that a change in one of these levels could lead to change in the others. Constituted in practices, gender establishes cultural parameters and institutional norms so as to socialize and shape identities. In turn, this controls and limits the practices that constitute gender. As Risman states, "Gender expectations are socially constructed and sustained by socialization, interactional expectations, and institutional arrangements. When individuals and collectivities change socialization, expectations and institutions, the gender structure changes."[15] According to Risman, transformations in socialization, institutional arrangements, or expectations could destabilize norms to the point of engendering structural changes in the family. For instance, change could occur if women overcome their economic dependence on men, if society redefines domesticity and breadwinning, *or* if society includes nurturance in notions of masculinity.[16] One example Risman provides is the case of single fathers, who begin to attach "mothering" attributes to their construction of gendered selves when forced to do child care. The case of single fathers indicates that institutional transformations could lead to individual (i.e., identity) transformations, which then break cultural parameters and institutional norms that socialize and shape identities.

Applying Risman's argument, the critical mass of women's emigration from the Philippines instigates institutional rearrangements that promise gender shifts in the family. However, as I establish in this chapter, I found this not to be the case. The ideology of women's domesticity retains its stronghold in the family. As I show, this happens because care practices in the transnational families of migrant women retain this ideology. I found that practices do not always conform to institutional structures or abide by institutional reorganizations. Instead, practices could produce contradictory constructions of gender. Moreover, contradictions between the constitution of gender in practices and its construction in institutional organizations may actually spur resistance to change and consequently retain gender inequities in institutionally rearranged families.

## Mother-Away Families

In the Philippines, scholars assert that women are less likely to leave their families than men are.[17] They make this claim on the basis of government figures, which indicate that more than half of women migrants are unmarried (approximately 56 percent) whereas the majority of male migrants are married (72 percent).[18] However, we cannot assume that unmarried women are without children. In actuality, I found unmarried women with children to be overrepresented in migrant communities, including in my current sample of thirty children of migrant mothers.[19]

The maintenance of the transnational families of migrant mothers generally relies on the work of extended kin. The survey of schoolchildren reflects their dependence. Only 20 of 94 children of migrant mothers expect their fathers to make sure they are ready for school, whereas 34 rely on either a grandparent or aunt to do so. In contrast, as I established in the previous chapter, the households of migrant fathers are more nuclear in structure.

For instance, 87 of 123 children of migrant fathers report that their mothers make sure they are ready for school every morning while only three report that extended kin do this work for them.

The guardianship of children also reflects the wider extended kinship base of the households of migrant mothers. While almost all the children of migrant fathers who participated in this study consider their mother to be their primary guardian, for the children of migrant mothers the guardians are more varied. Most children of single mothers (16) usually identified a female relative as their primary guardian, but some of these children are in contact with their biological fathers. In my sample of children who do have contact with their biological fathers (22), only 11 children identify their father as their primary guardian. Notably, most of them also name another female relative as a co-guardian.

The families of migrant mothers also represent more varied class backgrounds than do the majority of the stable middle-class families of migrant fathers. This heterogeneity is reflected in the occupations of migrant mothers, which include low-skill, semi-professional, and professional jobs, and the diversity of their destinations, which encompass nations in Asia, the Americas, Europe, and the Gulf region. In contrast, the fathers of the children in my study were mostly seafarers. The jobs of the fathers left behind in the Philippines also reflect the wide range of their class status. Nine of their fathers hold low-wage jobs, for instance as drivers and security guards. Others hold higher-status occupations (e.g., college professor, military officer, and research scientist). Notably, only two fathers are jobless in the Philippines.

## The Division of Labor in the Transnational Family

Regardless of duration of separation or class status, the children of migrant mothers face greater difficulties than do the children of migrant fathers. As I noted, this fact is not necessarily due to the inadequacy of care in mother-away transnational families. Instead, this is because the provision of care in these families reinforces the conventional division of labor in the family. These practices perpetuate conventional notions of mothering among children and concomitantly establish a standard of care that disagrees with the reconstitution of mothering initiated by the rearrangement of their households.

In this section, I show that children face difficulty accepting the reconstitution of mothering in transnational families because caring practices in the family reinforce the ideology of women's domesticity. I describe the care work performed by fathers left behind in the Philippines, migrant mothers, eldest daughters, and finally extended kin. Care practices reinforce "normative gender behavior."[20] As a result, the provision of care in mother-away transnational families perpetuates conventional notions of mothering. This conflicts with the reconstitution of mothering initiated by the rearrangement of their household, specifically the expansion of mothering to include breadwinning and the removal of the mother from the domestic sphere. Notably, the destabilization and internal contradiction in gender that we find in the transnational families of migrant mothers do not lead to drastic transformations in the gender ideological beliefs of children. This suggests that gender could persist against the transformations enabled by its destabilization in the institutional rearrangement of the family.

## Absentee Fathers

According to children, fathers do not perform much caring work in the transnational family of migrant mothers. Findings in my survey of schoolchildren reflect this emotional distance. Only 18 of 94 children in mother-away families identify their father as their favorite family member, while 61 of 124 children in father-away families view their mother as their favorite family member. Generally, fathers do not increase their share of the household responsibilities in spite of the greater economic contributions of migrant women to the family. Thus, mother-away transnational families face a "stalled revolution" similar to the one identified by Arlie Hochschild in the 1980s among dual income earning couples in the United States.[21] Men do not respond to the increase in women's labor market participation by increasing their share of household responsibilities; instead, they leave women burdened with the "second shift." Similarly, men in the Philippines still expect migrant mothers to nurture their children even from a distance. This is true regardless of the added earnings of women and even despite their *greater* earnings than men's.

Moreover, men forgo the physical caring responsibilities that migrant mothers surely cannot perform due to their geographical distance by passing this work on to other women in the family (for example, daughters, domestic workers, or extended kin). For instance, none of my interviewees report that they relied on their father for their primary care as adolescents. Instead, other women cared for them. By rejecting women's work, fathers left behind in the Philippines do their share of gender boundary work in the family: they resist the redistribution of labor forced by women's greater economic contributions to household income and thereby help keep the conventional gender division of labor intact. This gender process works against the physical removal of mothers from the domestic sphere.

Notably, the more tenuous the father's position is in the labor market, the more likely he is to reject women's household work. Most fathers are like the physically present but emotionally absent father of Isabelle Tirador,[22] who leaves most of the caring responsibilities in his family to domestic workers, extended kin, and his oldest daughter. His youngest daughter Isabelle cannot help but express her frustration over this: "It's annoying. I cannot help but feel resentful, because I feel abandoned. It's because my father is here but he does not care. He does not support us, especially when it comes to school." The division of labor in Isabelle's family still follows gender conventions. Despite her greater earnings and despite her geographical distance, her mother is still more responsible for nurturing her children than is Isabelle's father. As Isabelle describes, "my mother is the one far away but she is the one who is close. It's because I think that my father is there physically but he does not care. He does not get involved with us. My mother, even if she is outside the country minds our business." In contrast, Isabelle's mom telephones her children regularly to stay familiar with the routine of their lives.

The inability of men to do care work hurts children, especially if families are without much support from extended kin. When the transnational families of migrant mothers maintain the division of labor of men as breadwinners and of women as nurturers, children often find themselves without much emotional support. Because children usually acknowledge the struggles that migrant mothers face at work outside the country, they hesitate to additionally burden migrant mothers with their emotional needs. Thus, they tend not to share their troubles with their mothers but instead keep their problems to themselves. One of these children is seventeen-year-old Nieva Lacuesta,[23] who was left under the care of her father and without much kin support after the death of her grandmother. Explains Nieva:

My mother calls and asks me if I have any problems, if I have a boyfriend. (Laughs). But I do not share with her any serious problems. I try to take care of them on my own. I try to carry the burden of solving my problems on my own, because I cannot help but think that she is already so far and I should not be there to only give her more problems. So, it's better if I carry my problems on my own than bother her all the way there.

Most children would not even consider sharing their worries with their fathers, I assume because many fathers have not made themselves available to provide emotional comfort to their children.

I do not mean to imply in my observations that men turn their backs completely to the needs of their children. Some men do care. The fact that some men clean and cook in the absence of women tells us that women's migration opens up the possibility of gender transformations in the Philippines. However, few men do housework. Moreover, when men do housework, they seem to downplay such work as temporary. The father of two daughters, Filipe Lacsamana states: "It's back to normal when she comes home. She does her work again. She cooks."

Among the children of migrant mothers, I met only four children whose fathers do a high level of women's work such as cleaning and cooking for the family. These men share certain characteristics that secure their masculine identity despite their performance of women's work. First, they all had a concrete house built for their families prior to the migration of their wives, including members of poorer families, who utilized government-subsidized housing projects to obtain a home in a less-populated area. Thus, fathers are not likely to be threatened by the greater earnings of women if they are secure in their masculine identity as the pillar of the home. Second, all the men who are likely to perform women's housework, surprisingly, carry a gun at work. If not in the military, they are police officers or licensed security guards, suggesting that men are less likely to feel emasculated when doing the dishes if they have a job that projects the masculine attributes of authority, control, and power.

If they have neither of these male attributes, men left behind in the Philippines are not likely to expand their household work to include female gendered activities. However, these attributes do not guarantee that men will do more housework. For instance, while men who have had a house built prior to their wives' migration are more likely to do housework than those who do not have a house, they are also more likely to afford to hire domestic workers. In my area of study, domestic workers receive on average the equivalent of US$20 a month for live-in employment. Most families I interviewed could afford more than one domestic worker to help run their households. Thus, the achievement of the masculine identity of being the *haligi ng tahanan* more than likely also translates into an ability to "buy out" of the work technically relegated to them in women's migration. This surely was the case for the college professor, stockbroker, research scientist, and business owners left behind by their wives in the Philippines whose children I interviewed. None of them were responsible for housework despite the absence of their wives.

The presence of domestic workers and attainment of a concrete house are not the only strategies used by men to avoid the expansion of male gender boundaries to include women's work. I also found that fathers tend to disappear once their wives migrate. They relocate to another area of the Philippines and in the process completely avoid the possibility that women's work would become part of their daily routine of family life. Rather than doing such work, they prefer to pass it onto other women, including paid domestic workers. This is the case for professional men, who mostly live elsewhere in the Philippines and not with their children. Nine children in my sample, more than half of those whose fathers were still involved in their lives, told me that their fathers worked elsewhere in the Philippines. These men include a stockbroker, a fabric machine operator, and a security guard in Manila, a college professor in Cebu, a fruit grower on the island of Mindoro, and a business proprietor on the island of Romblon.

By disappearing, men seem to resist the reconstitution of gender in the family that is instigated by women's migration, perhaps because they still insist upon essentialist notions of gender. According to one father I interviewed, men discipline and women care. Carmelo Ledesma, the earlier cited military officer and father of two whose wife works as a nurse in Saudi Arabia, explains:

The role of the father is to discipline the child. Right?. . . . While the father also is the one who will provide for the financial needs of the family, then the mother takes care of their emotional needs. That is why it is good that their mother always calls them. She gives them guidance, and she does this even if it is very expensive to talk on the telephone. But it is very important for my sons to hear from their mother, to get advice from her, or just even hear her voice. This is necessary to uplift them.

In the Ledesma household, like in most mother-away households, the migrant mother still bears most of the caring work assigned to women as the "light of the home," as she is expected to "uplift" the emotions of her children, even cross-nationally by telephone.

When I asked Carmelo about his feelings regarding the extension of his wife's responsibilities to include those traditionally defined to be his, he responded without hesitation that he did not mind her greater earnings as long as she did not contest the gender hierarchy in their household. As he stated, "I am fine with that matter. This is because my wife is submissive. . . .

I mean, it is not always me who makes decisions. We often reach an agree-ment. But if we do not agree, then . . . it is my decision." The Ledesma household, it seems, has yet to witness a gender revolution inspired by the greater earnings of his wife outside the country.

However, Carmelo Ledesma was also one of the four men who extended their work to include that of women. Unlike most fathers, he cooks and he cleans his comfortable three-bedroom home in the city center. He provides more care than other fathers of the children in my sample do, but he, like the three other fathers who provide care, does it in a way that does not expand definitions of fathering to include acts of nurturing. As his son told me, he runs his household as if it were a "barracks" with his sons as "soldiers" in boot camp. As a military officer, he acts with authority and his sons know that they must obey his command at once. He makes "intensive disciplin-ing" part of the daily routine of his household so as to instill his masculin-ity against the threat posed by the earning power of his wife.

Men do the boundary work of keeping gender conventions in the family intact, it seems. They maintain the gendered division of labor in the family by limiting the work they do to that traditionally assigned to men. Hence, they reject any work perceived by themselves or others to be women's work, at the risk of leaving this work undone. For one example, as we saw in the case of Nieva Lacuesta's family, men avoid any responsibility for their chil-dren's emotional security.

I do not mean to imply here that the institutional rearrangement of the household has not forced some men to take on certain aspects of women's work. One man who has had to is actually Nieva's father, Lurenzo Lacuesta. Lurenzo had to quit his job as a security guard in Manila upon the sudden death of his mother. Prior to her death, she had been responsible for the care of her two grandchildren, since her daughter-in-law was working as a do-mestic in Israel. Against his will, Lurenzo now found himself saddled with all of the domestic chores required to care for his eleven-year-old son.[24] But despite having to take on domestic responsibilities, Lurenzo still does not think of himself as doing women's work; instead, he considers his house-work to be an extension of his duties in the military. He told me, "This is just the skills I learned during my military training as a soldier. I was trained to do this work as a soldier." We can imagine that Lurenzo as a soldier can only perform domestic chores that do not involve the emotional labor of af-fection. This surely limits the extent of care work that his eleven-year-old son and seventeen-year-old daughter receive in the absence of their mother.

However, men in the absence of women sometimes cannot completely avoid female-gendered care work. Involved are usually mundane tasks that are often overlooked; however, they carry with them in their performance far-reaching gender implications. They include grocery shopping, attending meetings at school, and doing various activities in public with their children, such as walking them to school. These activities underscore and make visible the absence of the mothers. Although men seem to resist the changes forced by the institutional rearrangement of their households, they sometimes find themselves with no choice but to adjust accordingly to their new household arrangements. This fact leaves us with a glimmer of hope that transformations in gender ideologies could eventually follow suit in the transnational families of migrant mothers.

## Martyr Moms

Contrary to media portrayals of their families, mothers do not abandon their children upon migration. They do not even pass down all of their gender responsibilities to other family members left in the Philippines. Instead, they not only reconstitute mothering by providing acts of care from afar, but also often do so by overcompensating for their physical absence and performing a transnational version of what Sharon Hays identifies as "intensive mothering."[25] They attempt to maintain intimacy from a distance. Thus, while men reject the work of nurturing the family from up close, migrant women struggle to nurture their children from a distance. Thus, in fact migrant mothers are responsible for ensuring the security, both economic and emotional, of their children. In this section, I illustrate how children recognize the ways that mothers nurture them from a distance. I show that children are more likely to accept the reconstitution of mothering in transnational households if they perceive that their mothers are *grieving* in the process of mothering them from afar. I found that the children who believe that their mothers suffer in migration have less difficulty adjusting to their transnational family life than those who do not.

From the descriptions given by their children, most mothers could be described as "super moms." I was often struck by the close involvement of transnational mothers with their children. In sharp contrast to migrant fathers, who tend to reduce their relationship with children to monthly remittances, mothers personalize their ties. To achieve some semblance of intimacy, they make regular communication part of the weekly routine of transnational family life. For instance, the mother of Cheryl Gonzaga[26] never fails to call her three children at three o'clock every Sunday afternoon. This routine has been in place since she migrated fourteen years ago and has yet to be disrupted by her relocation from one country to the next, from Bahrain to the United Kingdom and most recently to Hong Kong. Cheryl's mother not only contributes a larger share to their household income, she also maintains a greater level of involvement with her children than does Cheryl's father. Once a low-wage worker, he now runs their family business—a fish pond located on a far-away island—and returns only once a month to see his children.

The caring work of Cheryl's mother does not go unnoticed by her children. Cheryl elaborates on this work:

Sometimes she calls three times a week. Especially if one of us (she and her two brothers) is sick, then she will call one day, then she will call again a day later. Sometimes she is busy. So she will only call on Sunday at 3 P.M. That is why we are all home on Sundays. This is when she checks up on us. She asks us if we are happy with our food. She is kind of strict. When it comes to our food and our health, she is strict. So it has been a couple of years since we stopped using MSG. We don't use that anymore because it is supposed to be bad for our health. . . . With MSG, I get a headache. According to my mother, MSG causes it. She would know, because she is a nutritionist.

In addition to providing health advice, she also plans their menu for the week. She talks to her children about their school, their teachers, and activities outside the classroom. She even gives them advice on their school projects. Thus without question she continues to perform her role as "mother" and tries to achieve intimacy in separation.

Migrant mothers achieve intimacy in other ways. Many rely on the cellular phone service of international text messaging to communicate with their children on a daily basis. Some children told me that they even wake up to biblical messages from their migrant mothers every morning. They receive doses of "my daily bread," as they called them. Text messaging is one system that mothers use to make sure that their children are ready for school in the mornings. Many are also like the mother of Cheryl Gonzaga and set up a routine of calling at particular times during the week. Other mothers send a *balikbayan* box every two months or so.[27] In the boxes would be clothes, goods, and toiletries such as soap and lotion that they purchase for their children. Finally, many mothers resort to dropping a letter in the post for their children on set periods of the month. Some children told me that they know when they can anticipate a letter from their mother.

Rodney Palanca,[28] for instance, has learned to expect a letter from his mother in the middle of each month. Describes Rodney: "I am excited to receive letters from my mom every month. I expect the letters to arrive on the 15th of each month. When it does not get there on the 15th, I worry by the following day. Then I cannot help but think that my mother must have forgotten about me." Such set routines enable transnational families to achieve a semblance of intimacy. Set routines establish expectations, such as those expressed by Rodney, and with these expectations come established standards of care for mothers to gain intimacy in the family.

Surely the achievement of intimacy brings rewards of greater closeness in transnational family life. The children of migrant mothers are less likely to feel a gap in intergenerational relations than the children of migrant fathers. Moreover, they are also more likely to experience "family time" in spatial and temporal distance. As Edriana Lingayen,[29] whose mother works as a nurse in Saudi Arabia, explains, "Family time is a little expensive for us because it entails an overseas phone call. But there are times when my mother and I share a laugh. Like once she bumped her head on a glass door while in a hurry. She could not stop laughing when sharing that story. Then she asks how is my boyfriend. That is what you can call family time." Moments of intimacy achieved in a transnational terrain do not go unnoticed by the children of migrant mothers.

Because of such experiences, many children easily describe their relationship to their mothers as "very close." For instance, Ellen Seneriches,[30] whose mother has worked as a domestic worker in New York for more than a decade, did not hesitate to describe her relationship to her mother as close:

We communicate as often as we can, like twice or thrice a week through e-mails. Then she would call us every week. And it is very expensive, I know. . . . My mother and I have a very open relationship. We are like best friends. She would give me advice whenever I had problems. . . . She understands everything I do. She understands why I would act this or that way. She knows me really well. And she is also transparent to me. She always knows when I have problems and likewise I know when she does. I am closer to her than to my father.

Although Ellen only lives three hours away from her father, she actually communicates more frequently with her mother and feels closer to her mother than to her father.

By nurturing across great distances, migrant mothers counter public opinion regarding their abandonment of children. However, they also go against the reconstitution of gender initiated by the institutional rearrangement of the family. They not only reinforce conventional gender norms, but do it in a way that heightens the gender expectations of children. Based on the stories of children, I found that migrant mothers seem to overact their performance of gender, as if to compensate for their physical absence from the family. The family of the earlier cited Carmelo Ledesma serves as a good example. According to the oldest son, Benjamin,[31] his mother acts as a super mom both at home and abroad. From afar, she calls on the telephone frequently and "advises her children on the best course of action" for "all" the problems that they encounter during her absence. Up close, she performs mothering even more intensively. Every single day that she spends in the Philippines, she "brings life to the home" by cleaning, serving breakfast in bed, preparing afternoon snacks without fail, and sitting by her children's side as they complete their homework.

Suggesting that these caring acts fulfill his expectations of mothering, Benjamin states with much longing in his voice: "When my mother comes home, she more than makes up for her ten months of absence. She makes up for all that is missing in two months. Everything is in order whenever she is home." Because mothers like Benjamin's nurture so intensively, children easily develop the unrealistic view that mothers have a natural inclination to always shower them with acts of love. Children often carry the "unnatural" expectation that mothers should perpetually be available to meet their domestic and emotional needs. The overperformance of mothering additionally promotes a traditional division of labor in the family: fathers discipline and mothers nurture. As Benjamin continues,

Emotional support is what you miss out on, because your mother is the one who knows more about what to do when it comes to the opposite sex. She knows how you should handle things like because a man is different from a woman. I often want to get advice from her about women. . . . And also the TLC [tender loving care] inside a house is what you look for when she is gone. A mother gives love differently.

As a result of their unrealistic gender expectations, in general children resist the reconstitution of mothering initiated by migration, reject the flexibility of allocating some of their mother's conventional duties to other members of their family—even women—and finally expect their mothers to be their primary nurturer despite all of their financial support. With these expectations, shortfalls in family life are bound to trouble the children of migrant mothers, regardless of the tremendous efforts that mothers make to achieve intimacy in the family. For instance, Cheryl Gonzaga complains, "there are still some difficulties." In particular, she has a hard time accepting the inaccessibility of her mother, who she expects should always be available to her.

Children accept their transnational family life with less difficulty if they do not doubt the love of their mothers. Significantly, the care provided by kin and fathers does not determine whether children find transnational family life adequate. Instead, it is the continued nurturing of mothers that sets apart children who find less dissatisfaction in the transnational family. Children frequently identified the love of their mothers based on their mothers' projection of emotions. Specifically, mothers must abide by "feeling rules" that follow the social order of gender in the family. Coined by Arlie Hochschild, "feeling rules" refer to the direction of emotions guided by social and ideological conventions.[32] In this case, mothers must use emotions to counter the threat posed by the distance of time and space to their fulfillment of conventional notions of mothering. The children I interviewed took note of how their mothers expressed grief, sorrow, and hardships and used these emotional displays as a way to measure their mothers' remorse over her decision to impose the geographical distance on their families. They do so in order to establish that the reconstitution of mothering is not a choice but instead a sacrifice.

Thus, mothers must demonstrate to their children that they suffer while they economically provide for them. For instance, the mother of Floridith Sanchez[33] elicits sympathy from her daughter when describing her work in Taiwan as one of continued hardship. As Floridith tells me, "My mom told me that she still works even when she is sick." "How does that make you feel?" I ask. "I cry." "You cry?" "Out of pity." Mothers continually remind their children that they struggle a great deal at work. Children often view this as a motive to reciprocate for their struggles. States another daughter of a domestic worker, Theresa Bascara: "My inspiration is my mother, because she is the one suffering over there. So the least I can do is do well in school."

For the earlier cited Ellen Seneriches, it is also the image of her suffering mother that compels her to reciprocate for her mother's income contributions:

Especially after my mother left, I became more motivated to study harder. I did because my mother was sacrificing a lot and I had to compensate for how hard it is to be away from your children and then crying a lot at night, not knowing what we are doing. She would tell us in voice tapes. She would send us voice tapes every month, twice a month, and we would hear her cry in these tapes.

Only with the image of her suffering mother can Ellen acknowledge the difficulties and sacrifices that her mother has had to make to be a "good
provider." This knowledge appeases the resentment that as Ellen mentioned
frequently arose in her before she understood that her mother's migration
had been a sacrifice for the entire family. The image of the martyr mother,
one that resonated throughout many of my interviews, shows that children
find comfort in their mother's grief over not being able to nurture them directly. The children of migrant fathers, however, were a different case; emotional security does not mandate an image of a suffering dad. Instead, the
view of their father as the "ultimate breadwinner" is enough to give them
the security of their father's love.

Children also determine maternal love based on the grief projected by
mothers over their forced separation. As Rudy Montoya[34] describes,

How would you describe your relationship to your mother? Very close. Because we want to see each other. Even on the phone, she would say that she
really wanted to see me. She misses me. She would say that I must be so
much bigger now and that she wanted to see how I looked like. I can just tell
in the way she talks to me, the way she says it on the phone. She gets very
emotional.

Rudy's mother is no exception. Regardless of the division of labor in the
transnational family—that is, whether fathers do housework or not, or
whether extended kin lend a hand or not—most children I interviewed feel
secure about their mothers' love based on their mothers' projection of grief.
However, this strategy of determining affection fortifies the gender boundary
contested by the institutional rearrangement forced by women's migration.[35]

The attempts of women to reconstitute mothering come into resistance
from family members in the Philippines. Without doubt, the rigidity of gender constructions in the family increases the caring work of migrant women,
as their economic contributions and the care provided by kin cannot over-
shadow the nurturing work children still expect of their mothers. The children impose stringent care expectations on migrant mothers. Mothers cannot just provide material security and demonstrate some semblance of
familiarity. To establish their love, migrant mothers must also nurture them,
care for them, and guide them from a distance, and often they must grieve
when doing so. To guarantee the erasure of doubt that looms over their love
for their children, mothers must suffer in the process of nurturing their
children from a distance. The role of "martyr mom," however, naturalizes
the maternalism of women and contests the gender reconstitutions insti-

gated by women's migration. To act as a martyr is to do the boundary work of keeping the care of the family the responsibility of women.

The image of the martyr mom is possibly an extension from the impression in Philippine public discourse that migrant domestic workers are martyrs of the nation. As Vicente Rafael explains, the label of "new heroes of the economy" that is bestowed upon migrant domestic workers extends from the image of their martyrdom and specifically the sacrifices (including the risk of death) that they endure to secure a smooth flow of remittances to their families and the nation.[36] In the Philippines, heroism as embodied in the national hero Jose Rizal is embedded in the messianic aura of martyrdom.[37] Like the national hero, migrant domestic workers evoke an "ethos of mutual caring, the sharing of obligations (*damayan*), and the exchange of pity (*awa*)."[38] Hence, the construction of domestic workers as heroes is subject to their suffering and likewise suffering is required for migrant women to be good mothers. While migrant fathers do not have to suffer to be a good provider, migrant mothers do. Thus it is gender that figures prominently in the construction of migrant women as "modern-day heroes" and "martyr moms."

## Dutiful Daughters

In his research on immigrant children in Los Angeles, Abel Valenzuela, Jr., observed that girls carry far more responsibility than boys in the maintenance of immigrant families.[39] They translate; they do advocacy work in financial, medical, and legal transactions; and they act as surrogate parents to younger siblings. As surrogate parents, the eldest children must assist younger siblings with schoolwork, help them get ready for school, baby-sit for them, and feed them. Doing these tasks frees the immigrant parents of time and allows them to increase their hours of paid labor and maximize the productive labor needed to reproduce their families. This strategy of familial cooperation extends to a transnational terrain. Daughters more so than sons enable migrant mothers to work, in this case not just outside the home but outside the country, for the financial benefit of the family. Dutiful daughters, as I refer to them, do more housework than fathers, who prefer to pass this responsibility on to other women in the family.

Among those I studied, families neither discriminate by age nor protect the youngest of children from doing housework. Eldest daughters do housework even in their adolescence. The large representation of eldest daughters in my voluntary sample of young adult children suggests that they have much to say about their family life and the responsibilities accordingly placed on them by their mothers' migration. Many assist in the daily maintenance of the household to reciprocate for their mother's efforts to provide for them economically. Generally, eldest daughters fall into two groups: those who resent this work and those who do not. The former tend to be those who do housework without the help of fathers or domestic workers, and the latter are those with fewer responsibilities because of the help of other family members.

The work of eldest daughters is often burdensome. Daughters experience a radical transformation in their daily routine and a sudden reduction in their quality of life. This drastic change is especially hard for daughters who come from poorer families that cannot afford to hire paid domestic workers, especially if the men do minimal work in the home. One such child is Barbara Latoza, a nineteen-year-old college student, who had to take care of two younger brothers at the young age of thirteen after her mother relocated to Taiwan.[40] She describes the change in her routine.

I had a very difficult time when my mother left. I am the oldest and I had to take over her work at home. I had a hard time adjusting and juggling my studies with my housework. I was still quite young. I was only in the seventh grade. . . . Before my mother left, I did not have to do anything when I got home from school. All the work at home would be done. Sometimes, I would play with my friends before I headed home. Then, my mother would call me at around 6 P.M. She would help me with my homework. Well, that stopped. (Laughs.) That stopped. . . . Now, my grades are not so good anymore. It is because sometimes I cannot study because of all the housework that I have to do. See, my father does not do anything at home. For example, as soon as my brothers are all at home, he leaves and will go to a neighbor's house and just start drinking and gambling. (Laughs.)

Interviewer: So who cooks dinner then?

Barbara: Sometimes I do it. By 4 P.M., when I get home from school, I start cooking. I clean too. But a big help is my auntie. I eat lunch at her house. She cooks lunch for my brothers and me.

I: And your father? Does he ever cook for you?

B: Never. Never.

While fathers could possibly assist in the care of their children, unfortunately they do not always lend a hand, especially if female kin are available to help with the household. As illustrated by the case of Barbara, many daughters look at their added work as a burden that results in overload.

Other children are more fortunate than Barbara and benefit from the help of other relatives. These children are less likely to grieve over their added responsibilities. Ellen Seneriches, for instance, became a surrogate mother when she was only ten years old, and her mother left her with three younger siblings to work in New York City. Unlike Barbara, Ellen views her extra work quite positively. She sees it as a way of reciprocating for the sacrifices made by her mother for the collective good of the family. As Ellen told me:

It was a strategy, and all of us had to sacrifice for it. . . . We all had to adjust, every day of our lives. . . . Imagine waking up without a mother calling you for breakfast. Then there would be no one to prepare the clothes for my brothers. We are going to school. . . . I had to wake up earlier. I had to prepare their clothes. I had to wake them up and help them prepare for school. Then I also had to help them with their homework at night. I had to tutor them.

Asked if she resented this additional work, Ellen replied: "No. I saw it as training, a training that helped me become a leader. It makes you more of a leader doing that every day. I guess that is an advantage to me, and to my siblings as well."

Unlike Barbara, Ellen benefits from the assistance of a paid domestic worker, who at the very least did the laundry for her family. Moreover, her father assists in the care of his children. For instance, he does the grocery shopping every week, unlike Barbara's father. The assistance of others surely pays off. Unlike Barbara, Ellen's schoolwork did not suffer as a result of her added household responsibilities. Viewing her added responsibilities as positive lessons in life, Ellen believes that these responsibilities allowed her to develop leadership skills. Notably, her high school selected her as the first ever female commander of its government-mandated military training program. Moreover, she graduated at the top of her class in both high school and college. Now a medical school student, Ellen hopes to someday follow her mother to the United States.

Indeed, most daughters report finding they gain skills from their added responsibilities. For instance, some daughters appreciate the opportunity to learn how to budget a household. In the absence of their mothers, they take responsibility to pay the wages of domestic workers, the utilities, and the groceries. Additionally, they learn how to complete the process of school enrollment on their own, securing without guidance the required vaccinations and course registration. They learn to make decisions with minimal intervention from adults. Moreover, they also do this work for their younger siblings. However, the trust placed in them sometimes results in conflict. Daughters find themselves with power over extended kin who depend on their mother's earnings. They also struggle against the temptation to abuse their mother's earnings by splurging. As is to be expected of teenagers, many but not all have done so. Overcoming such temptations is one of the lessons they learn from early independence.

Eldest daughters face greater challenges when their mothers migrate than when their fathers do. Likewise, sons find themselves with extra responsibilities when their fathers leave the country, but their workload does not come close to that of daughters such as Barbara and Ellen. This clear-cut gender division of labor across generations has implications for the socialization of children, since the gendered division of task assignments to children usually molds household work patterns in a later age.[41] Without doubt, men's rejection of particular household tasks such as budget management, cleaning, cooking, and child rearing reproduces gender norms that socialize children in the everyday. The performance of this work by daughters further enforces this socialized pattern of gender against its forced reconstitution in mother-away transnational families.

## Overextended Kin

In the United States, numerous studies have repeatedly concluded that men's household participation has only slightly improved over the years, despite the remarkable increase in the rate of women's paid employment.[42] Likewise, as I have shown, the dramatic departure of mothers from the Philippines to work overseas has not resulted in an increase in men's household work in transnational families. Examining dual wage earning couples in the United States, sociologist Harriet Presser identifies as a solution and advantage for women the maintenance of different work schedules from their male partners. She notes that their absence from the home forces men to increase their share of household work. As Presser observed, "The more hours husbands are not employed during times when wives are employed, the more likely husbands are to do housework that is traditionally done by females, breaking traditional gender expectations."[43] However, this is certainly not the case in the Philippines, where the disappearance of women has not resulted in men's doing a greater share of the household work. The reason is that other women besides daughters cushion men from taking on more household responsibilities. I specifically refer to female extended kin, many of whom feel the cultural pressure to act as guardians to younger kin who are at risk of being without maternal guidance in transnational families.

The passing down of care work among women is exemplified in the linguistic terminology that the children use toward female extended kin. Many children refer to their aunts or grandmothers as "mother." They would distinguish one as "mommy" and the other as "mama" or sometimes "*nanay*," which means mother in Tagalog. Indeed, children are well aware of the extensive care work provided by female relatives. They acknowledge and credit their efforts by name and title. As one child told me, "I do not refer to my auntie as 'auntie,' but instead I call her 'mama' and my mother, I call her '*mamang*.'"[44] Many children do the same, including Roan Leyritana,[45] who kept on explaining himself when he spoke about his mother and aunt during the course of our interview. Roan said, "I am much closer to my mommy, oh, I mean to my auntie, than to my mother." Indeed, the aunt does more than her fair share of mothering work for Roan. Undaunted by the distance, twice a month she travels by bus for over ten hours from her home in a remote province to visit Roan in the city center. She does so to keep track of his performance in school. Notably, the efforts of surrogate fathers in father-away families to provide care in lieu of the absence of migrant men do not even come close to the efforts of female kin in mother-away families. Thus, they do not earn the title of "father" from children in migrant families.

In my previous research, I established that the migration of women usually results in the international division of reproductive labor. By this I mean that women pass down their care responsibilities to less and less privileged women in a global terrain. However, this process of the "care chain" not only frees men of household work but also results in tensions and strains between women.[46] Indeed a relationship of inequality between women exists, not just one of mutual cooperation against patriarchal constraints. As migrant domestic workers free their women employers to pursue more rewarding careers outside the home, women in the Philippines likewise free migrant domestic workers to do the same. This process is not without costs. While the women in the middle of the care chain suffer from having to raise their children from a distance, the women at the end of this chain have to endure the hardship of overwork.

Female kin left behind in the Philippines are often bitter and frustrated over their unwanted responsibilities. One such woman is Claudia Hizon, the guardian of two college-age girls, who often sighed heavily in exasperation when talking to me about the caregiving responsibilities given to her by her cousin, who works as a nurse in the United States. Claudia describes her role in the lives of her two nieces to be "like a mommy"; she feeds them, washes their clothes, and cooks their food every day. She states: "I do whatever they need to be done. They always call out to me when they need something, just me." Aggravating Claudia's resentment is the minimal work done by the children's father in the Philippines, who, while not divorced or even separated from the migrant mother, remains emotionally distant from his children. Claudia says with frustration: "The father does not work. For example, when something is broken in the house, he often cannot help, not even with the clothes hanger. He does not do anything at all in the house." Although she would rather return to her home province, Claudia stays and looks after the children left under her care. She, not the father, drives them to school. She, not he, attends their school meetings. Finally, she is the one whom they run to for any of their emotional needs. Claudia tells me that she does not do this work out of financial necessity but out of worry for the welfare of her nieces, who she fears would be neglected if left under the care of their father.

Another aunt in a similar situation is Quirina Belleza, who helps look after the three children of her brother and his migrant wife. Quirina does not rely at all on the remittances sent by her sister-in-law in Hong Kong, because she herself receives a greater monthly allowance from her husband, who works as a seafarer. Still, Quirina does a significant amount of household work for her brother's family. As she tells it,

Before, I would wonder why I was willing to carry them all on my shoulder. I would ask myself that question. Why do I make all these sacrifices? I would ask that too. I only have one child, and yet I make all these sacrifices. Oh, sometimes I would just be overwhelmed by the work. There would be piles and piles of clothes that I need to sort. I would need to clean after so many people. I have to cook before a certain time. I would cook lunch right before noon. When they all get home, all the food is cooked. My schedule would be, I would take my child to school, then I would go to the market, then I would cook. Then after the food is cooked, I would take food to my child at school. But the food for Phoebe and her siblings would be there waiting for them.[47] I take care of everything. The only thing their mother needs to do is give them an allowance. Then, I take care of all the needs in the household. I do this because I do not want the studies of the children negatively affected, which it could be if they had household responsibilities at home.

Quirina helps run two transnational households—one initiated by her husband's migration and the other by her sister-in-law's departure for Hong Kong.

In the first household, she performs "intensive mothering" for her son. For instance, she prepares a home-cooked lunch for him to eat at school every day. This practice is quite common among the wives of migrant men, who do so as a way of reciprocating for the efforts of their "ultimate bread-winner" husband. In addition, Quirina helps maintain the transnational household of her brother, who plays the most minimal of roles in his children's lives. In the latter transnational household, the division of labor is distributed only between women. The mother provides for her children economically while Quirina, as an aunt, looks after their other caring needs. With the burden of nurturing multiple households, Quirina's extended family unit clearly has left her with too many responsibilities.

Extended kin, as we see with the cases of Claudia Hizon and Quirina Belleza, do not always welcome their new responsibilities with open arms. Instead, they view this work not as a responsibility that is rightfully their own, but as a burden and cultural expectation that they have no choice but to fulfill. Unfortunately, they meet this cultural expectation not always without strain. I spoke to thirteen female guardians who assist in mother-away transnational families. Many of them are aunts who have families of their own or grandmothers who feel they are too old to raise children. Notably, most of them sobbed during the course of our interview. They are often overextended by their duties and responsibilities to care for the children of migrant parents. Thus, it is dangerous for us to romanticize extended kinship ties and celebrate their work as a symbol of collective family unity, one that goes against the heteronormative structure of nuclear households. In assisting migrant mothers, female extended kin bear the brunt of persistent gender inequalities that free men of household work and in the process they perpetuate the responsibilities bound to them.

If they are so overworked, why do women left behind in the Philippines still provide care? Significantly, not all extended kin need the financial support of migrant women, a fact that lessens their incentive to take on additional family responsibilities; however, it does not necessarily deter them from doing so. The aunt of the earlier cited Roan, for instance, is a business proprietor and landowner not in need of the monthly remittances of her sister, Roan's mother; even so, she takes on the role of surrogate mother in his life. Regardless of financial incentives, cultural expectations of familial cooperation seem to dictate the caring practices of extended kin. The male guardian of Gailanie Tejada, a twenty-three-year-old college student whose parents both work in the United States, explains: "I never really chose to be anyone's guardian. Just that, you know, this responsibility had to fall on my lap because I was here most of the time. And it was like, hey, you know, they are my nieces. I just feel responsible. . . . but it wasn't really my responsibility because I was not their parent."

In addition, the affinity among women that develops from resentment over how little work men do also motivates female kin to provide care in transnational families. They pity the children, whom they see as those who unduly suffer from the lack of male efforts to reciprocate for the work of migrant women. As Quirina Belleza, the earlier cited guardian and aunt of Phoebe Latorre,[48] exclaims in frustration, "You cannot help but feel resentful. He should be taking care of his children, especially in the evening when they come home from school. He should make sure their clothes are ready for school the next day. He should make sure they finished their homework. He should be attending their meetings at school." Phoebe's father does not do any housework at all but spends most of his time drinking and gambling with neighbors next door. Because of his irresponsibility, Quirina finds herself saddled with mothering responsibilities that she does not see as rightfully hers. As she herself clarifies, "This responsibility is not mine." Clearly, she resents this duty and blames the weight of it on her brother's neglect of his share of household work.

However, she finds herself with no choice but to do this work, because of sentiments of *pakikisama* (mutual obligation) in the family. She acknowledges that Phoebe and her siblings would not be able to go to college without the earnings of their mother and that she as an aunt would not want to see the efforts of her sister-in-law to go in vain. She goes on to state:

You would not be able to help but feel pity, at the situation. Even if you try to stop yourself from taking on the work, you can't do it. You will do the work. How could the mother look after them when she is so far away? You cannot get that out of your mind. You cannot help but think that you have to do the work so she sees her children are okay after all these years. They would be bigger when she gets home. And she will see they are okay and she will know that you are the one who took care of them for her.

Certainly, sentiments of mutual cooperation among extended kin motivate female kin to assist in the maintenance of transnational households. As Quirina adds, "Among me and my siblings, the problem of one is the problem of all."

But even if they are willing to do care work, extended kin would not sacrifice their own personal happiness to meet family obligations. Aunts usually ease their workload upon marriage. Phoebe's aunt, who gives greater priority to her own son than to her brother's children, did so. However, the fact that female kin would be less able to provide care does not necessarily mean that fathers would do more work. Quirina complains: "It is a lot harder now that I have a husband. So I was telling their father that he should be the one disciplining his children, especially now that I have my own family. And I do not really know what he is doing all the way in Cabugao [a distant province]."

The fact that female kin in the Philippines free men of housework leads to contradictions of gender in the family, because it conflicts with migration's promotion of gender boundary crossings. Gender contradictions emerge not only because mothers pass down their caring work to other women, which maintains the ideology of their domesticity; in addition, they emerge out of the social pressure imposed by extended kin to conform to normative gender behavior. As sociologist Judith Lorber observes, "people go along with the imposition of gender norms because the weight of morality as well as immediate social pressure enforces them."[49] In the transnational families of migrant mothers, extended kin tend to assert the normativity of conventional nuclear families. Extended kin are usually part of non-transnational nuclear families or are of the older generation. Scott Coltrane observed that families embedded in dense kin networks face greater social pressure to conform to gender conventions.[50] This I found to be true among the families of migrant mothers.

Extended kin tend to label the families of migrant mothers as not the right kind of family, especially those of single mothers, who make up a considerable portion of migrant women. For instance, consider one interviewee, Lourdes Dumangas,[51] the only child of a single mother working in the United States. Lourdes's grandmother describes the circumstances of her birth as a "*disgrasya*" or "accident," an "embarrassment" that she and her husband feel should not be talked about publicly. Similarly, the extended kin of Rudy Montoya, also a child of a single mother, hold to the ideal of the nuclear household and consider Rudy to be more prone to deviant behavior despite the care that they provide him. His uncle states: "I thank God that he really cared for [Rudy]. That he did not indulge in drugs, not indulge in juvenile delinquency. . . . Based on my observation, an illegitimate child and those children without parental guidance [i.e., children in transnational families] are prone to such kind of vices. This is because nobody guides them. So, they resort to some vices, which lead them to destruction." Extended kin like Rudy's uncle often romanticize the care that biological parents provide children. They consider the substitute care that they give to be an insufficient replacement of parental love. Thus, they assume that children in non-nuclear families are naturally more prone to deviance.

In other instances, I found guardians questioning the ability of fathers to nurture their children. Voicing her disapproval, the earlier cited aunt Quirina Belleza, for instance, asks in judgment and disbelief: "Can you believe that it is only the father who manages the home? *Is that wrong?* A man is different." Extended kin do not hide their disapproval of transnational and other non-traditional families from the children they are caring for, who do take note of their opinion. As Nelida Yarra[52] states, "My aunt blames my mother for my father's failures in life."

The gender conventions projected by extended kin most likely perpetuate the "stalled revolution" that confronts the outmigration of women from the Philippines.[53] The aunt of Phoebe Latorre, for instance, sees the caring work that she reluctantly performs on behalf of her sister-in-law as work that cannot completely replace what Phoebe's mother herself could provide for her children. Mirroring the views of Phoebe's aunt, children tend to have greater care expectations of their mothers than they do of their fathers, even if the fathers remain in the Philippines. Thus, mothers seem to face pressure to nurture their children directly despite the distance, because violating gender boundaries of mothering risks stigma and the judgment of kin.[54]

## Conclusion

In this chapter, I've described the caring work of various members of the transnational families of migrant mothers. To capture the essence of their care work, I refer to them as absentee fathers, martyr moms, dutiful daughters, and overextended kin. Absentee fathers only do the most minimal of care work. Conversely, martyr moms do more, but they often mourn in the process of doing care work from a distance. By mourning, mothers portray that they would much rather be at home with their children then earning a living outside the country. This picture often helps their daughters cope with the burden of taking on most of the housework that the mothers have left behind in the process of migration. Dutiful daughters, as I refer to them, do more housework than their fathers do. Finally, extended kin provide a great deal of care to the transnational families of migrant mothers. Yet, I found that extended kin are not without resentment of their responsibilities. In fact, they tend to be overextended, doing more work than the fathers, who usually provide only the bare minimum of care. In reconstituting the family's division of labor, fathers tend to pass on the caregiving responsibilities of children to other women, including daughters, extended kin, and even the migrant mothers themselves. This is done at the expense of women, as men's freedom from this work strains relations between women, particularly causing tensions between the overworked daughters and female extended kin, who often need to hear that migrant mothers are suffering, too.

The transnational families of migrant mothers embody contradictory constructions of gender. Migration places women outside the domestic sphere and increases their income-earning power. Moreover, the geographical distance imposed by migration helps denaturalize particular mothering acts, making them doable by men and other women in the family. Nonetheless, the caring practices in these families also recreate conventional gender ideologies that seem to be more fitting of modern nuclear families, thereby contradicting the gender ideology promoted by the family's transnational arrangement. Unfortunately, the contradiction of gender that embodies the transnational families of migrant women does not necessarily destabilize the gender structure. It also does not necessarily engender the formation of more egalitarian gender relations in Filipino families. Instead, the internal contradictions of gender, as I show more extensively in the next chapter, may reinforce the ideology of women's domesticity as they could exacerbate the emotional difficulties of children. I illustrate in the next chapter that sentiments of abandonment dominate children's views about their intergenerational relations with their migrant mothers. This is so for children whose mothers nurture them from a distance, children whose extended kin provide care, and children whose fathers are present in their lives. To ease these problems, family members frequently reinforce traditional gender ideologies, and in the process fail to adapt ideological views that support the reconstituted form of mothering imposed by migration.

Institutional rearrangements thus do not necessarily instigate gender transformations. Indeed, my discussion of caring practices in the family indicates that practices do not always conform to structures or abide by institutional reorganizations. In the case of transnational families, contradictions of gender fuel negative perceptions of migrant mothers and hide the degree to which children do receive care. This tells us that gender expectations could still guide practices so as to slow down the changes enabled by institutional rearrangements.[55] This is certainly the case in the transnational families of migrant mothers, whose members confront social pressure from community and kin to recreate the traditional family against its reorganization. The backlash against these families, and men's resistance to the changes encouraged by the rearrangement of their households, tells us that hegemonic beliefs win over the possibilities for change that emerge from the internal contradictions of gender in the family.

# CHAPTER 6

# Gendered Care Expectations: Children in Mother-Away Transnational Families

The problems children identify in mother-away families include a lack of intimacy, feelings of abandonment, and a commodification of mother-child bonds. Although they are sources of real emotional injury for children, we should not merely accept these problems at face value. We should understand and tackle them in the context of the social conditions that shape them, one of which is the gender paradox of a simultaneous encouragement and discouragement of gender boundary crossings.

As I established in the previous chapter, paradoxes of gender do not necessarily result in a contradiction of views that ruptures gender belief systems. They may also exacerbate the social pressure on members of transnational families to uphold gender boundaries and recreate the "family" in daily practices. Not immune from such pressure, children whose mothers migrate uphold even stauncher moral beliefs about the family than those of other children in migrant families. These children uphold standards of mothering that maintain gender conventions, including the need for mothers to nurture them in close geographical proximity. The high value given to keeping women inside the home raises the expectations of children of migrant mothers to an unrealistic level, unavoidably leading them to a sense of disappointment and a feeling that care in their families is inadequate.

In this chapter, I argue that the challenge for transnational mothers to conform to gender norms, which they inextricably contest spatially, aggravates the difficulties encountered by their children. It seems that the more that transnational families diverge from the conventional nuclear family, the more problems children have to confront. This observation extends my previous discussion on emotions and gender in transnational families.[1] I had argued that gender and its boundaries aggravate the emotional difficulties of the children of migrant domestic workers. Building on this idea, I now situate the emotions of children in relation to practices of caring work in the family.

This chapter begins with a discussion of the gender parameters on which children base their standards of care. I establish that the care expectations of children mirror those of a child in a conventional nuclear household with a stay-at-home mother and breadwinner father. Thus, migrant mothers are often left in a no-win situation, their geographical distance from their children making it nearly impossible for them to meet the children's care expectations. I next describe the difficulties faced by children in the context of their notions of gender. I conclude with a discussion of how the work of fathers in the home, as well as a greater acceptance by the community of non-nuclear households, can help facilitate the ideological acceptance of the reconstitution of mothering in transnational families.

## Gender Boundaries in Mother-Away Families

The children of migrant mothers express greater problems regarding their transnational family life than the children of migrant fathers do. Hearing parts of my interviews with the children of migrant mothers, one could easily have assumed that they have received no care at all. In various ways, they talk about the inadequacy of care in their families. Children whose mothers not only send a monthly remittance but also call once a week claim that they have been "abandoned." Children whose aunts help them with their homework almost every night allege that they received inadequate guardianship. Generally, children uphold biological-based views on mothering, and because they do they believe that it is impossible for mothers to provide care from a distance. Moreover, they insist that the work of extended kin, even including those whom they call "mom," does not adequately substitute for the nurturing acts performed by biological mothers.

Children underplay the quality of care that other kin could provide them, arguing that, at most, extended kin could share only what children consider "obligatory" and "reluctantly performed" care, such as feeding, clothing, and providing them with security. Roan Leyritana, the seventeen-year-old son of a migrant worker of more than eleven years, who was introduced in Chapter 5, exclaims: "What is right is for [my mother] to be by my side." He continues, "The love that I received from a father and mother was not enough. I received a lot of love from my aunts and my grandmother, but that was it." Roan grew up in a close-knit family. His aunt took an active role in his parenting—walking him to school every day, meeting with his teachers, helping him with his homework, and generally spending much quality time with him while his mother toiled as a domestic worker in Kuwait. Nonetheless, the care that he received was not enough for Roan, even though his mother also visited him quite frequently in the Philippines, because of Roan's belief that his aunt would naturally perform acts of mothering with less emotional attachment than his mother would. Although he has yet to experience the same intensive caring acts from his mother that he has received from his aunt, Roan assumes that the acts of walking him to school, helping him with his homework, cooking him breakfast and so on must just *naturally* be better performed by his mother. Thus, Roan—like other children—presumes the naturalness of mother-child bonds.

Similarly, the affection of fathers is believed not to be interchangeable with those of mothers. For instance, Phoebe Latorre states: "I do not know if I could identify the love of my parents when I was growing up. We should have grown up with her [i.e., the mother]. Then, she would have been the one taking care of us, of our needs."

Interviewer: And your father? Doesn't he live with you? Did he take care of your needs?

Phoebe: Sort of, but surely the way a mom takes care of you is different from the way a father does. Isn't that right?

Children often assume that the division of labor between mothers and fathers is natural. Fathers discipline and mothers nurture. Fathers provide financial stability and mothers ensure emotional stability. Not surprisingly, Phoebe still wants her mother at home, regardless of the fact that her mother left behind an alcoholic and jobless husband to work in Hong Kong, calls frequently enough to know the weekly routine of her children, has taken on the role of "pillar of the home" by building a house for her family, and finally has financially supported all of her children through school.

While migration's reconstitution of mothering entails the expansion of the duties and obligations of mothers, the efforts of migrant mothers to redefine mothering do not always meet with recognition. Rosette Cabellero,[2] a nineteen-year-old whose single mother works in Qatar, recognizes the material gains her family receives from migration. As she tells me, "We were able to have a house built. Then, we were able to buy appliances." Rosette, whom I visited in her home three hours from the city center, lives in a modest cement home with her blind grandmother, who has been her primary guardian since her mother departed for the Gulf region. According to Rosette, their new home, even though it is still without flooring, is a far cry from the bamboo hut that formerly stood on their land. Despite the visibility of the material gains that the migration of her mother has extended to their family, Rosette still considers mothering received from a distance to be "not enough."

As she poignantly told me, good mothering requires constant nurturing. When I ask her to elaborate on what she meant, Rosette says: "I want to touch her, touch her hands, hug her, kiss her. That is what I want." She continues: "What I want is, for example, what I see with other children. I see their mothers get frantic whenever they get hurt. They rush to their child's side, apply ointment on the wound. On my own, I do not get that attention. Then your mother should also brush your hair. You do that on your own without her." Children expect mothers to perform acts of the most intensive mothering. In fact, the expectations described by children like Rosette reflect picture-perfect moments of a mother and child bonding, a kind of intensive nurturing not expected or received by some children growing up in the proximity of their mothers. However, the longing for such moments of intensive mothering among children like Rosette also suggests that what are easily overlooked and insignificant gestures of affection in everyday life are starkly absent in the lives of children in transnational families. This tells us that the children of migrant mothers are denied daily acts of nurturing from those who they assume are their rightful caregivers.

The care expectations of children such as Rosette undeniably follow a grid of gender conventions. Children generally expect to feel the emotional labor of their mothers, much more so than they do that of their fathers; yet, in most cases, only the intimacy achieved in the daily routine of family life—which is denied transnational families—can provide such reassurances of love. The care expectations of children such as Rosette reflect this desire to be nursed by their mothers. Without doubt, using physical intimacy, or moments of togetherness, as a measure of the quality of life in the family places mothers and their children in a no-win situation; nevertheless, I found that a great number of children do so.

These remarkably high care expectations haunt the families of migrant mothers and burden women as they toil in other countries. Mothers may provide for their children economically, but not to the extent that it would free them, even if only partially, of the responsibility to nurture the family.

Expressing the shortfalls of distance mothering, Marinel Clemente asserts this "lack" in her mother's love when she states:

My mother's love was not enough. I would have wanted her next to me, so that I could feel her love. I feel it, but only a little bit. I know she loves me because she is working hard over there. She is working hard so that we could have everything we want and everything we need. Even when she is sick, she continues to work. . . . But still, I want her to be with me here every day. It's because since I was small it was only my grandparents showing me love. She was not here.

Children recognize the economic contributions of their mothers, but they do not accept this form of care, which clearly steps outside of gender boundaries, as a rightful form of mothering or a kind of mothering that frees mothers of the responsibility of nurturing their children in proximity.

As I noted earlier, these children are not likely to accept a reconstituted form of mothering, one that redefines mothering to be that of a "good provider," because their moral beliefs regarding the family tend to be stauncher than those of other groups of children. For instance, they have a less flexible definition of the "right kind of family." This view is reflected in the earlier cited comments of Theresa Bascara, who holds in high regard the conventional nuclear family with a father and mother, which she considers the norm as opposed to her "un-whole" family. She states: "A family, I can say, is whole if your father is the one working and your mother is only staying at home. (Pauses.) It is OK if your mother is working too, but somewhere close to you, not somewhere far away." Theresa's views on the family contrast quite sharply with the more flexible definition given by the children of migrant men. Despite receiving care, either from extended kin or from other surrogate parental figures, children of migrant mothers idealize the conventional nuclear family more so than other children. This is the case for the children of either single or married migrant mothers.

One of these children of a single mother is Binky Botavara,[3] the daughter of a domestic worker in Los Angeles. Binky asserts that a "mother's love is just different." She elaborates:

The image of the mother is different from the father's. No one could ever replace a mother's love because the role of the mother is really different. See, it's like the father can never completely portray the role of a mother. It's really different. The love we can get from a mother is really different.

Interviewer: What do you mean?

Binky: The mom?

I: Yes, what image do you have of a mother?

B: It's because my mom understands us emotionally. A mother is everything and the father is different. I mean they are not very emotional. In contrast, a mother gets everything, even the smallest things. You just feel their affection naturally.

Sentiments such as those held by Binky illustrate the ideological stranglehold of the modern nuclear family among members of the transnational families of migrant mothers. Many believe that mothers nurture and do so naturally. Not surprisingly, the children of migrant mothers are more likely to describe their families as "broken," which is a term often used in Philippine public discourse to refer to the "deficiencies" of non-nuclear households. I would point out, however, that families tend to be "broken" not through lack of care but because the transnational rearrangement of their households threatens the organization of gender in society.

## *Abandonment and Other Emotional Insecurities of Children*

Children of migrant mothers entertain feelings of abandonment more so than the children of migrant fathers. This is the case among the children of married mothers whose husbands do not reciprocate for the economic support of their wives or ex-wives. It is also true among the children of single mothers, even if extended kin shower them with love.

Nineteen-year-old Nilma Loberiza,[4] the daughter of a stay-at-home dad who does not contribute much work to the family and a migrant mom who labors in Saudi Arabia, has one wish, which is for her mother "to come home." As she tells me, it is because "so we feel it." When I asked her "Feel what?" she responded, "We feel as children what it is like to be with our mother." The story of Nilma and her family mirrors those of Phoebe Latorre and many other children. Her mother emigrated from the Philippines ten years earlier to do domestic work in Saudi Arabia, leaving three children. They are now all college graduates except for Nilma, who is still enrolled in school, under the charge of an alcoholic and jobless father but also under the care of a grandmother and aunt. In the last nine years, her mother has returned to the Philippines only twice.

While surely aggravated by the infrequency of her mother's visits, the melancholy sentiments of Nilma are not caused by the absence of care in her life. Her aunt acts as her second mother, and she talks to her mother at least once a week. Nilma additionally recognizes the difficulties that her mother has faced with her employers, who refuse to give her mother vacation time to visit her family in the Philippines. Yet the case of Nilma tells us that recognizing the financial contributions of mothers to the family, understanding how work demands limit the ability of mothers to spend greater time with their children, and acknowledging the security provided by trustworthy kin do not override a child's idealization of the care and love provided by a mother. This idealization could be influenced in part by the fact that Nilma's father, like most of the other men whose children I had interviewed in the Philippines, has not taken a significant amount of responsibility for the work left behind by his migrant wife.

The longing for greater intimacy raises the question of what the children imagine they are being denied by the physical absence of their mothers from the Philippines. Without doubt, the children seek familiarity with their mothers. However, they also seek to achieve an assumed household normativity, the "proper" order of gender, and with both of these, they assume, naturally will come familiarity as well as guidance and care. To be part of a transnational family is not to be normal. This assumption underlies most descriptions of the family by children of migrant mothers. As Rocil Relocio states,

I have a lot of problems. Like sometimes, especially when you are still young, you need to have your parents around, right? You know that it's different. You see that other kids are growing up with their parents. You often wonder how it would feel like to have your mother by your side. . . . I need her. You just know it's different. She's not there and all I can do is write to her or call her.

In longing to reunite their transnational families, children seek to capture an idealistic scenario of the nuclear household with the return migration of mothers.

Yet, it is not only a nuclear family that children are denied in migration, but more significantly the greater familiarity that one could only achieve from moments of togetherness. For instance, Theresa Bascara, who identifies time to be the one thing most lacking in her relationship with her mother, asserts: "I can say that there is still something lacking. It's like, there is something missing in our relationship." What is it? I ask her, and she answers: "Time. It's just that is missing and lacking in our relationship." By achieving greater time together, Theresa hopes to achieve greater familiarity. She continues: "Telephone calls. That is not enough. You cannot hug her, kiss her, feel her, everything. You cannot feel her presence. It's just words that you have. What I want is to have my mother close to me, to see her grow older, and when she is sick, you are the one taking care of her and when you are sick, she is the one taking care of you." For Theresa, opportunities to provide small acts of care in moments of togetherness would fulfill her desires of family life. Moreover, the familiarity of seeing each other "grow older" is what she feels migration denies her family.

Another child sharing her sentiments is Lourdes Dumangas,[5] the seventeen-year-old college student. Her mother has worked as a nurse in New York since 1982, and Lourdes fears that she and her mother will never be close. As Lourdes sadly recounts, "It is very hard to fix. Maybe it was possible ten years ago, but now 17 years later. . . . What if I follow her to the USA next year? It's not like you can assume that you can establish a bond, fix the bond in one year, because seventeen years is a very long time. She did not see me grow up." The infrequency of her mother's visits to the Philippines without doubt aggravates Lourdes's negative impressions of transnational families. Unlike most other mothers not restricted from travel by an undocumented status or reasons of financial hardship, the mother of Lourdes has returned only once to the Philippines. Yet, like other women, it is the stigma of single motherhood that deters her from returning more frequently.

As the cases of both Theresa and Lourdes demonstrate, the children of migrant mothers are more likely to hold feelings of abandonment than the children of migrant fathers, partially because they spend less time together. As I noted in the Introduction, fathers return on average at least once a year but mothers usually only once every two years. However, it is not only the factor of time that enforces the greater adversities felt by the children of migrant mothers; there is also the double standard of care expectations in the Philippines. From the children's perspective, fathers can establish their love and support simply by sending monthly remittances and interspersing them with customary telephone calls. In contrast, mothers must maintain the most intimate involvement in their lives. These different expectations designate more emotional work for migrant women, who must make more of a concerted effort to demonstrate their love to their children. However, the unrealistically high standards of care work placed on migrant mothers are so difficult for them to meet that even the most cared-for children, for instance Roan Leyritana, still question the love of their mothers. Just on the basis that they receive mothering from afar and not up close, they cannot help but develop feelings of abandonment. As Roan tells me, he often wants to ask his mother: "Do you love me, Ma?"

Mothers must do it all, I could not help but think during my interviews with many of their children. I remember Rudy Montoya, the nineteen-year-old college student whose single mother works in Hong Kong to support an expansive extended clan. During our interview, Rudy frequently contradicted himself and interchangeably described his relationship with his mother to consist of "abandonment" and at the same time of the "deepest love." Rudy recognizes his mother to be more than a "good provider" for his family. He tells me:

As I was growing up, I realized that she is the best, that I would never replace her for anyone. I realized that if she did not work abroad, I would have no hope for my life. She sent me to school. She makes sure that all of my needs are taken care of. She really wants to satisfy all of my needs. She really gives me everything, and tries to fulfill all my needs and make me happy. And it is really important to her that I complete my education. That is what she tells me over and over again, how important it is that I study, that she works in Hong Kong for my sake. She tells me that all the time.

It seems that his mother tries to allay his fears of abandonment by frequently reminding him of her financial provisions to the family and by communicating with him regularly.

Yet, despite recognizing the economic contribution of his mother, Rudy still also views himself as having been abandoned and says that his mother should have provided him with better care. As he insists, "Before I had told you that my mother really loves me, yet you could say that my mother abandoned me, because it is just right that she is the person with you as you are growing up. She is the person who should scold you. She is the person who should give you advice." For Rudy, his extended kin's support and his mother's efforts to provide him with distance mothering cannot completely diffuse his feelings of abandonment, making it hard for me not to think that gaining the full security of maternal love is nearly impossible for children in the transnational families of migrant women. Rudy's mother surely has scarcely abandoned him; it seems more accurate to say that these children struggle not so much with their mothers' abandonment, as with their mother's abandonment of the "proper" order of gender.

Holding onto the most conventional notions about the family, children identify the lack of time together as the most egregious aspect of transnational family life. They do so regardless of the efforts of mothers to maintain open and regular communication with them, which, as I had noted in the previous chapter, ironically also reinforces the idealization of stay-at-home mothers. Greater frequency of returns also does not seem to ameliorate the problem significantly. Thus, mothers who visit the Philippines every year still confront the pressure to spend more time with their children. However, we can safely assume that they face this problem less than mothers who have had less opportunity to return home. Even so, a mother who is able to and does visit her children regularly may still be defined as as much of a "bad mother" as someone who seldom visits.

Notably, extended durations of separation do not mechanically result in feelings of abandonment. For instance, acts of intensive distance mothering could diffuse this threat. This is the case for twenty-one-year-old Ellen Seneriches, who at the time of our interview had not yet seen her mother in nearly eleven years. Despite this long separation, Ellen says she does not feel abandoned at all, not because of the physical support of kin or the care of her father, but because her mother manages to always "be there." As Ellen describes:

I realize that my mother loves us very much. Even if she is far away, she would send us her love. She would make us feel like she really loved us. She would do this by always being there. She would just assure us that whenever we have problems to just call her and tell her. (Pauses.) And so I know that it has been more difficult for her than other mothers. She has had to do extra work because she is so far away from us.

Ellen herself recognizes the extra work mothers must do to compensate for their distance. It is an expectation that does not exist for migrant men, whose migration does not question the "proper" order of gender in the family.

With abandonment come feelings among children that migration denies them the guidance of their mothers, whose attention undoubtedly is diverted to other families in the new world reproductive order. Children often feel jealous of their mother's wards. One such child is Floridith Sanchez, the eighteen-year-old daughter of a domestic worker in Taiwan. Expressing her frustration, Floridith states: "It's irritating. I get jealous. I feel these kids are so much better off with my mother taking care of them than me her real child left alone here. But my father tells me that if she was not doing that then we would not have any money." Floridith is not alone in her sentiments. Many children feel that they lose love due to the diversion of their mother's care. Moreover, the emotional absence of fathers also cannot help but aggravate the frustrations of children.[6]

With their families directly shaped by the gendered political economy of globalization, children of migrant workers are forced to make certain sacrifices. For instance, they are forced into maturity and independence, which are responsibilities they do not always welcome. This is the case for Nelida Yarra, the eighteen-year-old college student, who complains about the independence she must practice without her mother nearby. Explains Nelida:

It's like I feel sorry for myself. I feel sorry for myself that I do not have a mother next to me, every time that I have a problem. I cannot be with her. I cannot talk to her. Or sometimes I cannot seek her advice. Of course, I did not feel what it is like to be parented by her, agghh, mothered by her. It's hard, very hard. You are forced to be your own mother. You become responsible. No one needs to tell you that you are too young to have a boyfriend. . . . You also try to act like everything is ok. So everyone thinks that even without my mother I am ok, but the reality is deep down I am not.

Holding onto ideal constructions of mothering, Nelida believes that mothers must always be there for their children, yet migrant mothers clearly cannot always be there.

With the view that mothers need to be there, children such as Nelida can easily claim that they do not receive sufficient guidance from their family. As she continues, "Of course, I lost the opportunity to receive advice from my mother. I lost out on that, plus the memories that we rightfully should have from being together. The good memories and also the opportunities that I would have grabbed if there were someone guiding me, explaining the process to me." I asked her if she could give me an example, and she replied: "Yes, if she were here, then I probably would be sexy, because she does not like me to be fat." I could not help but smile hearing Nelida's comments. I don't believe Nelida is fat, but I consider her comments to refer not solely to her weight, but more generally to her confidence level over her physical appearance, which she believes would not be so low if she received more reassurance about it while growing up. Not denying the losses incurred by children in women's migration,[7] sentiments of receiving "not enough" care in the absence of intimacy must be understood within the rubric of globalization but also in the context of gender boundaries. The fact that the families of migrant mothers question conventional gender norms aggravates the emotional losses of children.

## The Commodification of Mother-Child Bonds

The labor migration of women pushes the gender boundaries of mothering, spatially placing women outside the home, and extending the duties of women to include those historically relegated to men; yet, as I have tried to show in this chapter, children resist gender border crossings in their families. In this section, I address the difficulties that children face in balancing their acceptance of the economic support of mothers with other forms of caring work that they still expect from them (e.g., emotional and physical support). My discussion focuses on the ways children accept their mother's economic contributions to the family.

The expansion of mothering to include providing for the family economically does not necessarily reduce the other caring responsibilities of mothers. This is partly due to the fact that migrant mothers are not really breadwinners but are so only by default. I addressed in an earlier chapter how mothers usually leave the country in the most desperate of situations. They are either impoverished, abused wives, or single mothers. Unlike migrant fathers, women, at least according to their children, do not leave the Philippines for adventure or career opportunities. This rationale makes women's migration more palatable to children, as it keeps gender boundaries of "good mothering" intact.

However, the economic urgency of migration alone does not guarantee that children will recognize the economic contributions of their mothers to the family. Migration is not an easy choice for women because according to the established gender boundaries of the family it translates into women's abandonment of their responsibilities. Hence, I found, the child easily questions the motives behind the mother's decision to choose labor migration as a strategy of family survival, even if the family had been fairly poor prior to migration. Without doubt, providing economic security to the family is one of the most tangible ways that transnational mothers can provide care for their children. Thus, in order to guarantee that they receive the credit they are due for doing this family work, mothers face the added task of having to constantly remind their children of their economic contribution to the family.

Migrant mothers must frequently remind their children of their economic provisions. We see this from the words of Rosette Cabellero and Barbara Latoza, when I asked about their mothers:

Rosette: My mother often tells me that she left as a sacrifice for us. She left so that we could study. She sacrifices her loneliness and homesickness for the sake of supporting us and meeting our needs. She left, because she wanted to give us everything.

Barbara: My mother always tells us to study hard. She tells us she is in Taiwan so that we could study, because that is the only thing she could give to us as a mother.[8]

The responsibility of providing for the family economically does not read similarly for migrant mothers and fathers, as we have seen. Migrant mothers must convince their children that they are doing so, while the children automatically assume it of fathers. As noted, this increases the emotional labor of women in the family.

Mothers sometimes take this greater pressure to the extreme and remind children of their economic contributions to the family quite excessively. This is the case in the family of Rodney Palanca, whose description of his relationship with his mother seems to boil down to the importance of education. This emphasis began at the moment his mother left the Philippines to work as a nurse in Saudi Arabia ten years previously. As Rodney tells me, "That day, well the night before she was supposed to leave, we were of course very sad. . . . She told us that no matter what happens, she would never take us for granted. She told us that she wants us to study while she works in Saudi [Arabia]. She wanted us to study hard. She wanted us to just study and study." Not only did the push for Rodney to study begin on the eve of his mother's departure, it has continued ever since. In every letter and every phone conversation, Rodney tells me, his mother urges him to study. Phone conversations between Rodney and his mother often concern school: lessons, tuition fees, housing costs, and various other educational expenses. In this family, the mother heightens the commoditized aspects of their relationship so as to emphasize that, in her reconstitution of mothering, migration does not disagree with the collective interests of the family.[9]

To emphasize her point, Rodney's mother uses the narrative of her own suffering to motivate her children to strive harder in school. I ask Rodney if he knows about his mother's life in Saudi Arabia. He replies: "She wrote to me recently that she underwent an operation. She said that she had a hard year. She often had to work standing for eight hours. Then, she did not like the people there. They were not like Filipinos. Then she said she was oftentimes crying. She said that she missed us. Then, she would tell us to study hard." In this family, the reduction of the mother-son relationship to a commodity exchange is reflected in the infrequency of her visits. The mother returns to the Philippines only once every five years, because of the need to maximize the economic gains of migration (according to her). As Rodney explains, "It's because she supposedly wants to secure the money she needs to pay for our education." Notably, these economic gains not only pay for the educational expenses of her children but also subsidize the losses incurred in her husband's farming businesses in Mindanao, specifically the losses from their fish pond and pineapple farm.

However, the reduction of the relationship between Rodney and his mother to a commodity exchange does not mean he is without other forms of care in his family. Rodney benefits from an extensive kin base, with an unmarried uncle whom he describes as caring for him like a father, and he also benefits from the presence of a doting grandmother and her sisters. Their support enables Rodney to reciprocate for the martyrdom of his mother. Describing his desire to do so, Rodney explains:

I am inspired by my mother. I sometimes think about how she reminds me to often study. If she is suffering and struggling in Saudi Arabia, then we have a need to also struggle in our studies. It's because, as she told us, it is not easy to acquire money. It is something one struggles for. So we cannot help but think that we also need to struggle toward what our mother supports us to do. This is because she is suffering over there for us to accomplish what we need to accomplish.

During our interview, Rodney expressed his desire to finish university soon, so that he could help expedite the end to his mother's suffering. He wishes for her to come home. Explains Rodney: "A personal relationship would be so much better, wouldn't it? You would get to know one another more than just telling stories of one another or writing letters to one another. . . . I just want a personal experience with my mother. Especially that I am much older now, I would like the opportunity to show her that I am responsible now." However, unbeknownst to Rodney at the time of our interview, his mother—terminally ill with cancer—had returned to the Philippines. But as it was close to the end of the semester, his mother did not want to break the news of her illness to Rodney, fearing it might disrupt his studies. His grandmothers informed me during the follow-up interview a year after I first met Rodney that they had followed his mother's wishes. They note: "We kept it a secret when she went home [from Saudi Arabia]." I was not able to do a follow-up interview with Rodney. I was actually afraid to do so, not knowing if I could cope with asking him questions about his mother's death. Clearly, the commodification of love in this family is manifested in the lack of consideration of the emotional needs of Rodney, who had not been given a choice to even say goodbye to his mother. This is not the case for all families. However, I did notice that the pressure for children to excel in school as a means of reciprocating for the struggles of labor migration was one of the biggest burdens for many of my interviewees. This, and the denial of closure to Rodney, forces me to ask to what extent the material gains of migration outweigh the emotional costs.

A zero-sum game does not exist in the allocation of love in all families. Yet, without doubt, in the family of Rodney it did. In most families, mothers perform intensive mothering without completely overriding the emotional needs of children. Mothers seem to do so in order to ensure that their children's acceptance of their efforts to reconstitute mothering will include their economic provisions from afar. Because children are not easy to convince, they do not easily accept the gender boundary crossings pushed onto the family by women's migration. Elda Legaya is one such child; she struggles to accept her mother's reconstitution of the gender division of labor in the family. Elda told me:

My mother calls and we talk on the phone. Then, she tells me, she tells me not to neglect my studies because I work here for your schooling. (Starts crying.)

Interviewer: (I pause.) May I ask why you are crying?

Elda: I just do not like it that she is so far away.

I: How often do you see her?

E: Every two years, for one month.

Elda is a seventeen-year-old who lives with her father, her eleven-year-old sister, and three older brothers. Her mother has been a domestic worker in Lebanon for eight years and returns home every two years for a month. When her mother is away, Elda is responsible for almost all of the housework in their family. Her father, a construction worker who earns the equivalent of $2.00 for a day's work, never lifts a finger at home, as he is left physically exhausted by the heavy manual labor he performs during the day. However, he does not need to work, as the $200 that his wife remits every month is more than enough to adequately provide for their family. Thus, it would be more logical and rational for him not to work outside the home but to do the housework more needed of him in order to care adequately for his children. However, he saddles all of this work on his daughter Elda. Surprisingly, Elda blames her mother's migration more than her father's stubbornness for her difficulties at home. It is evident that children do not always see the economic contributions of their mothers as justifying a reduction in the mothers' care work or a greater need for their father to do care work.

Gender transformations have seeped into Philippine society, however, even if only slightly, as more women enter the workforce, leave the Philippines, and support their families economically. In some cases, children are slowly beginning to realize and accept the work of their mothers outside the home, as well as take note of the economic support of their mothers and the material gains they have accordingly accumulated from such support.

Children perceive these gains not only via private education but also through homeownership. For instance, some families saw their lives improve from abject poverty in the slum areas of the city to modest home ownership in safer neighborhoods. Other families have also secured enough funds to demolish their bamboo homes and begin building ones made of solid concrete. Children also recognize their mother's economic contributions in smaller ways. Some children describe the improved quality of their meals, the greater comfort of home life enabled by their acquisition of appliances, and the higher quality of life allowed by greater disposable income. With their mothers abroad, they can now afford to go to the movies or eat in a restaurant. These material comforts enable children to expand mothering, even if only slowly, to include breadwinning.

Even so, children can only recognize these economic gains when mothers interject their performance with multiple acts of intensive mothering as well as demonstrations of grief and gloom. Thus the reconstitution of mothering to include the role of "good provider" must come with acts that maintain the maternal duty of nurturing the family. When it does, children are also more likely to accept the challenges imposed by geographical distance on emotional ties. This is the case for the earlier cited Ellen Seneriches, who finds comfort in separation from the image of her mother weeping in despair over their forced separation. But as we have seen, the retention of women's maternal duties upon migration also results in their being blamed more frequently rather than non-productive men for the emotional difficulties that children face in transnational families. A tension in mothering and fathering thereby exists in mother-away migrant families. The economic breadwinning of women comes with the continued responsibility of women, specifically biological mothers, to nurture the family. This contradiction in turn justifies the disappearance of the men left behind in the Philippines, who by refusing to do housework saddle other women, including their daughters, with this labor.

*The Achievement of Emotional Security*

Not all children of migrant mothers suffer from emotional insecurities as a result of the distance of time and space in their families. As I insisted in the previous chapter, emotional security in mother-away transnational families seems to rely on the maintenance of gender. Keeping inside gender boundaries assures children of their mothers' love, weakens feelings of abandonment, and motivates children to reciprocate for the financial contribution of their mothers to the family. Maintaining gender boundaries is done in multiple ways, and most prominently through the performance of intensive mothering in a transnational terrain; however, there is a limit to the emotional security that children can achieve via this avenue, as it still maintains the view that mothers are better caregivers when in proximity than they are when geographically distant.

Yet additionally, I also found that the cooperation of community and other kin can help children achieve emotional security while contesting gender boundaries. When fathers take on more nurturing responsibilities in the family, children are less likely to frown upon their household arrangement. When community and extended kin speak positively of the efforts of migrant women to reconstitute mothering and accept the role of women as good providers, then children are able to find greater comfort from the economic need for their mothers to raise them from a distance. Children no longer hold their mothers accountable to higher standards of transnational parenting than they do their fathers. Thus, they would not expect mothers to call more than twice a week but find it comparable for fathers to call only twice a month. Some children whom I met in the Philippines have come to accept the gender contestations instigated by the reconstitution of mothering forced upon their families by labor migration, and they have usually achieved this with the help of kin and community.

However, these children did not constitute the majority of my interviewees. Most of the children had yet to accept their family as the right kind of family. The view of most echoes those expressed by Rudy Montoya and Roan Leyritana, who reject transnational household arrangements and consider the material gains brought into such households not to be worth the emotional costs of distance and unfamiliarity. In response to my question on whether or not they would raise their children in transnational families, Rudy states: "Probably not. I do not want my children to have the same experiences in life as me. What I want is for us to be together. . . . I want more emotional and physical companionship from my mother." Roan concurs, saying: "Even if we are only poor, as long as we are together. . . . Of course, I know what it feels like to be left behind by your parents, like my mother. I would never do that to my children." Children like Rudy and Roan would rather be poor and destitute in the Philippines than raise their children in a transnational family. They, like most children of migrant mothers, could be labeled as traditionalists, as they would prefer to stay in the country and work alongside their families. Realists—by which I mean children who have realistically come to accept the dismal opportunities available in the domestic labor market and know that they would most likely also have to search for work outside the country in order to adequately sustain their families in the future—are in the minority. Notably, only a handful of my interviewees fall into this latter category.

Daughters, more so than sons, are likely to become traditionalists. In our survey of schoolchildren, thirty-nine daughters of migrant mothers expressed unwillingness to be separated from their children, and only twenty-four daughters accepted that in the future they are likely to leave their children behind in the Philippines.[10] In contrast, nineteen sons of migrant mothers said they would realistically leave their children in the country and only fifteen said they would not. Similarly, the daughters of migrant fathers, more so than sons, were also more likely to hold onto traditional beliefs regarding the family. Of seventy-one daughters of migrant fathers participating in our survey, fifty-seven would never leave their children behind in the Philippines and only fourteen would do so.[11] In contrast, twenty-seven out of fifty sons of migrant fathers were comfortable with the realistic option, while only thirteen would prefer to work in the Philippines alongside their children. This tells us that the children of both migrant fathers and migrant mothers subscribe to gender boundaries of the family. More daughters preferred the traditional practice of nurturing children close by, and more sons held onto the tradition of the father maximizing breadwinning in the greater labor market opportunities outside the country.

The stubbornness of gender norms does not bode well for children in transnational families. As I have insisted repeatedly, staunch moral views that subscribe to gender convention run counter to the smooth adjustment of children and hinder their achievement of emotional security. In some families, the acceptance of a reconstituted form of gender and mothering has significantly helped children resolve the emotional insecurities engendered by their household rearrangement. The direct help of extended kin and members of the community in redefining mothering assists children a great deal.

One daughter of a migrant mother who has received the benefit of acceptance and support from kin and community is Bea Lemana, who for a long time saw her mother's migration as an act of abandonment. A widow, Bea's mother left Bea and her brother in the care of their maternal grandparents to be a domestic worker in Taiwan. Only with the reassurance of kin and community could Bea begin to accept her new household arrangement. As she states,

I remember when my mother first left, my classmates and teachers would speak to me. It was because I was always sitting alone. . . . I did not want to talk to anyone. I was always crying. So my teachers spoke to me. They asked me why I was sad and why I did not want to make friends. I told them that it was because my mother is selfish. She went to Taiwan and she did not even tell us [she and her brother]. Then, they and my friends told me that my mother went to Taiwan for my sake and for my brother's sake. She went there to support my studies. And then, my grandmother and grandfather also kept on telling me that was the case.

However, kin and community do not usually comfort the children of migrant mothers, but instead they often criticize migrant mothers for deciding to raise their children from a distance. Migrant mothers are usually derided, and this process further strains the already tenuous ties between migrant mothers and their children. Children may be constantly taunted with unconstructive comments that establish the wrongfulness of transnational mothering, such as "mothers should not go outside the country," "how could your mother just leave you here," or "good mothers stay with their children." In most cases, community and kin frown upon the decision of mothers to seek labor migration as they consider this decision a threat to the "Filipino family." Exempted and protected from this more hostile view, Bea was able to resolve the reconstitution of gender in her transnational family life more smoothly than have many other children. The fact that Bea's mother was a widow most likely made Bea's family an acceptable exception to the negative view of transnational families.

Influential members of the community, including educators and religious clergy, could help children adjust to transnational family life. They could do so by directly counseling children or by recognizing transnational families during sermons or lessons that they give concerning the family. The mere acknowledgment of the existence of transnational migrant families would be of great reassurance to children. It would not only validate their existence but also help begin to place these families within the norm. Educators and religious clergy could also help by facilitating the formation of support groups for children. For instance, Nieva Lacuesta, the earlier cited child whose mother works in Taiwan, was better able to cope with her mother's migration after her teacher made the effort to introduce her to another child who shares her experience. Describes Nieva:

Before, I used to wonder all the time if it was really necessary for parents to leave the country, only to work. In my perspective, there were many jobs available here, like in an office. Why do parents have to leave, then? I used to think that. Then, I started to better understand why parents leave after I met someone whose father works abroad. I remember, at the back of my school, there was this shed house. She went there with my teacher. My teacher wanted to introduce us. It was because I used to cry every day for about three months. I used to cry. Then, I was getting skinnier and skinnier. So my teacher brought this girl over and we talked. She explained the situation to me. I remember I did not agree with her and we fought. But she explained to me that life in the Philippines is very difficult. She explained that one could not earn as much money in the Philippines as they could in other countries. Then she told me all these other things that I now forget. But she was the one who convinced me that parents have no choice but to work abroad. She was the reason why I started to understand why my mother had to work abroad.

Support groups for children in transnational families could facilitate the smoother adjustment of children with their reconstituted family life. They also could provide a forum in which children could begin to understand the decision of parents, especially mothers, to migrate; they could find comfort from those who share their experiences; and together they could identify coping strategies for building strong intergenerational ties cross-nationally. Unfortunately, such groups did not exist in my area of study, even in schools where administrators estimate that more than 25 percent of students are members of transnational migrant families.

Finally, fathers could assist children with dealing with the migration of mothers and help them accept transnational mothering. Just as the wives of migrant fathers double their family work so as to better accommodate the effects on children of the geographical distance of migrant men, the fathers could do so in mother-away families. Such efforts from men are few and far between. I hardly ever heard children speak of fathers sitting them down and talking to them about the decision of mothers to seek migrant work. The silence and absence of men could backfire against them. Children do not always express sympathy toward fathers or view them as having been wronged by women whose migration has threatened their breadwinner status. In fact, children more often critique than sympathize with their fathers, whom they feel need to grow up and accept the economic reality of the greater need for women's work outside the country. Reiterating the views of many, Nelida Yarra states: "In my family, it is my mother who works. My mother works and my father acts like he is a prince. So I am angry at him. I am very angry at him." Like many children, Nelida frowns upon her father's lack of effort to find work, disapproves of how little work he does at home, and disrespects him for what she sees as his failure as a father. As the case of Nelida demonstrates, the inability of fathers to reconstitute fathering in ways that balance and reciprocate the efforts of mothers to perform transnational mothering is usually not acceptable to children.

## Conclusion

Children of migrant mothers are not without problems, from insecurities over maternal love to, among others, the commodification of family ties. Gender shapes these problems, since they are aggravated or even created by existing gender boundaries. For instance, children who in fact receive ample care may still view themselves as receiving "not enough" care, only because the caring work in their families is not done directly by their biological mothers. In acknowledging the existence of emotional difficulties in the families of migrant mothers, I do not mean to call for a return to the nuclear family. Doing so dangerously suggests that nuclear families are problem-free. This is not the case, particularly for the families of migrant mothers, as many of them decided to leave the Philippines in the first place to escape irresponsible men. A call for a return to the nuclear family also ignores the fact that most families of migrant mothers had never been nuclear families. By acknowledging the problems of children in mother-away transnational families, I raise the question of how the community can increase responsibility for their welfare. Fathers surely need to reshape gender beliefs about fathering and expand their familial duties and obligations to include those traditionally associated with women. Support groups and networks at schools and churches should also exist for members of transnational families. The need to institutionalize their presence in the public sphere remains a challenge in Philippine society, but a step toward inclusion of them would tremendously help children cope with the emotional challenges of transnational family life.

# The Overlooked Second Generation:
# The Experience of Prolonged Separation
# in Two-Parent Migrant Families

*Rhacel Salazar Parreñas*
*with Cerissa Salazar Parreñas*

[When I was seven years old,] my mom went to Malaysia first, for one to two years. Then she went to Saudi Arabia and then from Saudi Arabia, she went straight to the U.S. When she went to the U.S., that was the longest—ten years—that we did not see each other at all. She came back and when we saw each other, I was already twenty-one years old. —Isabelle Tirador[1]

This chapter focuses on the experiences of children in two-parent-abroad transnational families, most of which are based in the United States, but some also in other countries that allow for the eventual permanent settlement of migrants and their dependents.[2] Examples of such countries are Canada and the United Kingdom. This chapter specifically addresses the issue of prolonged separation, which is a common reality, but not one exclusive to children in two-parent migrant households.[3] The issue of prolonged separation takes into account the differences in transnational family life engendered by the geographical location of the migrant parent.

Migrants in countries where they may become eligible for permanent migration, for instance, the United States, experience longer separations from the children they leave behind in the Philippines. In contrast, migrant parents in countries where they are restricted to temporary status, for instance, Singapore, could expect to see their children at the end of each of their labor contracts. As noted earlier, the labor contracts of most migrant domestic workers are for two years, and those of professionals (e.g., engineers and nurses) include an annual vacation back to the country of origin. Ironically, the reward of permanent migration usually comes at the expense of the prolonged separation of families. In the case of the United States, migrant parents cannot return to the Philippines because they are either un-documented or "out of status" while their application for legal residency is still pending with the Immigration and Naturalization Service (INS). Also, children cannot visit their parents because of the difficulty that Filipino nationals have obtaining a tourist visa for various high-end destination countries of the diaspora, meaning countries that potentially allow for the permanent membership of migrants into their national body.[4]

The sacrifice of prolonged separation for the purpose of family migration does not always end with the reward of permanent migration, however. In the case of Isabelle's family, her younger brother has been able to follow their mother to the United States, but Isabelle and her older sister have yet to qualify for family-based migration. The forced separation of migrant families such as those of Isabelle's seems to go against the grain of the identity of the United States, as well as other countries, mostly in the West, that similarly pride themselves on their humanitarian tenets and priority for "family values."

Family separation is associated more often with illiberal destinations such as Singapore and Taiwan, because such countries restrict granting Filipino migrant workers the status of temporary contract workers.[5] Migrants are also not allowed to bring dependents into these countries. Ironically, however, children can visit their migrant parents more easily in destinations with illiberal regimes such as Hong Kong and Singapore than they can in liberal countries such as the United States. The reason for this is not only that Hong Kong and other such destinations are closer to the Philippines, but also that it is legal for Filipino children to enter a destination such as Hong Kong while it would be nearly impossible for them to go a liberal country like the United States. Likewise, migrant parents in transnational households can more easily come back to visit their children in the Philippines if they work in a country where they are only temporary contract workers, versus a country where they are working in hopes of eventually attaining citizenship. This is so because migrant parents usually return to the Philippines at the end of their labor contracts; if they were working in other countries they would have to wait a significant number of years to achieve landed status or permanent membership before they could secure re-entry after a visit to the Philippines.

These two different constructions of "partial citizenship"[6] lead to two different experiences of transnational family life, distinguishing those able to reunite, even if only for a short time, from those unable to do so. In the first group are usually families with workers based in illiberal countries where Filipino contract laborers are denied access to permanent migration. This group would include the families of domestic workers under contract in the Gulf region or another Asian country. The second group is based in liberal countries where workers aspire to relocate with the entire family unit. Most of these families are based in the United States.[7] In these families, extended separation defines transnational family life and parents and children often do not see each other for more than a decade. In recent years, more than 75 percent of immigrant admissions were made under family preference provisions.[8] If we consider that family reunification is the benchmark of U.S. immigration laws, then we could easily assume that only undocumented migrant workers would be unable to reunify with their families. However, this is not the case; Isabelle and other children who share her experience of prolonged separation are mostly the children of legal residents of the United States.

What legal entanglements prevent children from reuniting with their immigrant parents? Their situation raises the question of the citizenship rights earned by labor migrants and the extension of such rights to their children. At some point or another, fourteen of the sixteen children I interviewed whose parents lived in the United States endured an extended period of separation from their parents. Although the parents of my interviewees had all entered the United States without proper documentation, they have since obtained legal status, via either marriage or employment. At the time of my interviews, ten of these children had yet to reunite permanently with their parents, even though their parents were all legal migrants. The average length of separation in these families is quite long, extending to 12.6 years. Of these ten children, six are members of two-parent-abroad transnational families. Focusing on their stories, this chapter explains how legal entanglements embedded in U.S. immigration policies could force the separation of migrant workers and their families. It then addresses the costs of prolonged separation to familial relations and identifies the particular struggles that arise for this group of children.

## The Loopholes in U.S. Immigration Laws

The overlooked second generation, meaning the children of migrant workers who are unable to join their parents in the United States, represents a gaping hole in U.S. immigration laws. Driven by economic incentives for low-cost labor, U.S. immigration laws serve as a valuable tool to satisfy labor shortages.[9] Nonetheless, the issue of how foreign families are affected by immigration laws arises. Specifically, do the laws accommodate the dependents of the workers who were sought to satisfy the labor shortages that hamper economic production? The case of the overlooked second generation denied entry to the United States tells us otherwise. This problem remains even with the establishment of family reunification preference categories in the Immigration Act of 1965. In fact, stopgaps and barriers, specifically waiting lists and the stringent determination of age eligibility by the INS, control the entry of the dependents of migrant workers even when these workers have been legally recognized to fill the employment needs of the U.S. economy.

In order to explain how immigration affects the overlooked second generation, I begin my discussion with the story of Sharon Seneriches and her family. To explain the circumstances behind the forced separation of her family, I then examine visa preferences and the process of implementation of these preferences in immigration laws. I show that maximizing immigrant labor exponentially increases the population of the overlooked second generation.

After twelve years in the United States, Sharon Seneriches, a domestic worker for a wealthy family in New York City, finally returned to the Philippines and reunited with the family she had left behind. Lacking proper documents, she had not been able to see her husband or children for more than a decade. Likewise, her children—who did not meet proper visa requirements to visit their mother—could not join her in New York City. The Seneriches family endured this long separation in hopes that eventually they would be reunified as a family in the United States. This sacrifice was made for the greater possibilities of economic mobility in the United States. In 2001, after obtaining her green card, Sharon triumphantly returned to the Philippines. Moreover, her new legal status allowed some of her dependents to obtain the visas needed to live permanently with her in the United States. After a two-month visit to the Philippines, Sharon returned to the United States, accompanied by her twenty-year-old daughter, JoAnn, her nineteen-year-old son, Mike, her eighteen year-old son, Peter, and her husband, Frederico.

Nonetheless, the migration of Sharon's family members did not come with complete joy, because the whole family did not qualify to go to the United States. The oldest daughter, Ellen, had turned twenty-two years old by the time she was considered. No longer considered a "child" under the immigration laws, Ellen now belonged in a preference category that requires a longer waiting period for entry to the United States. She qualified for entry as an unmarried adult child of a U.S. permanent resident. In this category, she would have to wait at least six more years[10] to receive a visa.[11]

Although left behind in the Philippines, Ellen still had the hope of eventually joining her family in the United States. However, for this Ellen has had to put her life on hold. For instance, she cannot marry the man whom she has been dating in the last two years. If Ellen were to marry her partner, her mother, who is a permanent resident, would no longer be able to petition for her entry. Alternatively, though, Ellen could be allowed to enter the United States legally as a skilled migrant.[12] With this in mind, Ellen has pursued a medical degree. However, she still has years of schooling and training to complete before becoming eligible. Finally, Ellen could apply for a tourist visa. This temporary measure would theoretically allow her to join her family during the holidays. Fortunately, Ellen did obtain a tourist visa to visit her siblings and parents in New Jersey. Since obtaining her tourist visa, Ellen has visited her family twice.

Ellen was not yet twenty-one when her mother petitioned for her entry to the United States. Although eligible at the time of her petition, Ellen still did not qualify to join her mother as did her younger siblings. Many minor children fall through the cracks in qualifying for higher preference categories because the age of the dependent child is determined on the moment of consideration of the petition, not on the day of filing. Therefore, a child petitioned by her migrant mother at the age of seventeen would be ineligible for immediate family reunification if the backlog extended the processing of visa applications past the year of higher eligibility. Sadly, Ellen's story is not atypical. This bureaucratic loophole affected many other children whom I met in the Philippines, among them twenty-four-year-old Andrei Montenegro, whose mother, after ten years in the United States, had yet to be granted legal permanent residency and remained on a temporary visa (H1–B) while working as a teacher.[13] At age twenty-four, Andrei was no longer eligible to join his mother in the United States, because adult children of H1–B visa holders do not qualify for family reunification.

Why do children like Ellen and Andrei find themselves unable to join their legal-migrant parents in the United States? For U.S. immigration laws, the economy is a higher priority than the family. It has been the case throughout history in the United States that immigrant labor generally benefits the economy. Periodically, large groups of workers have been brought into the United States under special conditions to fill shortages in agriculture, manufacturing production, and services. We see this in the early twentieth century with the recruitment of Chinese and other Asian laborers, with the labor of Mexican braceros in agriculture and manufacturing in the mid-twentieth century, and with the recruitment of nurses in the 1970s and 1980s.[14] Other examples are the increase in the number of labor migrants allowed in the United States after the 1990 Immigration Act and the influx of high-tech professionals in the 1990s.[15]

Nevertheless, when U.S. production needs for the work of migrants are low, the effects of anti-immigration kick in. This is illustrated by the opening and closing of U.S. borders to Asian immigrants historically. As the demand for labor increases, so too does the flow of Asian immigrants. Similarly, as the demand for labor decreases, nativism, meaning sentiments of anti-immigration hostility in the host society,[16] kicks in to block the flow of Asians into the country.[17] As early as the 1800s, this pattern of inclusion and exclusion began for Chinese laborers.[18] Initially, these workers immigrated to California to work in gold mines and later on to build the transcontinental railroads.[19] Throughout this period, Chinese migrants were depicted as perpetual foreigners who posed a threat to mainstream American society.[20] Even though business owners benefited from Chinese labor, they eventually gave in to a massive labor union campaign against foreign workers.[21] As the economic downturn continued in the 1800s, the anti-Chinese movement eventually culminated into the Chinese Exclusion Act of 1882.[22] This illustrates the dominance of economic incentives, or pro-production forces, in immigration laws.

The economic drive behind U.S. immigration laws still remains today, as shown for instance by the implementation of anti-family measures along with pro-production laws. In recent years, the increase in the use of temporary visas (e.g., H1–B visas) for admitting skilled workers but not their families attests to this pattern of the limited integration of migrants in the United States.[23] In globalization, receiving nations such as the United States incorporate immigrants under the logic of the "opposite turns of nationalism," meaning the simultaneous denationalization of economies and renationalization of politics.[24] According to political economist Saskia Sassen, nation-states maximize production in the global economy by lifting borders and welcoming the flow of capital, information, and labor but simultaneously closing these borders when it comes to the permanent integration of immigrants and refugees.[25] Integrating labor migrants but not their dependents lessens the wage requirements of these workers. Therefore, excluding their dependents guarantees a flexible reserve army of cheap labor for the economy and maximizes the benefits provided by foreign workers.[26]

As mentioned, to accommodate the production demands of the U.S. economy, temporary visas are granted in increasing numbers to prospective labor migrants willing to fill labor shortages in the United States. In 1998, Congress passed legislation increasing the number of H–1B visas to as many as 142,500 in the next three years. Due to big business pressure, Congress further increased the annual allotment of H1–B visas to 195,000 in 2001, 2002, and 2003.[27] The H1–B visa grants temporary residency to people who could fill particular "specialty [professional] occupations" but ties these workers to a particular employer.[28] Essentially a form of bonded labor, H1–B visas deny the migrant the "free-worker" rights articulated in the Contract Labor Law of 1885, which banned the importation of any form of contract labor in the United States.[29] Without the flexibility to switch employers, these workers cannot bargain for better wage rates or working conditions.

H1–B visas maximize the production capabilities of the migrant worker, however, without any consideration for the reproduction needs of their family, that is, without consideration or accountability for the resources needed by the worker's family to reproduce as a self-sustaining unit. H1–B visas restrict the conditions of entry of children and spouses of the migrant worker to a non-working status. This fact, coupled by the low wages[30] of most H1–B visa holders, promotes the formation of split-apart family units for these migrant workers. In other words, their low wages coupled with the inability of their immediate relatives to contribute to their family income make it more likely for them to leave families in sending communities, where the lower costs of living could afford them a higher quality of life.[31] This is the case for at least two children whom I had met in the Philippines, including the aforementioned Andrei Montenegro, who has yet to permanently reunite with his mother after ten years of forced separation.

The parents of most of the children I met had not been skilled workers in the United States. Thus, they did not qualify for an H1–B visa. Instead, most were low-wage service workers caught in the legal tangle of remaining "out of status" while their petition for permanent residency under the Labor Certification Program was pending with the INS.[32] Migrant domestic workers qualify for permanent residency under the Labor Certification Program.[33] Under this program, employers can sponsor the permanent migration of a foreign worker if they are unable to attract "native" workers to fill their specific labor needs. While their petition for labor migration is pending at the

INS, potential migrants are technically out of status. During this time, they are unable to leave the United States and visit their families in the country of origin with assurance of re-entry. Instead, they must stay employed by the sponsoring employer, and are thus placed in a position of bonded servitude. Moreover, they are unable to sponsor the migration of their families or attach the names of their spouses and dependent children to their pending application, because technically they could still be denied immigrant status. According to a volunteer at the New York-based grassroots organization for Filipino domestic workers, Damayan, migrant domestic workers sponsored under the Labor Certification Program stay out of status for close to ten years. To obtain immigrant status via the Labor Certification Program, Sharon Seneriches had to wait seven years to receive her green card. During this time, her children—in limbo as well—also waited, with the hope that their mother would receive legal status before they became too old and thus ineligible to join her in the United States.

Despite the continued use of temporary visas and the indentured servitude embedded in the process of labor certification, humanitarian concerns do shape immigration laws. Over time, the United States refined its posture over the immigrant population; in 1965, amendments to the Immigration and Naturalization Act completely removed the national-origins quota system created in the 1920s.[34] Instead of broad exclusionary practices, the government introduced a layered preference system giving priority to immediate relatives of U.S. citizens. Immediate relatives were defined as (1) spouses, (2) unmarried minor children, and (3) parents of adult citizens. This system limited remaining relatives by the number of available visas and divided them into a hierarchy of categories based on their relationship with the citizen or the permanent resident.[35] The categories are:

1. At the top, adult unmarried sons and daughters of citizens.
2. Spouses and unmarried children of lawful permanent resident aliens.
3. Professionals who possess exceptional ability in the arts or sciences. In order to qualify, one needed to show proof from the Department of Labor that the potential immigrant did not diplace an available worker.
4. Married adult children of citizens.
5. Siblings of adult citizens.
6. Workers who can satisfy U.S. labor shortages.

7. Displaced persons fleeing from a Communist or a Middle Eastern country or persons uprooted due to a national catastrophe.[36]

While this preference system is still in place, the individual categories have been changed. In the 1980s, the seventh preference was eliminated. Moreover, the third and sixth preferences were incorporated into an employment-based scheme in 1990, and more visas were allocated for the use of permanent residents.[37]

Even so, the principle of upholding family values still remains. In the mid-1990s, attempts by conservative legislators to limit family-based migration to spouses and minor children were met with vehement criticism from most lawmakers. One of them was Senator Edward Kennedy, a Democrat from Massachusetts, who passionately argued for the importance of setting family values as the moral ground defining the incorporation of recruited immigrant laborers to the United States. Senator Kennedy argued, "We are saying that we want your skills and ingenuity but leave your sisters and brothers behind. We want your commitment to freedom and democracy but not your mother. We want you to help rebuild our inner cities and cure our diseases but we do not want your grandchildren to be at your knee. We want your family values but not your family."[38] With most legislators agreeing with Senator Kennedy, efforts to restrict family preferences to spouses and minor children were denounced. The legislative support this evidences for keeping families intact in migration leaves us to assume that forced family separation should not be an issue for migrants legally residing in the United States. However, as I later explain, loopholes do exist. Moreover, the imposition of annual per-nation limits results in extended waiting lists that eventually disqualify the entry of dependents.

The 1965 Immigration Act implemented the humanitarian goal of family reunification. As I noted earlier, the available visas, 75 percent were designated for relatives of U.S. citizens and permanent residents specified into "preference" categories.[39] These preference categories do not include immediate relatives of U.S. citizens, who are not subject to a quota.[40] Framers of this law also thought to balance the flow among various nations and set an annual limit of 20,000 immigrant visas for each country outside of the Western Hemisphere, regardless of the country's population.[41] Thus, India would be allocated the same amount of visas as Madagascar.[42] However, migrants from England or any other European nation would not be bound to the same nationality limit. However, because Mexican migrants benefited more than other countries from this non-numerical restriction, Congress in 1976 enacted legislation that imposed a 20,000 per country numerical limitation on the Western Hemisphere.[43] This was a year after visa usage rates for Mexicans reached approximately 40,000. By imposing this nationality-based limit, lawmakers ensured the diversity of immigrants but also prevented a flood of certain nationalities, particularly those from Mexico and from Asia and the Pacific.

Coupled with the elimination of the national quotas act, the 1965 Immigration Act's allocation of the majority of immigrant visas for family members of U.S. citizens suggested a turn toward reproduction and a move away from production in the U.S. immigration landscape. However, the implementation of a 20,000 limit per country, regardless of the size of the country, leads to deficiencies such as backlogs. Specifically, this limit created a backlog of potential migrants from the more populous countries awaiting reunion with their family members in the United States. According to the State Department, this backlog has placed close to 4 million individuals on the visa waiting list to reunite with family in the United States.[44] The families of Isabelle Tirador and Ellen Seneriches are affected by this backlog. The pro-production and anti-reproduction stance in the implementation of immigration policies is indicated by the issuance of temporary visas to these prospective migrants, but reserving them for workers in demand by the economy.

Due to its nationality-based limit, the 1965 Immigration Act unintentionally disqualifies certain immigrants from family reunification, imposing an anti-reproduction consequence particularly on larger migrant populations. The greater the threat of an overflow from a given country, the greater the likelihood of a backlog imposed on the migrants from that country. Hence, the backlog for family reunification tends to be longer for migrants from high migrant source countries such as Mexico and the Philippines.[45] Thus, the process of legal migration inadvertently results in the alienation and racial exclusion of those seeking to reunite with family. It also acts as a mechanism of population control.

The evolution of the immigration scheme has not resolved the problem of backlogs and family separations. Beginning in 1990, the immigration scheme underwent major revisions. The visa limits per country were still in place. Now, however, family-sponsored and employment-based immigrants occupy two distinct categories. Family-sponsored immigrants are given only four preference categories: (1) unmarried adult children of citizens; (2) spouses and unmarried children of permanent residents; (3) married children of citizens; and (4) siblings of citizens. These changes drastically altered the immigration scheme with respect to employment-based immigration. There are now five different preference groups: (1) workers with extraordinary or outstanding ability; (2) members of a profession with an advanced degree; (3) skilled workers and professionals; (4) special immigrants; and (5) employment creation via entrepreneurship.[46]

While the immigration scheme regularly undergoes change, what remains constant is the prolonged family separation created by backlogs for certain migrant countries. For example, in 1993, sisters and brothers of U.S. citizens from the Philippines had a waiting period of thirteen years.[47] In 2002, the waiting period for this preference category was twenty-one years.[48] For unmarried adult sons and daughters of U.S. citizens, the wait could take as long as nine years.[49] These lengthy waiting periods reflect the deficiencies in U.S. immigration laws.

Exacerbating the backlog is the narrow definition Congress gives with respect to "immediate family." According to this definition, spouses and minor, unmarried children of citizens and the parents of adult citizens are not restricted by visa limitations. However, other family members are not so lucky. For example, regardless of their minor status at the time of the filing of the immigrant petition, unmarried adult children of permanent residents do not qualify for immediate family reunification. Moreover, spouses and minor children of permanent residents still fall within the visa preference system, and are subject to prolonged separations.[50] According to the State Department, they constitute approximately 45 percent of individuals on the visa waiting list to reunify with family members in the United States.[51] Adult children of U.S. citizens have to wait years to receive approval.[52] Sharon Seneriches's family is an example of such a split-household scenario.

The backlog caused by current and past immigration schemes calls into question the adequacy of the laws in accounting for migrant workers' families. The operative effects—pro-production and anti-reproduction—prolong the separation of families from migrant-heavy countries. Despite prolonged separation, the U.S. economy continues to benefit from the labor of workers such as Sharon Seneriches. In the 1980s, the nursing shortage was a crisis.[53] In response to the demand for nurses, Congress enacted the Immigration Nursing Relief Act of 1989 (INRA), granting permanent residency to foreign nurses working in the United States on temporary visas for the next five years.[54] At the time, 75 percent of the foreign nurses were from the Philippines.[55] While Congress passed INRA, a process granting accelerated permanent residence, it neglected to deal with the prolonged waiting periods facing the family members left behind in the Philippines.

The historical evolution of the immigration laws reveals that immigration policies have been heavily driven by economics, but such laws have not addressed the unintended consequences to the overlooked second generation. Given the state of the current laws, the susceptibility of backlogs from migrant-heavy countries and the failure to address these backlogs make prolonged periods of separation in migrant families even more likely. The overlooked second generation falls through the cracks because of an anti-reproduction, or anti-migrant family, discourse that affects the implementation of immigration policies. The predicament of the Seneriches family illustrates that U.S. immigration laws are deficient when it comes to reconciling migrant workers and their families. This deficiency in U.S. immigration laws is of particular concern to countries with a large in-flow of immigrant workers of non-European stock. Indeed, families of migrants from the Philippines—the second-largest sending community of immigrant workers to the United States—are more likely to confront the reunification difficulties of the Seneriches family than most other migrant ethnic groups. This suggests that family exclusion is more likely to concern migrant populations that pose a greater threat of foreign invasion, due to the backlog generated by per-country limits in admittance of family members, which lengthens in time the larger the foreign migrant population from a particular country.

## The Difficulties of Prolonged Separation

Every year tens of thousands of Filipinos enter the United States as permanent residents. In 2001, the United States admitted 53,154 immigrants from the Philippines. The annual numbers have fluctuated anywhere between 30,000 and 65,000 in the last ten years.[56] If Filipinos enter as work-based migrants, not all migrate with their complete family units and if they come in as family-based migrants, not all reunifications represent complete family units. The case of the Seneriches family supports this point. Moreover, these numbers do not include visa overstayers, that is, migrants who illegally overstay their temporary visas in the United States. There are an estimated 95,000 undocumented Filipino migrants working in the United States.[57] We can assume that many of the undocumented workers who happen to be parents left their children in the Philippines. After all, most of the parents of the children I met in the Philippines had at one point been undocumented workers in the United States.

The fact that not all of the family members of individuals who contribute to the U.S. economy can come to the United States raises questions about the quality of such individuals' family life, at both ends of the migration spectrum. Looking at the receiving end, in a previous study I addressed the emotional difficulties undergone by transnational mothers and the added pressures of raising children from a geographic distance.[58] At the sending end of the migration spectrum, a different set of problems confronts those children growing up without their parents. In this section, I address the particular difficulties that children in two-parent abroad transnational families who experience a prolonged period of separation from their parents encounter.

I found that children in these transnational families are more likely to suffer from poor guardianship than are children whose parents can more easily return to the Philippines. Although they represent very few of my sample of sixty-nine interviewees, the handful of children who dropped out of school had all been members of two-parent-abroad transnational families that experienced prolonged periods of separation. These children are not necessarily neglected or abandoned by their parents, as they are usually left under the guardianship of extended kin or older siblings. However, parents unable to return to the Philippines are not in a position to monitor their situation.

One such child who received inadequate guardianship and eventually dropped out of school is Jeek Pereno, a twenty-five-year-old merchandiser for a large department store. He feels that his life deteriorated as a result of his transnational household arrangement. Although his mother more than adequately provided for her children in the Philippines—managing with her meager wages first as a domestic worker and then as a nurse's aide to send them $200 a month and even purchase a house in a fairly exclusive neighborhood in the city center—Jeek still feels abandoned by his mother and emotionally insecure about his relationship with her. He generally feels that he lost out not having received enough discipline growing up without his parents. His mother has not returned once to the Philippines since leaving for New York in 1983.

Jeek's parents relocated to New York when he was only eight years old. He, along with his four-, twelve-, and thirteen-year-old brothers, was left under the care of their aunt. In 1991, two of his brothers—the oldest and youngest—joined their mother in New York, a few months after their father passed away. Complications with the U.S. Embassy have since prevented Jeek and his other brother to join their family in New York, and his mother has not once returned to visit them in the Philippines. In reaction to my surprise over this fact, Jeek solemnly replies: "Never. It will cost too much, she said." Feeling abandoned in the Philippines, Jeek is without the assurance that only a visit and not her weekly phone calls could adequately provide after seventeen years of separation. Jeek's mother had not been able to return to the Philippines while she was an "out-of-status" migrant awaiting her green card via the Labor Certification Program. This process took her more than ten years. Then, if she was like the mothers I had spoken to in Rome and Los Angeles, she probably feared returning to the Philippines to confront the emotional difficulties built up in her children after such a long separation.[59] Insecurity plagues Jeek and his sense of self. Lacking complete reassurance of his mother's love, Jeek is also without an emotional outlet to process his insecurities.

Jeek: I talk to my mother once in awhile. But what happens, whenever she asks how I am doing, I just say okay. It's not like I am really going to tell her that I have problems here. . . . It's not like she can do anything about my problems if I told her about them. Financial problems, yes she can help. But not the other problems, like emotional problems. . . . She will try to give advice, but I am not very interested to talk to her about things like that with her.

Interviewer: You sound like you resent your mother.

J: Yes. Of course, you are still young, you don't really know what is going to happen in the future. Before you realize that your parents left you, you can't do anything about it anymore. You are not in a position to tell them not to leave you. They should have not left us. (Sobs.)

I: [I ask if we should end the interview, but he insists that we continue.] So does your mother know that you feel like this?

J: No, she doesn't know.

I: Do you get emotional support from anyone?

J: As much as possible, if I can handle it, I try not to get emotional support from anyone. I just keep everything inside me.

During the interview, I could not help but think of Jeek as a sealed bottle, one filled with so much pent-up emotion and just about ready to explode. Aggravating Jeek's emotional insecurities is his assumption that his mother's absence represents her lack of care. This assumption also prevents Jeek from expressing his emotional needs. Left without an outlet to release his insecurities, Jeek has had no choice but to repress his pent-up emotions, a reality which aggravates his feelings of resentment against his mother.

His belief that his mother did not care enough to make sure that he and his brothers received adequate surrogate parental support in her absence also aggravates Jeek's feelings of abandonment. Left under the care of his aunt— who had a family and children of her own—Jeek feels that he did not receive sufficient guidance growing up without his mother.

J: While I do know that my aunt loves me and she took care of us to the best of her ability, I am not convinced that it was enough.

I: Why not?

J: Because we were not disciplined enough. She let us do whatever we wanted to do.

Not having had a disciplinary figure in his life, Jeek feels that his education had suffered. One of Jeek's biggest regrets in life is not having concentrated on his studies. Having only completed a two-year vocational program in electronics, Jeek doubted and continues to doubt his competency to pursue a college degree. At twenty-five, Jeek feels stuck with no mobility, but only the limited option of turning from one low-paying job to another in the future.

Jeek is not alone in feeling the lost opportunity resulting from his parents' migration. One of his counterparts is Norbert Silvedirio, a twenty-one-year-old college dropout whose mother and father have worked in New York City as domestic workers for more than thirteen years. Like Jeek, Norbert also relates how his schooling suffered from the lack of guidance brought about by parental absence.

I remember that I was in Grade 2 [when my parents left for the U.S.]. I was just left on my own. I was the one who looked after myself. [My older siblings] would just hand me my allowance and it was up to me to budget it. . . . I would go to school every day but in high school, I would only go to class once in a while. I was always at the billiard hall. (Laughs.) . . . I think it would have been better if I grew up with them around. There was no one around to guide me. I just did what I wanted to do. I would go to school if I felt like it. My [older brother] would try to tell me to go to school but I never really listened to him.

Without the option of following their parents to the United States, children

such as Jeek and Norbert could only depend on what they feel had been inadequate guardianship from kin who did care but were most likely too
overextended to show the extent of their care. For Jeek and Norbert, the experience of inadequate guardianship is an unintended consequence of U.S.
immigration policies, as it results from their ineligibility for family reunification and/or the position of their parents as "out-of-status" migrants.

In addition to poor guardianship, children in two-parent-abroad transnational families also find themselves with the greater responsibility of having
to manage the distribution of the emotional labor of their guardians. They
fear overburdening kin with the responsibility of securing their emotional
well-being. Twenty-three-year-old Gailanie Tejada, whose parents work as a
teacher and nursing aide in the Washington, D.C., area, lives in her mother's
ancestral home with two uncles, an aunt, and her grandmother. Although
she has the security of a dense network of kin, Gailanie does not feel comfortable enough to expect unconditional amounts of emotional labor from
each one of them. Instead, she feels compelled to consciously make sure that
she does not overburden any one of them with her problems. She explains:

I am very close with my uncle. So, if I have problems, I talk to him and then
it's like I distribute my problems. Of course, they are only my uncles so if
you lean on them too much, they eventually give in. So I have to spread it
out. It's like, I would go to my aunt and tell her about a problem and then
next time I will go to an uncle. It's like that. I go from one to another. . . . It
is because I do not want to be a burden to them. Because I have a lot of problems, and I feel if I stick to one uncle then it's like I am expecting too much.
I do not want them to have a difficult time taking care of me.

Equally distributing the responsibility for their care is a form of labor that
children in two-parent-abroad transnational families share with others who
equally rely on the work of extended kin. This tells us that children do not
always feel that extended kin can be expected to provide as much care as
would a parent. Moreover, the conscious monitoring of the distribution of
emotional labor in the family speaks of the early maturity of children and
their sense of responsibility for ensuring the smooth maintenance of
transnational households.

Finally, the legal entanglements that keep transnational families apart
commonly result in a bifurcated transnational household that divides children between the First and Third World. As I have shown, not all children in
transnational families can eventually join their parents in the United States.
Only younger children usually gain this right, while older children often

find themselves disqualified by age. This had been the case for Ellen Sener-iches and Isabelle Tirador. Each of them has one or more younger siblings in the United States. Due to this bifurcation, parents are not in a position of be-ing able to provide their children with the same options for mobility. Chil-dren in the Philippines are without question denied the benefits of a secure labor market and the greater potential for mobility available in the First World. Thus, the bifurcated family system usually results in resentments and tensions between the children left behind in the Philippines and those able to migrate to the United States.

Jason Arandil, a twenty-four-year-old short-order cook in Texas, can be described as one of the lucky ones. His parents qualified to remain in the United States under the Labor Certification Program by providing their la-bor as "sewing machine operators and handstitchers."[60] Jason followed his parents at the age of seventeen, approximately ten years after they first left the Philippines and entered the United States as tourists. Of their eight chil-dren, they could reunite in the United States with only two; the rest were past the cut-off age, and no longer eligible to join them as "minor children" of legal permanent residents. To negotiate the difference in opportunity that they as parents could provide for their children, the parents of Jason recently purchased land for each one of their children left behind in the Philippines but did not do the same for the two able to join them in the United States. They figured that their two other children could take advantage of the higher wages granted their labor in the United States and if they so choose could eventually afford to buy their own land in the Philippines.

While the efforts of Jason's parents to help balance the unequal footing between their children could arguably seem fair, i.e., in light of the eco-nomic disparities and difference in opportunities between the Philippines and the United States, this did not come without resentment for Jason, who complained:

My parents bought some properties over here for my sisters, well for my sisters and brothers. So I was so very jealous about it. How about us? They think that because we are in the United States, we could work over there and buy our own property. But they do not work over here, and then they have properties bought for them. How about us? We work and we work. And we get nothing. It probably would be better if I were also in the Philippines, then I would also be given a house and lot, and a car. So, in the United States, we struggle and we do not even have a car. We do not own a house.

Jealousy and resentment are more likely to occur in families in which children occupy extremely disparate structural locations. A low-end service worker like Jason feels that he also lacks opportunities in the United States, albeit differently than do his college-educated siblings left behind in the Philippines. He blames his low-end position and his lack of skills for mobility in the U.S. labor market on the poor guidance he had received while left behind with his older siblings by his migrant parents at the young age of eight.

Yet, regardless of their intentions and regardless of the circumstances in transnational families, it is nearly impossible for parents to give exactly the same opportunities or help to their two sets of children in the First and Third Worlds. Jason is not without financial support from his parents, as he does still live with them in Texas. However, as his resentment indicates, the different treatment of children makes it difficult for him not to (mis)read the different actions of his parents to mean the greater worth of one set of children over the other. Appeasing these insecurities adds to the labor of parents, who must carefully negotiate through the disparities imposed on their family by the legal entanglements in U.S. immigration policies.

## Conclusion

Barriers impede the full integration of immigrants into U.S. society; the overlooked second generation attests to this fact. In immigration studies, there is a growing interest on the lives of the children of immigrants, or the "immigrant second generation," and researchers insist that their experience is indicative of the extent of integration and acceptance of minorities in the U.S. population.[61] As the children of immigrants, those left behind in the Philippines and other sending countries surely must be made part of this category called the immigrant second generation. Without doubt, their inability to enter the United States attests to the continued exclusion of immigrant workers in this country.

Although immigration laws are premised upon work-based and family-based preference categories, work-based entry does not categorically result in the entry of the dependents of the worker. The problems of the overlooked second generation illustrate the cost of the government's neglect of backlogs and preoccupation with the growth of the U.S. economy. Nativism, in other words, xenophobia, is at work in this process, because backlogs are more likely to affect the most representative migrant populations, such as migrant Filipinos, who continue to enter the United States to fill the nation's labor market needs but have no guarantee of complete family migration. Although the U.S.'s liberal tenets purport to support family reunification and human and civil rights discourse opposes forced family separation, the families of migrant workers still often find themselves forcibly separated and disqualified from receiving the benefits that their working members have rightfully earned.

As a solution, I propose that the immigration laws that concern the dependents of legally permanent migrant workers in the United States should be revised. I do not necessarily mean loosely advocating for an open-border policy or questioning the government's preference to restrict the number of immigrants allowed into the United States. Instead, my proposed solutions would give greater consideration to the rights earned by those who contribute to the economic growth of U.S. society and to the extension of their citizenship rights to include family reunification. For instance, I favor giving the immediate families of migrant workers entering under H1–B visas temporary working visas as well. This would drastically reduce the likelihood of migrant families being split apart geographically, because the increased wage-earning power of the migrant family could help them to afford the higher cost of living in an advanced capitalist country such as the United States. In other words, migrants would feel less compelled to form transnational families, with the migrant worker in the United States and the rest of the family left behind in the sending country. Moreover, if my proposals were implemented, someone like Andrei Montenegro, an only child, would be given the option of growing up in the United States with his mother.

In addition, officials should not use the backlog that is caused by the annual limit imposed on countries when granting family-based visas to dependent children of legally permanent migrant workers against families. This change could be made without increasing the annual numerical limits imposed by the law if the cut-off age of eligibility of family-based migrants was decided when the petition was filed, not when the petition was considered. In this way, families such as Sharon Seneriches's would not be penalized for having come from a heavy migration-sending country such as the Philippines.

Prior to 1965, many Asian migrants to the United States left behind their spouses and children due to stringent immigration laws.[62] As a result, the number of split households increased exponentially.[63] In these households, relationships were unusually dichotomous, one spouse laboring in the United States and the other responsible for domestic work in the homeland. With the preference categories given to family-based migration in the 1965 and 1990 Immigration Acts, many assumed that split households would no longer be a reality. If such families still existed, we assumed that they were split by choice. However, the dynamics of the overlooked second generation fly in the face of this assumption. Nativism still managed to lurk beneath the liberal-leaning 1965 and 1990 immigration laws, which increased the population of Filipino migrants in the United States, but alarmingly also led to prolonged transnational household formation.

# The Persistence of Gender

In the Philippines, thousands of children grow up spending little time around their parents. Labor migration has as its consequence the rise of split-apart households, that is, transnational migrant families with members located in two or more nation-states. Transnational families pose numerous challenges to the development of close family relations; these include the risk of emotional distance between migrant parents and their children, the overburdening of extended kin with care responsibilities, the threat of strains in marriages, and the danger of inadequate parental guidance of children. I do not wish to deny the added risk of emotional rifts in transnational families, nor do I reject the possibility that geographical distance in these families may engender emotional injuries.

However, I did find that gender plays a role in shaping transnational family dynamics and exacerbating or sometimes even creating these problems. Thus, as a solution to the problems of transnational families, I would support greater acceptance of the malleability of gender. By this I mean the incorporation of egalitarian views of men's and women's roles in the family, the rejection of views that naturalize differences between men and women, and finally the adoption by families of a forced reconstitution of gender through the organizational rearrangement of their households. These measures would ease the emotional tensions that mar transnational family relations.

## Global Inequities

In making such an assertion, I do not ignore the structural factors that cause the formation of transnational households. An ideal solution would of course be to give migrant families the option of family reunification, in other words, to give them the choice to live in close geographical proximity with one another, with the guarantee of economic mobility and security. This would be possible in either the sending country or the receiving country of migration. In the sending country, this option could be made possible only if the country (such as the Philippines) were not saddled with foreign debt. This could become an option in the receiving country if it were to institute truly family-friendly immigration policies.

As I discussed in Chapter 1, globalization engenders the formation of transnational families, and leaves the average family in the Philippines without an adequate supply of either public or private care resources. Without doubt, foreign debt relief for poor countries such as the Philippines would increase social welfare provisions, and in so doing it would also possibly deter individuals from turning to the option of labor migration as a means of supporting their children. Likewise, another possible way to ameliorate the risks posed by geographical distance on the family is to make migration policies less restrictive in host societies, many of which, whether deliberately or not, deny entry to the families of migrant workers.

Entry restriction occurs in host countries with illiberal regimes in Asia and the Gulf region. In these countries, the dependents of Filipino labor migrants do not qualify for family reunification, since the migrants themselves are only temporary residents of these nations. More surprisingly, nations with liberal regimes such as those found in North America have also promoted the formation of transnational households via loopholes in policies that allow for the eventual reunification of families. For instance, as I discussed in Chapter 7, domestic workers sponsored via the Labor Certification Program in the United States remain out of status for an average of ten years. During this time, the children they left behind in the Philippines are not eligible to join them in the United States because of the risk that their petition for residency may still be denied by the INS. This results in long and continued separations for the families of migrant workers in the United States.

Another cause of lengthy separations is the greater concentration of undocumented workers in these countries. In contrast, migrants working in nations with illiberal regimes more often are documented workers with temporary residence visas that grant them the flexibility to return to the Philippines. Among the children I met in the Philippines, the length of continuous separation for those with at least one migrant parent based in a "liberal" nation such as the United States averaged more than a decade. For children with both parents abroad, prolonged separations often resulted in greater emotional insecurity as well as lack of discipline.

By calling for a reevaluation of gender practices and norms in transnational families as a solution to the emotional injuries of transnational family life, I do not wish to override the significance of giving families the choice to live in close proximity with one another. I also do not wish to downplay the major economic and racial inequalities that force the organizational reconstitution of families into transnational households. However, I do want to call attention to the ways that the constitution of gender—particularly in the care practices that maintain transnational families—does not ease but instead aggravates or even creates the problems that forced geographical separation imposes on family relations.

## The Persistence of Gender

Transnational families in their organization invite the reconstitution of gender relations. The conventional division of labor suited for patriarchal nuclear households, with breadwinner father and homemaker mother, is quite difficult to maintain in these households. This is the case in the families of both migrant fathers and migrant mothers. Both kinds of transnational families find it difficult to follow the conventional gender script that relegates mothers to performing the role of the *ilaw ng tahanan* (light of the home, or she who brings radiance to the home). Likewise, it is not conducive for fathers to be solely the *haligi ng tahanan* (pillar of the home, or he who makes the home stand). Moreover, it seems that following gender conventions in both types of households aggravates the emotional injuries of children. Thus, it would seem more beneficial for families to rearrange the division of labor in their families and for members to reconstitute their gender ideologies so as to accommodate the transformations engendered by spatial distance.

In the case of father-away households, women who perform only the role of the *ilaw ng tahanan* and do not in their performance incorporate male-ascribed responsibilities such as the disciplining of children run the risk of raising wayward youth. At the same time, migrant fathers would be ill-advised to perform only "distance fathering" as a *haligi ng tahanan*, that is, the authoritarian economic provider of the family. Migrant fathers who fail to incorporate nurturing qualities more often ascribed to mothers risk aggravating the emotional distance and unfamiliarity that geographical separation imposes on intergenerational ties in their families. Thus, as I discussed in Chapter 4, migrant fathers must in addition to their economic provision include more nurturing acts of kindness and sensitivity to their children so as to secure closer ties.

In the families of migrant mothers, children struggle to accept the reconstitution of mother as more of an economic provider and less of a caretaker of the home. Consequently, children who recognize the economic contributions of their mothers may still consider themselves to have been "abandoned" in migration. This is true regardless of the work done by extended kin (i.e., whether they do a lot of caring work or not). Aggravating feelings of abandonment is also the invisibility of fathers in mother-away families. Fathers rarely do housework, and in avoiding such labor they are doing gender boundary work. Indeed, female extended kin do the work left behind by migrant mothers more often than fathers do.

Most of the children of migrant mothers whom I met in the Philippines actually maintain little or no contact at all with their fathers, as these men tend to disappear. I assume that men do so in order to avoid the work left behind by migrant women. Men should nurture their children, however, as more and more women economically provide for them. Moreover, migrant women should still nurture (and they do) in order to maintain the close relations that they have sustained despite their geographical distance. The intimate ties mothers sustain with their children via their constant communication should be mirrored with like efforts by fathers remaining in the Philippines. In this way, children could come to see the responsibility of nurturing the family as belonging to both men and women. Finally, community and kin should help the families of migrant mothers in this effort by supporting the reconstitution of gender in their families. As we saw in chapters 2 and 5, community and kin unfortunately tend to uphold the ideal of the biological mother as the caretaker of children.

In households of both migrant mothers and migrant fathers, the expansion of either mothering or fathering means the achievement of closer intergenerational ties. In father-away families, migrant fathers who not only provide economically but also nurture tend to achieve more emotionally fulfilling ties with their children in the Philippines than those who only act as authoritarian disciplinary figures around their children. Likewise, migrant mothers who not only relegate the emotional care of their children to other relatives but assist them in doing so achieve closer ties with their children than migrant women who reduce mothering to the role of economic provider.

Following the same logic of the expansion of parental responsibilities for both men and women in transnational families, not only must mothers who care for the homes of migrant men impose discipline and authority on their children, but fathers left behind by migrant women must in turn nurture their children and care for them. Crossing the boundaries of the gender ideology of separate spheres, via the mutual expansion of men's and women's gender responsibilities, accommodates the caring needs created by migration's reorganization of the family better than does a division of labor that maintains gender boundaries. Such a strategic shift in the performance of gender, while requiring more work from all care providers, leads to fewer emotional rifts and greater tolerance of geographical distance.

Unfortunately, most families refuse to reorganize gender, which remains stubbornly static in the families of both migrant mothers and fathers. As I established in Chapter 3, income-earning migrant women often downplay the expansion of mothering to include the role of good provider, considering it to be an act of desperation. In so doing, they establish the inherent inadequacy of such an option for household arrangement. As we saw in Chapter 5, they further reinforce this inadequacy by maintaining images of martyrdom and suffering in their performance of transnational mothering. Moreover, transnational mothering is seen as not a choice, but a necessity. The persistence of gender conventions also manifests itself in the performance of fathering by migrant men. As we saw in Chapter 4, many men can act only as authority figures around the children they rarely see, since they often assume that this is what they ought to be doing to fulfill their role as a good father.

In various ways, the performance of mothering and fathering in transnational families does not question but instead maintains gender conventions. Fathers and mothers both resist the crossing of gender boundaries that is encouraged by the structural rearrangement of households in migration. This tells us that institutional rearrangements do not dictate the behavior of individuals. In other words, institutions do not overdetermine actions but only encourage set behavioral patterns. Encouragement of change could also face resistance from other sources, because the family as an institution does not exist in a vacuum. This tells us that organizational arrangements of institutions do not singularly determine the actions that constitute gender. Pressure from kin and community to uphold gender conventions, cultural pressure to meet moral standards of gender in society, and the resistance of men to expand their work are all factors that limit the possibility of greater gender transformations resulting from the formation of transnational families.

We have also seen that transnational families maintain gender conventions through an unequal distribution of labor between men and women. In keeping with gender boundaries, transnational families demand more work from women, whether abroad or in the Philippines. This is the case in both father-away and mother-away families. In both, I found that the work of men tends to narrow in its scope, while the work of women expands. Thus, although it is true that individuals cross gender boundaries, I found that inequalities of gender distinguish the scope of boundary crossings of men and women. Women add male-ascribed responsibilities to definitions of mothering, but men rarely add to their responsibilities that are traditionally assigned to women. It is also the case in Western societies that few men mother. Some scholars speculate that this may be due to economics, as income disparities between genders make it more conducive for men to stay outside the home.[1]

In the families of migrant men, mothers left behind often complain about having to simultaneously mother and father children in order to fill the vacuum created by the absence of fathers in their daily lives. In contrast, migrant men rarely if ever consider nurturing to be one of their fathering responsibilities. Thus, they are less likely to cross gender boundaries than migrant mothers. Women appear to be much more secure with their gender identities than men, who are less likely to challenge the boundaries that limit their performance of gender and the boundaries that set the tone of their relationships in society.

In either type of household, the reconstitution of gender would create closer intergenerational ties in the family. However, gender practices more often than not fail to conform to the transformations encouraged by the institutional reorganization of families. Instead, gender remains stubbornly conventional in both father-away and mother-away families. This works to the detriment of children, who I find still need to denaturalize concepts of mothering and fathering and at the same time realize that the division of labor in the family is a malleable construction that conforms to ideologies and structures in society.

### Future Studies

In this study, I did not focus on the experience of family reunification. Still unanswered is whether or not migrant fathers and their children are able to ease the emotional gap that confronts them upon the return migration of men; whether migrant women achieve a more egalitarian division of labor upon their permanent return home to the Philippines; and finally whether close familial relationships develop between parents and children that experience a prolonged duration of separation. What happens to these families, and the options parents have for raising children, is worthy of future study. When I completed my field research in the Philippines, the children who participated in this study had yet to reunify with their parents permanently. Since I left in April 2002, some children informed me that they themselves sought employment outside the country after they completed college. Those who migrated to the United States opted to bring their children, usually still infants; those who migrated to destinations with illiberal state regimes usually could not.

It would be interesting to see the end result of the sacrifices of the transnational migrant families in my study. Will we eventually see more families reunify permanently in the Philippines? Or will we see a greater number of second-generation transnational families? In future generations we will be able to see whether or not families were able to overcome the lack of resources in poor countries via migration and whether the sacrifice of transnational family formation was well worth it for the financial security of future generations. Equally compelling will be the examination of gender relations in these future generations.

Specifically, we need to address the question of whether there are differences in intergenerational relations as determined by the degree of gender boundary crossing in the family. Moreover, we need to examine whether the recognition of women as economic providers will lead to better intergenerational ties and, similarly, whether the efforts of fathers to engage in acts of nurturing will be rewarded by closer relationships. Likewise, will the expansion of gender responsibilities of either men or women lead to stronger ties in transnational families? Finally, will we see a backlash against the refusal of men to recognize the economic contributions of women to the family and nation?

## The Gender Paradox of Globalization

Gender tensions mar the smooth adjustment of families in the formation of transnational households in the Philippines. These tensions are not restricted to the Philippines, or for that matter exclusive to nations in the global south with similar struggles in migration. Families in the global north also experience gender tensions in the reconstitution of households. We see them in women's struggle to balance work and family life in the last thirty years. In globalization, we find that the increase in women's work outside the home has not been met with a decrease in their responsibilities inside the home. This impediment to the advancement of women remains a challenge for feminist scholars.[2]

In globalization, a gender paradox defines the labor of women. Globalization simultaneously pushes women to work both inside and outside the home. This is true for women in both poor and rich nations in the global economy. This contradictory positioning of women vis-à-vis the home emerges from the doubling of women's work, which is caused, first, by the increase in women's labor market participation, one partially caused by the decline in men's wages in the last thirty years as well as the need for women's self-fulfillment; second, by the refusal of men to acknowledge the income contributions of women with an increase in their household work; and, third and finally, by the failure of the state to respond to the different set of caring needs of dual wage-earning or single-parent households (in other words, non-patriarchal nuclear households). The problems of women in the home are not just caused by gender inequalities in the family. In addition, regressive state welfare policies ignore the economic dependence of families and markets on women's productive labor.

This study closely examines the gender paradox that confronts the labor market participation of women based on a case study of migrant families in the Philippines. In the beginning of this study, I had assumed I would find a marked reconstitution of gender ideological beliefs in the Philippines, a country highly dependent on the foreign currency generated by migrant women's earnings and a country where a significant number of children grow up with their mothers living away from home. What I found was a "stalled revolution," similar to what Arlie Hochschild had observed of dual-income families in the United States in the 1980s, which stunts the reconstitution of gender forced by women's migration.[3]

The ideology of women's domesticity remains quite intact in the Philippines. This ideology has been recast to be performed in a transnational terrain by migrant mothers. Likewise, it is promoted by the absence of fathers. Finally, it is encouraged by the cultural traditions espoused by community and kin. Still, accepting the gender boundary crossings initiated by women's migration, and accordingly meeting this crossing with the expansion of the gender boundaries of men, could only benefit families. It would not just lessen the emotional upheavals endured by transnational family members in the Philippines, but by example it would also pave the way for women's equality in globalization.

INTRODUCTION

1. Pierre Bourdieu, *Masculine Domination* (Stanford, CA: Stanford University Press, 2001), 27.

2. Judith Butler, *Gender Trouble* (New York: Routledge Press, 1990), xv.

3. Sarah Fenstermaker, Candace West, and Don H. Zimmerman, "Gender Inequality: New Conceptual Terrain," in *Doing Gender, Doing Difference: Inequality, Power and Institutional Change*, eds. Sarah Fenstermaker and Candace West (New York: Routledge, 2002), 30.

4. Providing an ethnography of the *bakla* community in New York is the ethnography by Martin Manalansan IV, *Global Divas* (Durham, NC: Duke University Press, 2003).

5. Judith Lorber, *The Paradoxes of Gender* (New Haven, CT: Yale University Press, 1994), 96.

6. The notion of the Panopticon was originated by Jeremy Bentham, who wrote in 1843 about architectural designs for prisons that maximize surveillance and control. An imposing tower looming over those surveiled (which yet is invisible to those on the outside looking in), the Panopticon has as its effect "to induce in the inmate a state of conscious and permanent visibility that assures the automatic functioning of power" (Michel Foucault, *Discipline and Punish* [New York: Vintage Books, 1979], 201). The subject is to internalize a sense that he is seen, yet he himself does not see. Foucault applied the idea of the panoptic machine to the disciplining of society, which extends to society as a whole via its institutions and apparatuses. The extensive disciplining of society then occurs through the monitoring of actions. See 195–228 for Foucault's theoretical discussion of the panoptic machine and surveillance.

7. Arjun Appadurai describes how in globalization disjunctures between economy, culture, and politics occur primarily through five dimensions of cultural flows that cross nation-state boundaries. These he calls ethnoscapes, mediascapes, technoscapes, financescapes, and ideoscapes. In this case, cultural disorganizations or ruptures in globalization occur via challenges to the proper gender order in the Philippines. See Appadurai, *Modernity at Large:*

*Cultural Dimensions of Globalization* (Minneapolis: University of Minnesota Press, 1996), 33.

8. Kanlungan Center Foundation, *Fast Facts on Labor Migration* (Quezon City: Kanlungan Foundation Center, 2000). Recent works that address or mention the formation of a Filipino diaspora include Ligaya Lindio-McGovern, "Labor Export in the Context of Globalization: The Experience of Filipino Domestic Workers in Rome," *International Sociology* 18(3): 513–34; Barbara Ehrenreich and Arlie Hochschild, eds., *Global Woman: Nannies, Maids, and Sex Workers in the New Economy* (New York: Metropolitan Books, 2003); and Katherine Gibson, Lisa Law, and Deidre McKay, "Beyond Heroes and Victims: Filipina Contract Migrants, Economic Activism, and Class Transformation," *International Feminist Journal of Politics* 3(3): 365–86.

9. According to Anthony Giddens, practices constitute structures but structures impose social rules and orders that shape the contours of practices. See his *The Constitution of Society* (Cambridge: Polity Press, 1984); and *Modernity and Self Identity: Self and Society in the Late Modern Age* (Stanford, CA: Stanford University Press, 1991). Scholars who incorporate a structuration perspective in their analysis of gender include Barbara Risman, *Gender Vertigo: American Families in Transition* (New Haven, CT: Yale University Press, 1999); and Robert Connell, *Masculinities* (Berkeley: University of California Press, 1994).

10. Robert Connell, *Gender and Power* (Stanford, CA: Stanford University Press, 1987), 95.

11. Ibid., 96.

12. Barrie Thorne, "Symposium: On West and Fenstermaker's 'Doing Gender,'" *Gender and Society* 9 (1995): 497–99.

13. Judith Butler, *Gender Trouble* (New York: Routledge, 1990), 141.

14. Republic of the Philippines, *1998 Regional Social and Economic Trends, Region VI (Western Visayas)* (Makati City: National Statistical Coordination Board, 1998).

15. Rhacel Salazar Parreñas, *Servants of Globalization: Women, Migration, and Domestic Work* (Stanford, CA: Stanford University Press, 2001) (hereafter Parreñas 2001a).

CHAPTER 1

1. This figure is based on records of the Philippine Overseas Employment Agency. Danilo A. Arao, "Deployment of Migrant Workers Increasing," *Ibon Facts and Figures* 23(8) (April 30, 2000): 8.

2. Interview with Father Paulo Prigol, the representative of Catholic Bishops' Conference of the Philippines and Scalabrini Migration Center, August 27, 2001.

3. For an excellent documentation of the use of social networks in the incorporation of women in migration and the labor market, see Pierrette Hondagneu-Sotelo, *Gendered Transitions: Mexican Experiences of Migration* (Berkeley: University of California Press, 1994).

4. Interview with representatives of the Commission for Filipino Overseas, October 4, 2001. In 1974, President Ferdinand Marcos implemented the "manpower exchange programme" as a state strategy of economic growth for the Philippines. Its goals were the development, promotion, and regulation of overseas employment. See Linda Basch, Nina Glick Schiller, and Cristina Szanton Blanc, *Nations Unbound* (New York: Routledge, 1994).

5. Ibon, "Mirrors of the Social Crisis," *Ibon Facts and Figures* 19(7) (1996): 2 (hereafter Ibon 1996).

6. The Tagalog word *ibon* means bird, suggesting the image of the group's having a "bird's eye view" of the socio-economic inequalities in the Philippines.

7. This trend is reflected in enrollment rates of public and private schools in my field research site. My survey of one private high school found that 21.92 percent of its students are children of migrant parents. In contrast, only 5.91 percent of students in one of the large public high schools in the area are children of migrant workers.

8. Ibon, "Debt Curse," *Ibon Facts and Figures* 23: 21 and 22 (November 15 and 30, 2000), 8 (hereafter Ibon 2000a).

9. Maitet Diokno-Pascual, "The Burdensome Debt" (2001), unpublished paper available at the Freedom from Debt Coalition, Quezon City, Philippines.

10. Rosario Bella Guzman, "The Economy Under Arroyo: Crisis and Bitter Pills," *Birdtalk: Economic and Political Briefing* (July 18, 2001): 3–18.

11. A. M. Mendoza, Jr., *The Record of a Non-Confrontational Debt Management Approach, State of the Nation Report* (Diliman, Quezon City: University of the Philippines Press and the Center for Integrative and Development Studies, 1992), 7.

12. Ibon 2000a, 8.

13. Diokno-Pascual 2001.

14. Ibid. Note that the Philippines was the first country subject to SAP. It was used as a testing ground for the wholesale liberalization of the economy and the removal of all protection of import substitution industrialization.

15. Rene Ofreneo, *Philippine Industrialization and Industrial Relations*, State of the Nation Reports 12 (Diliman, Quezon City: University of the Philippines Press and the Center for Integrative and Development Studies, 1995).

16. Ibon, "The Export Strategy," *Ibon Facts and Figures* 21:13 and 14 (July 15 and 31, 1998), 5 (hereafter Ibon 1998).

17. Ibid.

18. Ibon, "The Creditors' Conspiracy," *People's Policy and Advocacy Studies Special Release* (September 1997), 9 (hereafter Ibon 1997b).

19. Ibid.

20. Guzman 2001, 4.

21. Ibid., 15.

22. Ibon, "In the Cycle of Debt," *People's Policy and Advocacy Studies Special Release* (September 1997), 8 (hereafter Ibon 1997a).

23. Saskia Sassen, "Women's Burden: Counter-Geographies of Globalization and the Feminization of Survival," *Journal of International Affairs* 53:2 (Spring 2000), 513.

24. Guzman 2001, 17.

25. Diokno-Pascual 2001.

26. Ibon, "The Neo-Liberal Prescription," *People's Policy and Advocacy Studies Special Release* (September 1997), 16 (hereafter Ibon 1997c).

27. Gina Mission, "The Breadwinners: Female Migrant Workers," *Women's International Network* 15A (1998).

28. Ida Monticello, a twenty-year-old marketing specialist, lives with her mother, who is a schoolteacher, and her four sisters, who are between the ages of twenty-two and thirty. Her father is a master mariner who has worked as a seafarer for more than thirty years.

29. Ibon, "National Budget: People's Budget?" *Ibon Facts and Figures* 23(21 and 22) (November 15 and 30, 2000), 4.

30. Ibid., 5.

31. Guzman 2001, 11.

32. Ibon, "Teachers of the New Millennium," *Ibon Facts and Figures* 23(8) (April 30, 2000), 5 (hereafter Ibon 2000c). Note that many debtor countries are forced to pay over 50 percent of government revenues to service the foreign debt. See Sassen 2000, 513.

33. Victoria Ilano is a stay-at-home grandmother helping care for three children between fifteen and eighteen years old; their father has worked as a seafarer for at least fifteen years. She helps her daughter-in-law with the care of these three children.

34. Arabela Gosalves is a retired manager of a department store. Her husband has lived in the United States since 1983, working as a car dealer. He sends Arabela $1,000 a month to cover the costs of raising their four children, who are now eighteen, twenty, twenty-five, and twenty-nine.

35. Rocil Relocio is a twenty-three-year-old medical student whose mother has worked as nurse in the United Kingdom since 1987. He and his twenty-one-year-old sister live with his father, an etymologist, in the Philippines. The father travels frequently to do his research.

36. Carmelo Ledesma is a retired military officer who lives with his two sons, aged eighteen and twenty. His wife has worked as a nurse in Saudi Arabia for at least thirteen years.

37. Tuition and registration fees average 20,000 pesos a semester at the university attended by Carmelo's sons.

38. Leotes Marie T. Lugo, "Search for Greener Pastures Continue [sic]," *Business World* (March 15–16, 2000).

39. Arturo M. Pesigan, Ruben N. Caragay, Marilyn Lorenzo, and Victoria A. Bautista, *Assessments of Primary Health Care in the Philippines, State of the Nation Reports 3* (Diliman, Quezon City: University of the Philippines Press and the Center for Integrative and Development Studies, 1992), 3, 4.

40. Structural Adjustment Participatory Review International Network (SAPRIN), "The Policy Roots of Economic Crisis and Poverty: A Multi-Country Participatory Assessment of Structural Adjustment" (Washington DC: SAPRIN, 2002), 152. Report available online at http://www.saprin. org/global_rpt.htm. Last searched on February 4, 2004.

41. Ibid.

42. Josette Piedad is a thirty-year-old mother of two. Her father, who worked as a seafarer, passed away when she was twelve years old. Her mother worked from 1982 to 1995 as a domestic worker in the Gulf region. See Abigail Bakan and Daiva Stasiulis, eds., *Not One of the Family: Foreign Domestic Workers in Canada* (Toronto: University of Toronto Press, 1997), for a discussion of the social boundaries that control the incorporation of domestic workers in Canada.

43. For extensive discussions of the stunted integration of migrant Filipina domestic workers in Canada, see the work of Geraldine Pratt, "Stereotypes and Ambivalence: Nanny Agents' Stereotypes of Domestic Workers in Vancouver, BC," *Gender, Place, and Culture* 4(1997): 159–77; and "From Registered Nurse to Registered Nanny: Discursive Geographies of Filipina Domestic Workers in Vancouver, B.C.," *Economic Geography* 75: 215–36.

44. Kanlungan Center Foundation, *Fast Facts on Labor Migration* (Quezon City: Kanlungan Center Foundation, 2000), 10, 12.

45. Ibid., 12.

46. See Parreñas 2001a; chapter 3 offers an extensive discussion of the international division of reproductive labor.

47. For an extensive discussion of the globalization of care work, see Barbara Ehrenreich and Arlie Hochschild, eds., *Global Woman: Nannies, Maids, and Sex Workers in the New Economy* (New York: Metropolitan Books, 2003); Noeleen Heyzer, Geertje Lycklama á Nijeholt, and Nedra Weekaroon, eds., *The Trade in Domestic Workers: Causes, Mechanisms, and Consequences of International Labor Migration* (London: Zed Books, 1994).

48. See Lugo 2002.

49. Rene E. Ofreneo, *Philippine Industrialization and Industrial Relations*, State of the Nation Reports 12 (Diliman, Quezon City: University of the Philippines Press and the Center for Integrative and Development Studies, 1995), 3.

50. Bureau of Labor and Employment Statistics, "Remittances from Overseas Filipino Workers by Country of Origin Philippines: 1997—Fourth Quarter 1999," *Pinoy Migrants*, Shared Government Information System for Migration, available at http://cmisd-web.dfa.gov.ph/pinoymigrants.

51. Paul Ong, Edna Bonacich, and Lucie Cheng, "The Political Economy of Capitalist Restructuring and the New Asian Immigration," in *The New Asian Immigration in Los Angeles and Global Restructuring*, ed. P. Ong, E. Bonacich, and L. Cheng (Philadelphia, PA: Temple University Press, 1994), 25.

52. Catherine Choy, *Empire of Care: Nursing and Migration in Filipino American History* (Durham, NC, and London: Duke University Press, 2003).

53. In 2000, 64.6 percent of women in the United Kingdom were in the paid labor force; there were 63.7 percent in the Netherlands, 57.9 percent in Germany, and 55.3 percent in France. Rianne Mahon, "Child Care: Toward What Kind of 'Social Europe'?" *Social Politics* 9 (2002): 350.

54. See Martin Conroy, *Sustaining the New Economy: Work, Family, and Community in the Information Age* (New York: Russell Sage Foundation Press; and Cambridge, MA: Harvard University Press, 2000), 138.

55. Scott Coltrane and Justin Galt, "The History of Men's Caring," in *Care Work: Gender, Labour and the Welfare State*, ed. Madonna Harrington Meyer (New York and London: Routledge, 2000), 29.

56. V. A. Goddard, *Gender, Family and Work in Naples* (Oxford and Washington, DC: Berg, 1996).

57. Conroy 2000, 137.

58. Arlie Hochschild with Anne Machung, *The Second Shift* (New York: Avon Books, 1989).

59. Shirin Rai, *Gender and the Political Economy of Development* (Cambridge: Polity Press, 2002), 101.

60. See Coltrane and Galt 2000; Hochschild 1989.

61. By welfare support, I refer to the government's accountability for the social and material well-being of its citizenry. See Jody Heymann, *The Widening Gap: Why America's Working Families Are in Jeopardy—and What Can Be Done About It* (New York: Basic Books, 2000).

62. Mary Daly and Jane Lewis, "The Concept of Social Care and the

Analysis of Contemporary Welfare States," *British Journal of Sociology* 51:2 (June 2000): 281–98.

63. Francesca Cancian and Stacey Oliker, *Caring and Gender* (Thousand Oaks, CA: Pine Forge Press, 2000), 116. See Jennifer Mellor, "Filling in the Gaps in Long Term Care Insurance," in *Care Work: Gender, Labour and the Welfare State*, ed. Madonna Harrington Meyer (New York and London: Routledge, 2000), 206.

64. Mellor 2000, 206.

65. Daly and Lewis 2000, 292.

66. Ruth Milkman, Ellen Reese, and Benita Roth, "The Macrosociology of Paid Domestic Labor," *Work and Occupations* 25(4) (1998): 483–507.

67. See Nancy Folbre, *The Invisible Heart: Economics and Family Values* (New York: New Press, 2001); and Joan Tronto, "The 'Nanny' Question in Feminism," *Hypatia* 17:2 (Spring 2002): 34–51.

68. Folbre 2001, 111.

69. Ibid., 110.

70. I acknowledge Kim W. West for making this analogy.

71. Tronto 2002.

72. Ibid., 48.

73. Marianne H. Marchand and Anne Sisson Runyan, "Introduction: Feminist Sightings of Global Restructuring: Conceptualizations and Reconceptualizations," in *Gender and Global Restructuring: Sightings, Sites, and Resistances*, ed. Marianne H. Marchand and Anne Sisson Runyan (London and New York: Routledge, 2000), 17.

CHAPTER 2

1. I thank Maria Ontiveros for making this observation.

2. Michele Lamont, *The Dignity of Working Men: Morality and the Boundaries of Race, Class, and Immigration* (Cambridge, MA: Harvard University Press; and New York: Russell Sage Foundation, 2000).

3. To illustrate her point, Lamont describes how white American workers shun as un-American those without the moral standards of the "disciplined self" and likewise how African Americans disdain uncaring individuals.

4. Belen Medina, *The Filipino Family*, 2d ed. (Diliman, Quezon City: University of the Philippines Press, 2001), 146. Most families require at least two incomes, because more than 70 percent of families live below the poverty line. See Mina Ramirez and Alfonso Deza, *When Labor Does Not Pay*, Occasional Monograph 9 (Manila: Asian Social Institute, 1997), 12; and Gelia T. Castillo, *Where Food and Population Meet: The Filipino Household Among Other Households* (Diliman, Quezon City: University of the Philippines Press and Center for Integrative and Development Studies, 1993), 13.

5. Medina 2001, 39.

6. Lucie Cheng, "Globalization and Women's Paid Labour," *International Social Science Journal* 160 (June 1999): 218.

7. Corazon Raymundo, "Demographic Changes and the Filipino Family," in *The Filipino Family and the Nation: A Collection of Readings on Family Life Issues and Concerns*, ed. University of the Philippines College of Home Economics (Quezon City: University of the Philippines, 1993), 20.

8. See chapter 4 of Parreñas 2001a.

9. See Rayna Rapp, "Family and Class in Contemporary America: Notes Toward an Understanding of Ideology," in *Rethinking the Family*, ed. Barrie Thorne and Marilyn Yalom (New York: Longman, 1982), 170.

10. Marjorie DeVault, *Feeding the Family: The Social Organization of Caring as Gendered Work* (Chicago, IL: University of Chicago Press, 1991), 15–18.

11. Lorber 1994.

12. Cynthia Fuchs Epstein, "Border Crossings: The Constraints of Time Norms in the Transgression of Gender and Professional Roles." Paper presented at the American Sociological Association Meeting, Washington DC, August 2000.

13. Judith Stacey, *In the Name of the Family* (Boston, MA: Beacon Press, 1996).

14. I thank Lok Siu for helping formulate this observation.

15. Alicia V. Sempio-Diy, "The Philippine Constitution and the Filipino Family: 'The Family Code,'" in University of the Philippines College of Home Economics (ed.), *The Filipino Family and the National Collection of Readings on Family Life Issues and Concerns* (Quezon City, Philippines: University of the Philippines, 1993), 1–15.

16. Republic of the Philippines, *1986 Constitution of the Republic of the Philippines* (Manila: Republic of the Philippines, 1986), Article XV, Section 1.

17. Republic of the Philippines, *The Family Code of the Philippines* (Manila: Republic of the Philippines, 1987).

18. In the prior civil code, women had to seek the approval of their husbands for their employment.

19. For example, the state constructs the services of women to the nation to include their maternal function. One constitutional provision states, "The State shall protect working women by providing safe and healthful working conditions, taking into account their maternal functions, and such facilities and opportunities that will enhance their welfare and enable them to realize their full potential in the service of the nation." Republic of the Philippines, *The 1986 Constitution of the Republic of the Philippines*, Article XIII, Section 14. This validates the classification of individuals on the basis of the biological differences between the sexes.

20. Republic of the Philippines, *The Family Code* (1987), Article 213.
21. Ibid., Comments.
22. Marije Meerman, *The Chain of Love* (Netherlands: VPRO-TV, 2001).
23. Both the Constitution and the Family Code stipulate that "the sanctity of the family" stands on the inviolability of marriage and the conjugal union of a man and (maternal) woman. The first provision of the Family Code establishes that "marriage . . . between a man and a woman . . . is the foundation of the family and an inviolable social institution whose nature, consequences and incidents are governed by law and not subject to stipulation." See Republic of the Philippines, *The 1986 Constitution of the Republic of the Philippines*, Article 1. Marriage is absolute once it has been recognized by the church or state.
24. Republic of the Philippines, *The Family Code*, Article 68.
25. Elizabeth Aguiling-Pangalangan, "The Family Under Philippine Law," in *The Filipino Family: A Spectrum of Views and Issues*, ed. Aurora Perez (Quezon City, Philippines: University of the Philippines Office of Research Coordination), 19.
26. According to the definition of a modern nuclear family, love and not property obligations bind marital ties. For the sake of love, fidelity is imposed as a legal obligation.
27. Republic of the Philippines, *The Family Code*, Article 69.
28. Ibid., Article 55.
29. These headlines appeared in the *Philippine Star* and the *Inquirer*.
30. Agence France Presse, "Ramos: Overseas Employment a Threat to Filipino Families," *Philippine Inquirer* (May 26, 1995).
31. Despite its push to retain the ideology of women's domesticity, the Family Code does advance the rights of women. For instance, the Family Code grants women—particularly wives—the autonomy to "exercise any legitimate profession, occupation, business or activity without the consent" of their husbands (Article 73). Under the pre-existing 1949 Civil Code, women did not have the right to participate in the labor market without the consent of their husbands. Acknowledging the constitutional provision that the state "shall ensure the fundamental equality of women and men before the law" (Article II, Section 12), the code also establishes that "the management of the household shall be the right and duty of both spouses" (Article 71). Despite the gains of women, the Family Code does still retain the figure of the father as the head of the household and gives him greater authority over children. Article 211 establishes that "the father and the mother shall jointly exercise parental authority over the persons of their common children. In case of disagreement, the father's decision shall prevail." See Republic of the Philippines, *The Family Code* (1987). For more readings on the gender transformations instituted by the Family Code, see Myrna Feliciano,

"Law, Gender, and the Family in the Philippines," *Law and Society Review* 28 (1994): 547–61; Center for Women's Resources, *Is the Traditional Filipino Family Still Surviving: The Women's Perspective on the Family Code* (Quezon City: Center for Women's Resources, 1989).

32. I thank Denise Segura for helping me advance this argument.

33. I base this claim on a survey of articles that appeared in Philippine dailies from 1995 to 1998. I obtained the newspaper articles from the library of the Philippine Overseas Employment Administration, which catalogues all media reports on migrant Filipino workers. For some examples, see Department of Social Welfare and Development, *Coping Capabilities of Solo Parents and Spouses of Overseas Workers* (Manila: Department of Social Welfare and Development, 1993); Francis Santamaria, "Problems Regarding Family Relations and Children of Migrant Workers," in *Filipino Women Overseas Contract Workers: At What Cost?*, ed. Ruby Palma Beltran and Aurora Javate de Dios (Quezon City: Goodwill Trading Company, 1992), 69–72; and Ramirez and Deza 1997.

34. Santamaria 1992, 69.

35. Marie Aganon, "Migrant Labor and the Filipino Family," in *The Filipino Family: A Spectrum of Views and Issues*, ed. Aurora Perez (Quezon City: University of the Philippines, Office of Research Coordination, 1995), 89. Blaming the difficulties experienced by children solely on the family, Aganon does not take into account the influence of other institutions on children's socialization. Moreover, she does not consider stigmatization as a possible source of "inadequate social development."

36. Graziano Battistella and Maria Cecilia Astardo-Conaco, *Impact of Labor Migration on the Children Left Behind* (Quezon City: Scalabrini Migration Center, 1996).

37. Ibid., 57.

38. Ibid., 65.

39. Various headlines reveal this propensity. While the headline "Overseas Job vs. Family Stability" equates transnational family life with instability, other headlines reveal the supposed causes of this instability. See Lorie Toledo, "Overseas Job vs. Family Stability," *People's Journal* (December 15, 1993), 4. For instance, the headline "Sleeping Beauty Gets Raped While Her Mom Works as a (Domestic Helper) in Hong Kong" points to the inadequate protection of children in these families. See Philippine Tonight Staff, "'Sleeping Beauty' Gets Raped . . . While Her Mom Works as DH in Hong Kong," *Philippine Tonight* (July 16, 1993). The insufficient guidance given children is pointed out four years later in the headline "Education of OFW's [Overseas Filipino Workers] Children Suffer [sic]." See Mac Cabreros, "Edukasyon ng mga anak ng OFWs nasasakripisyo (Education of children of OFWs suffer [sic])," *Abante* (June 23, 1997), 5. Finally, the absence of emo-

tional security is reported a year later, in an article by Lynette L. Corporal entitled "OFW's Kids Emotionally Troubled," *Manila Standard* (August 18, 1998), 1.

40. Lorie Toledo, "Child Sexual Abuse Awareness," *People's Journal* (February 19, 1996), 4.

41. Susan Fernandez, "Pamilya ng OFWs maraming hirap (Many hardships in the families of OFWs)" *Abante* (January 27, 1997), 5.

42. Elected representatives of a district, *barangay* captains are similar in function to city council members.

43. My research assistant and I gathered interviews with officers of each of these organizations and conducted focus-group discussions with members of five organizations. I arranged the focus-group discussions weeks ahead of time and with the cooperation of officers arranged to hold discussions with the most active members of each organization. Focus group discussions ranged from four to fifteen individuals in size. They were approximately one hour in length. The discussions addressed problems and issues that family members regularly confront in running transnational households, for instance, issues concerning the reintegration of the migrant parent and the struggle of raising children single-handedly or from a distance.

44. The government consistently reports that fathers are more likely to migrate than mothers. For instance, one survey indicates that 56 percent of migrant women workers are single and married men make up 71 percent of male migrants. Yet, these figures do not account for single mothers or undocumented workers. See Maruja Asis, "The Return Migration of Filipino Women Migrants: Home, But Not Home for Good," in *Female Labour Migration in South-East Asia: Change and Continuity* (Bangkok: Asian Research Centre for Migration, Institute for Asian Studies, Chulalongkorn University, 2001), 31.

45. The families of migrant mothers could not share their own perspectives as they were conspicuously absent in the discussion group. I also could not observe whether these claims ring true for the children of migrant women growing up under the care of their fathers or other relatives in this specific town.

46. We visited four parish churches in the area and interviewed parish priests to document how they address the issues of the family and migration. I selected parishes in different districts of the city and parishes that had parishioners representing various class backgrounds.

47. We conducted interviews with guidance counselors in eleven elementary and high schools in the area. We spoke to counselors in both private and public schools. The interviews were approximately one hour in length.

48. I had not followed up on the situation of these boys or sought to compare the school performance of children with migrant parents and those

without. A survey I conducted of 228 children of migrant fathers and mothers shows no difference in the school performance of the children of migrant mothers and migrant fathers. While 23 percent of 124 children of migrant fathers admitted to failing at least one subject, 28 percent of 94 children of migrant mothers admitted to doing so. Notably, four out of ten children of two-migrant parents reported failing at least one subject since the migration of their parents.

49. Excerpt taken from a handout distributed to high school students for a class on family values.

50. June Principe, Corazon Garcia, Cersencio Viernes, Carlos Asuncion, Trinidad Flores, *Technology and Home Economics for Secondary Schools*, rev. ed. (Quezon City: FNB Educational, Inc., 1999), 13.

51. Ibid., 14.

52. Pope John Paul VI, *Pastoral Constitution on the Church in the Modern World, Gaudium et Spes* (Pasay City, Philippines: Paulines Publishing House), 80.

53. It wasn't until I was reading the lesson plans from area high schools that I was struck by the fact that this precise definition was given by the Pope in the publication *Letters to Families from Pope John Paul VI* (1994), a popular text that teachers in the area refer to for their family values courses. See Pope John Paul VI, *Pastoral Constitution on the Church in the Modern World, Gaudium et Spes* (Pasay City, Philippines: Paulines Publishing House).

54. However, children often reduced notions of mothering and fathering to biology-based definitions.

55. Principe et al. 1999, 27.

56. See chapter five, "The Children of Immigration in School," in Carola Suarez-Orosco and Marcelo Suarez-Orosco, *Children of Immigration* (Cambridge, MA: Harvard University Press, 2001).

57. I acknowledge Nina Eliasoph for bringing my attention to this gender paradox that occurs in the public sphere.

CHAPTER 3

1. Among my sample of sixty-nine young adults, four had returned from the United States to go to school in the Philippines; two are children of fathers who left their mothers to start a new life in the United States; one is a child of a migrant mother who needed to escape a philandering husband; fifteen are young adult children of migrant parents who left to "provide for the family"; twenty-five have parents who migrated to "escape poverty"; eleven are children of parents motivated by career advancement; and another eleven are young adult children of parents who faced labor market difficulties in the Philippines.

2. See Medina 2001, 143; and Maria Emma Concepcion Liwag, Alma S. dela Cruz, and Maria Elizabeth Macapagal, *A UNICEF and Ateneo Study: How We Raise Our Daughters and Sons: Childrearing and Gender Socialization in the Philippines* (Quezon City: United Nations Children's Fund and Ateneo Wellness Center, 1999), 16.

3. Interviewees introduced me to these traditional gender concepts.

4. Medina 2001, 146.

5. Lucie Cheng, "Globalization and Women's Paid Labor in Asia," *International Social Science Journal* 160 (June 1999): 218.

6. Medina 2001, 148.

7. Ibid., 151.

8. Liwag et al. 1999.

9. Medina 2001.

10. Scott Coltrane, *The Family Man* (Oxford: Oxford University Press, 1996), 157. Also see Hochschild 1989.

11. Grace Aguiling Dalisay et al., as cited in Medina 2001, 144.

12. Medina 2001, 151.

13. Judith Gerson and Kathy Peiss, "Boundaries, Negotiation, Consciousness: Conceptualizing Gender Relations," *Social Problems* 32(4) (1985): 317.

14. Ibid.

15. Jean L. Potuchek, *Who Supports the Family? Gender and Breadwinning in Dual-Earner Marriages* (Stanford, CA: Stanford University Press, 1997), 27–28.

16. Theresa Bascara is the eighteen-year-old daughter of a never-married woman who has worked in Hong Kong as a domestic worker since 1984. Theresa and her twenty-year-old sister live in a big household under the care of her grandmother and with the support of a large clan of maternal kin. Her mother financially supports her entire household, giving them approximately $250 per month, and even without the benefit of a paid holiday she manages to visit the Philippines every two years, even if for only fifteen days.

17. Ibid., 54.

18. Among these children, four mentioned that their fathers had migrated for the sake of providing for their education, while another four gave "building a house" as the primary motive of their father. Another three children—two of a migrant mother and one of two migrant parents—cited "greener pastures," with eventual permanent migration for the entire family as the long-term goal. Finally, another four children in this category gave achieving security as the parental motive for migration. Of this last group, two are the children of two migrant parents and one is of a migrant mother.

19. See Jesse Bernard, "The Good Provider," *American Psychologist* 36:1 (1981): 1–12.

20. Caridad Candado lives with three siblings and her mother, who is a schoolteacher. An aunt assists them with daily household chores.

21. Gregoria Tremania is a law student who lives with her stay-at-home mother and two younger siblings, who are eight and seventeen years old. She has a twenty-eight-year-old sister who works as a nurse in Connecticut. Employed as a seafarer for twenty-eight years, her father is a high-ranking officer, a chief mate.

22. Rodney Palanca is a nineteen-year-old student whose mother migrated to Saudi Arabia in 1990. He grew up in the southern Philippines with his twelve-year-old brother and fourteen-year-old sister under the guidance of their father.

CHAPTER 4

1. Erlinda Gaylan is a nineteen-year-old college student who lives with her seven-year-old sister and stay-at-home mother. Her father had been employed outside the country for at least fifteen years at the time of our interview.

2. By maternal acts, I follow Sarah Ruddick's line of thinking to refer to nurturing acts of people-centered care. Sarah Ruddick, "Maternal Thinking," in *Rethinking the Family: Some Feminist Questions*, ed. Barrie Thorne with Marilyn Yalom (New York: Longhorn, 1982), 76–94.

3. Note that only two migrant fathers in my sample had left their wives for another woman in their country of destination.

4. Sharon Hays, *The Cultural Contradictions of Motherhood* (New Haven, CT: Yale University Press, 1996).

5. Ibid., x.

6. Bernard 1981, 4.

7. Ibid., 10. Bernard states that "tender loving care was not one of the requirements. Emotional ministrations from the family were his right. Providing them was not a corresponding obligation."

8. Medina 2001, 145.

9. Castillo 1993, 14–16.

10. National Statistical Coordination Board, *Men and Women in the Philippines: A Statistical Handbook* (Manila: National Statistical Coordination Board, 1999), 115.

11. See chapter 5 of Coltrane 1996.

12. Bernard 1981.

13. Danica and her siblings live with their stay-at-home mother. Her father is a chief engineer, the highest-ranked officer operating the machinery in the lower level of a shipping vessel.

14. Most children whose fathers work outside the Philippines cannot complain of major disruptions initiated by migration in the routine of family life, because the fathers of many of them have been working outside the Philippines for as long as they can remember.

15. Claudio Regala is a twenty-year-old student who lives with his eighteen-year-old sister and his mother, a college professor.

16. Kiara is an eighteen-year-old college student. Her mother is a public schoolteacher and her father is an unranked seafarer. She lives at home with her mother and her four-, six-, and eleven-year-old siblings.

17. Kenneth rents a room in a boarding house near his college but frequently returns to his parents' home in the provinces. His mother is a schoolteacher, and his father has worked in the Middle East as a craft maintenance mechanic for more than ten years. His siblings work in Manila and the United States or still attend school in the area.

18. Leonardo Monfort is a twenty-one-year-old college student. His father—now a captain—has worked as a seafarer since his birth. He now lives with his grandmother but grew up in Manila with his mother and three brothers.

19. Ton-ton lives at home with his stay-at-home mother, both his maternal and his paternal grandparents, a fifteen-year-old brother, a sixteen-year-old sister, and a slew of cousins and household help. His father has worked as a chief engineer in a shipping vessel for more than fifteen years.

20. See Article 211 of the 1986 Family Code of the Republic of the Philippines. It states: "The father and the mother shall jointly exercise parental authority over the persons of their common children. In case of disagreement, the father's decision shall prevail."

21. Suzette is a nineteen-year-old college student who lives at home with her stay-at-home mother and twenty-year-old brother. Her father is a trained mechanical engineer who works as a project manager for an oil company in Saudi Arabia.

22. Clara Maria Tantoco is an eighteen-year-old college student who rents a room in a boarding house near the university. The oldest in her family, she returns to the provinces almost every weekend to spend time with her nine-year-old sister and her three brothers, who are seven, twelve, and fourteen. Her stay-at-home mother cares for her siblings while her father, an unranked seafarer, works outside the country.

23. Adelaida Quilaton is a stay-at-home mother of two teenaged daughters, who are fifteen and seventeen. Her husband has worked on a ship for more than seventeen years.

24. A proportion of a seafarer's salary is paid directly to family members in the Philippines. Most households in my sample received a 50 percent salary distribution, but some seafarers allot 60 percent of their monthly salary to their families in the Philippines.

25. Ilonah Monticello is the mother of five daughters, who are between twenty and thirty-one years of age. Her husband has worked as a seafarer for more than thirty years. All of her daughters, even those who are married

with children, still live with her in their large, three-level home in the center of the city.

26. A popular brand of nourishment drink.

27. Caridad is an eighteen-year-old college student who lives with her siblings, her mother, and her aunt in the Philippines while her father works in Brunei as an auto mechanic. Her father has worked outside the country for more than six years. Her mother supplements the earnings of her father with her wages as a schoolteacher.

28. Bethamay Roncesvalles is a twenty-year-old college student whose mother works as a teacher. His father is a high-ranking seafarer who has worked outside the country for more than twenty years.

CHAPTER 5

1. See Pierrette Hondagneu-Sotelo, *Doméstica* (Berkeley: University of California Press, 2001); Parreñas 2001a; Nicole Constable, *Maid to Order in Hong Kong* (Ithaca, NY: Cornell University Press, 1997); and Christine Chin, *In Service and Servitude* (New York: Columbia University Press, 1998). In the case of Sri Lanka, it is reported that three-fourths of female emigrants are married women. See Michelle Gamburd, *A Kitchen Spoon's Handle* (Ithaca, NY: Cornell University Press, 2000), 39.

2. Pierrette Hondagneu-Sotelo and Ernestine Avila, "'I'm Here, But I'm There': The Meanings of Latina Transnational Motherhood," *Gender and Society* 11(5) (1997): 548–71.

3. Shellee Colen, "'Like a Mother to Them': Stratified Reproduction and West Indian Childcare Workers and Employers in New York," in *Conceiving the New World Order: The Global Politics of Reproduction*, ed. Faye Ginsburg and Rayna Rapp (Berkeley: University of California Press, 1995), 78.

4. See Rhacel Salazar Parreñas, "Transgressing the Nation-State: The Partial Citizenship and 'Imagined (Global) Community' of Migrant Filipina Domestic Workers," *Signs: Journal of Women in Culture and Society* 26(4) (2001): 1129–54 (hereafter Parreñas 2001b).

5. Barrie Thorne, "Feminism and the Family: Two Decades of Thought," in *Rethinking the Family: Some Feminist Questions*, ed. Barrie Thorne and Marilyn Yalom, rev. ed. (Boston: Northeastern University Press, 1992), 10.

6. For instance, see Parreñas 2001b; Hondagneu-Sotelo and Avila 1997; and Rajiman et al. 2003.

7. Gamburd 2000, 241.

8. Maruja M. B. Asis, "Overseas Employment and Social Transformations in Source Communities: Findings from the Philippines," *Asian Pacific and Migration Journal* 2/3 (1995): 345.

9. Ibid., 345.

10. Battistella and Astrado-Conaco 1996, 56.

11. Ibid., 57.

12. Sarah Fenstermaker and Candace West, eds., *Doing Gender, Doing Difference: Social Inequality, Power, and Resistance* (New York: Routledge, 2002); Judith Butler, *Gender Trouble*, 10th anniversary ed. (New York: Routledge, 1999).

13. The concepts of "doing gender" and "gender as a performance" are so similar in their formulation of the constitution of gender in practice that we need to clarify the differences between the two. The concept of "doing gender" establishes that gender practices are socially situated acts that reproduce social structures. Gender acts create boundaries. Similarly, Judith Butler asserts that the repetition of gender creates boundaries of a core ("heteronormative core") with individuals falling inside or outside this core. However, in contrast to Butler, Sarah Fenstermaker and Candace West speak of gender boundaries as conceptualized by actions that are inherently fixed by gender, with certain actions ascribed to men or women. In other words, they must accordingly perform these acts to stay in the norm. Thus, Fenstermaker and West assume the association of particular actions with women prior to and during the moment of their construction. In other words, men and women are born into a social context. In contrast, Butler starts with no presuppositions regarding gendered acts.

14. Risman 1999.

15. Ibid., 152.

16. Ibid., 127.

17. Asis 2001, 31. Asis uses figures released by the Philippine Overseas Employment Administration in 1992 and 1993.

18. Ibid.

19. See Parreñas 2001a.

20. Fenstermaker, West, and Zimmerman 2002, 30.

21. Hochschild 1989, 11–21.

22. Isabelle Tirador is a twenty-three-year-old college student. She has one older brother and one sister. Prior to working as a nurse in Singapore, her mother worked in Saudi Arabia for five years and then the United States for ten years. Her father runs an auto shop in Manila. Her parents are legally separated.

23. Nieva Lacuesta is seventeen years old. Raised by her grandmother, who recently passed away, Nieva now helps her father care for her eleven-year-old brother while her mother works as a domestic worker in Israel. Her father has worked as a security guard in Manila for most of the time that her mother has worked in Israel.

24. Nieva lives in a boarding house in the city center and therefore cannot take on much household work except on weekends.

25. Hays 1996, x.

26. Cheryl Gonzaga is a nineteen-year-old college student with two older brothers still in school. Her mother—a domestic worker—has been outside the country for at least fourteen years, first in Bahrain, then in the United Kingdom, and during the past four years, in Hong Kong. Cheryl and her siblings live with an aunt. Her father lives in another island, where he takes care of property he acquired using his wife's earnings.

27. *Balikbayan* means "return migrant." Remittance agencies that cater to the Philippines also offer cargo service in the diasporic community. Cargo packages from the United States take on average one month to reach the Philippines by sea and one week by air.

28. Rodney Palanca is a nineteen-year-old college student who lives with his maternal grandmother during the school year and returns home to his family in Mindanao during the summers. He has a fourteen-year-old sister and a twelve-year-old brother. His mother has worked as a nurse in Saudi Arabia for the past ten years. Unlike some other mothers, she returns to the Philippines infrequently. She has returned to the Philippines only once.

29. Edriana Lingayen is a twenty-year-old college student whose mother works as a nurse in Saudi Arabia and whose father is a police officer in the Philippines. She lives in her mother's ancestral home with her grandparents and aunt; her father lives with her younger brother across town. Her mother has worked outside the country for more than twelve years.

30. Ellen Seneriches is a twenty-two-year-old medical school student. Her mother has worked as a domestic worker for a wealthy family in New York City for more than a decade. Ellen grew up under the care of her father along with three younger siblings, who are now twenty, nineteen, and eighteen years old.

31. Benjamin Ledesma is a twenty-year-old student who lives with his brother and father in a comfortable middle-class neighborhood. They live next door to their grandparents, who often assist them with daily household maintenance.

32. Arlie Hochschild, *The Managed Heart* (Berkeley: University of California Press, 1976). Also see Arlie Hochschild, *The Commercialization of Intimate Life: Notes from Home and Work* (Berkeley: University of California Press, 2003), 97–100.

33. Floridith Sanchez is eighteen years old, the youngest of four children. She and her siblings live in their father's ancestral home with their grandparents and father. This family relies heavily on the caring work of an aunt, as the father does no housework of any sort. The mother returns to the Philippines every two years for one month.

34. Rudy Montoya is a nineteen-year-old son of a domestic worker in Hong Kong. He grew up under the care of his grandparents and uncle, whom

his mother supported financially through college. His mother started working in Hong Kong when Rudy was only six years old. She returns to the Philippines on average every four years, after completing two labor contracts.

35. Notably, its "parodic repetition does not expose its phantasmatic effect" and thus disagrees with Judith Butler's recognition of potential gender transformations occurring in this phantasmatic exaggeration of mothering. See Butler 1990.

36. Vicente Rafael, "Your Grief Is Our Gossip: Overseas Filipinos and Other Spectral Presences," *Public Culture* 9 (1997): 267–91. For a discussion on the iconic use of the martyr in the representation of women in the Philippines, see Neferti Tadiar, "*Himala* (Miracle): The Heretical Potential of Nora Aunor's Star Power," *Signs* 27 (2002): 703–42.

37. Jose Rizal was executed by Spanish colonialists by firing squad.

38. Rafael 1997, 275.

39. Abel Valenzuela, "Gender Roles and Settlement Activities Among Children and Their Immigrant Families," *American Behavioral Studies* 42(4) (January 1999): 728–30.

40. The mother of Barbara Latoza works as a domestic worker in Taiwan. Her parents are only high school graduates and thus without many options for mobility in the Philippines. Barbara's family lives near the ancestral home of her mother. The grandmother and an aunt assist in their care. Barbara's father is unemployed.

41. Mick Cunningham, "Parental Influences on the Gendered Division of Housework," *American Sociological Review* 66 (April 2001): 184–203.

42. See Harriet Presser, "Employment Schedules Among Dual-Earner Spouses and the Division of Household Labor by Gender," *American Sociological Review* 59(June 1994): 348–64; Hochschild 1989; and DeVault 1991.

43. Presser 1994, 362.

44. *Mamang* means mother in the local dialect.

45. Roan Leyritana, is a seventeen-year-old college student whose never-married mother has worked outside the Philippines for eleven years, first as a domestic worker of eight years in Kuwait, then as a bookkeeper in the United Kingdom for the last three years. On average, she visits her son every two years and usually stays for one month.

46. Arlie Hochschild, "The Nanny Chain," *American Prospect* 11(4) (2000). Available from http://www.prospect.org/print/V11/4/hochschild-a.html. Last verified on February 4, 2004.

47. Phoebe and her siblings commute home to eat lunch.

48. Phoebe Latorre lives in an extended household with her father, three brothers, and numerous extended kin. A college graduate, her father cannot find work and can only subsidize his wife's earnings by driving a passenger jeepney. Phoebe and her immediate family recently began to make arrange-

ments to relocate to a house financed by her mother, who returns to the Philippines every year for one- or two-week visits with her family.

49. Lorber 1994, 23.

50. Scott Coltane, *Family Man: Fatherhood, Housework, and Gender Inequity* (New York and Oxford: Oxford University Press, 1996). See also Chapter 5.

51. Lourdes Dumangas is a seventeen-year-old college student whose mother has worked in the United States as a nurse since 1982, the year she was born. The stigma of single motherhood motivated Lourdes's grandparents to push for her mother's migration and has also deterred her from returning more frequently. Lourdes's grandparents raised her as if she were their own child, and her mother has returned to the Philippines only once. Lourdes has yet to visit her mother in the United States.

52. The mother of Nelida Yarra has been a domestic worker in Taiwan for the last three years; previously, she worked abroad for ten years in various countries in the Middle East. Her mother is the breadwinner of her family and has not returned to the Philippines since she started work in Taiwan. Her father works as a tricycle driver. The low-wage work of her parents does not reflect their level of educational attainment. Both have college degrees. The mother is a trained chemical engineer, and the father completed his course work in maritime education. They rely on their extended kin for care as they live with three aunts and their paternal grandmother.

53. Hochschild 1989, 11–13.

54. See Cynthia Fuchs Epstein, "Border Crossings: The Constraints of Time Norms in the Transgression of Gender and Professional Roles." Presented at the American Sociological Association Meeting, Washington, D.C., 2000.

55. Risman (1999) acknowledges that gender expectations do slow down possible changes in either practices or institutions, but notes that institutional change can also transform expectations.

CHAPTER 6

1. This chapter continues a discussion on emotions, gender, and transnational family life that I addressed initially in chapter 5 of *Servants of Globalization*.

2. Rosette Cabellero tells me that her father has three wives and at some point lived with two of them simultaneously, including her mother, who is his third wife. Unhappy under such circumstances, the mother left the Philippines. Since she left, Rosette's father has not provided them with financial support. Rosette is now nineteen years old and lives with her maternal grandparents and her two brothers aged sixteen and eighteen. Her

mother left for Qatar four years ago and has yet to have the financial means and opportunity to visit her children in the Philippines.

3. Binky Botavara is a twenty-four-year-old mother of two young children. She lives with her partner in the Philippines; she has chosen not to marry him, however, in order to remain eligible for migration to the United States via the first preference category as an unmarried adult child of a citizen. Her mother left her and three older and one younger siblings under the care of her father when Binky was twelve years old. The mother obtained legal status in the United States when Binky was eighteen years old.

4. Nilma Loberiza is a seventeen-year-old college student with two older sisters and two older brothers. During the past nine years, they have grown up under the care of their father, a stay-at-home dad, while their mother worked as a domestic worker in Saudi Arabia.

5. Lourdes's mother has surprisingly returned only once to visit her daughter in the Philippines, when Lourdes was eleven. We can speculate that the stigma attached to single mothers in the Philippines discourages them from returning, along with the emotional distance that has developed between them through years of separation.

6. Floridith and her three older siblings live in their father's ancestral home with their grandparents and their father. Although physically present, the father does not do any caring work or even any housework. Instead, Floridith and her siblings rely more on the support of their aunt and their mother, who returns to the Philippines every two years for about one month.

7. The children identified a number of other tangible losses. For instance, they complained about the awkwardness of beginning to menstruate without their mothers in the Philippines, not knowing their correct bra size until after they had graduated from college, and not getting the most basic guidance in grooming.

8. Barbara Latoza is nineteen years old. She grew up with her father and two younger brothers, who are now twelve and fifteen years old. Their mother has been a domestic worker outside the Philippines for at least six years. The mother recently relocated to Taiwan after completing five years of work in Malaysia. The father is unemployed. The mother has returned to the Philippines twice since she first left the country.

9. See my *Servants of Globalization*, chapter 5, for an extensive discussion of the commodification of relationships in transnational families. Also, I acknowledge Kiko Benitez for pointing out the common use of education as a marker for commodifying love in the Philippines.

10. Among the thirty-nine daughters of migrant mothers who are unwilling to be separated from their children under any circumstance, there are

twenty who are not averse to labor migration and idealistically hope to eventually work outside the country alongside their children.

11. Thirty children, while not willing to leave their children behind in the Philippines, would prefer to work outside the country when they grow older.

1. Although I use her case as an example, I note that Isabelle Tirador is a member of a mother-away transnational household, not a two-parent transnational household.

2. This chapter builds tremendously on a co-authored article with Cerissa Salazar Parreñas, "Workers Without Families: The Unintended Consequences," *Asian Law Journal* 10:2(2003): 143–59. Portions of this chapter are direct excerpts from the article.

3. Among my interviewees, those in two-parent-abroad transnational families are mostly based in countries with liberal regimes. Thus, they usually experience prolonged separations. Rarely do migrant men in father-away families seek employment in liberal countries. Most work as contract laborers in the Gulf region or as seafarers and can usually see their children every year or two. Thus, they are hardly represented among families that experience continuous, prolonged separation. Finally, migrant women in mother-away families are more evenly distributed between nations with liberal and illiberal regimes. Notably, as I addressed in Chapter 6, the more extended separations endured by members of these families do not necessarily result in greater strains between mothers and their children.

4. See chapter 2 of my *Servants of Globalization* for a discussion of the hierarchy of destinations in the Filipino diaspora.

5. See Parreñas 2001b: 1134–35. Also see Constable 1997; Pei Chia Lan, "Political and Social Geography of Marginal Insiders: Migrant Domestic Workers in Taiwan," *Asian and Pacific Migration Journal* 12(1–2): 99–125; Brenda Yeoh and Shirlena Huang, "Negotiating Public Space: Strategies and Styles of Migrant Female Domestic Workers in Singapore," *Urban Studies* 35(3): 583–602.

6. Partial citizenship refers to the denial of full citizenship to migrant workers in both sending and receiving nations of migration. Whereas receiving nations restrict the membership of migrant workers, sending nations such as the Philippines usually cannot protect the rights of their deployed migrant workers as they lack jurisdiction to do so. See Parreñas 2001b.

7. The issue of prolonged family separation seems unlikely for those who are legal residents of the United States. Since the 1924 immigrant law that granted preference over all others for the migration of spouses, minor

and adult children, and parents of U.S. citizens and legal permanent residents, family ties have been the strongest basis of U.S. immigration. See Katherine Donato, "Understanding U.S. Immigration: Why Some Countries Send Women and Others Send Men," in *Seeking Common Ground: Multidisciplinary Studies of Immigrant Women in the United States*, ed. Donna Gabaccia (Westport, CT: Greenwood Press, 1992), 159–84. This law was later reinforced by the defense of the family reunification system, which the Select Commission on Immigration and Refugee Policy annunciated in its 1981 report. It states: "The reunification of families serves the national interest not only through the humaneness of the policy itself, but also through the promotion of the public order and well-being of the nation. Psychologically and socially, the reunion of family members with their close relatives promotes the health and welfare of the United States." See Bill Ong Hing, *Defining America Through Immigration Policy* (Philadelphia, PA: Temple University Press, 2004), 104.

8. U.S. Immigration and Naturalization Service, *1995 Statistical Yearbook* (Washington, DC, Government Printing Office, 1997); Bill Ong Hing, *Making and Remaking Asian America through Immigration Policy, 1850–1990* (Stanford, CA: Stanford University Press, 1993).

9. See William R. Tamayo, "When the 'Coloreds' Are Neither Black nor Citizens: The United States Civil Rights Movement and Global Migration," *Asian Law Journal* 2(1) (1995): 6. His article describes the massive deportation of Mexican migrant agricultural workers once demands for their labor subsided. Addressing the use of Filipina nurses to satisfy a nationwide shortage of registered nurses is Enid Trucios-Haynes, "Temporary Workers and Future Immigration Policy Conflicts: Protecting U.S. Workers and Satisfying the Demand for Global Human Capital," *Brandeis Law Journal* 40(967) (2002): 990–98.

10. Six years is an estimate based on interviews conducted with community members waiting for their visas in the Philippines.

11. For the estimated length of waiting lists per immigration preference category, see U.S. Department of State, Bureau of Consular Affairs, vol. 8, publication no. 56, *Visa Bulletin* (April 2003), available at http://travel.state.gov/visa_bulletin.html. Verified last on February 4, 2004. This bulletin shows that there are longer waiting periods for immigrant visas for adult unmarried sons and daughters of permanent residents than for minor children of permanent residents.

12. See Susan Martin et al., "U.S. Immigration Policy: Admission of Highly Skilled Workers," *Georgetown Immigration Law Journal* (16)619 (Spring 2002). The article describes the contributions of skilled immigrant workers to the United States. Also see Kitty Calavita, "Gaps and Contradictions in U.S. Immigration Policy: An Analysis of Recent Reform Efforts," in

*The Immigration Reader: America in a Multidisciplinary Perspective*, ed. David Jacobson (Malden, MA: Blackwell Publishers, 1998), 92–110; for a discussion of the provisions to increase highly skilled workers in the Immigration Act of 1990, see 103–06.

13. See Mark Krikorian, "Captive Workers: A Disturbing Trend in Immigration Policy," *Center for Immigration Studies Bulletin* 3, available at http://www.cis.org/articles/1998. Last verified on February 4, 2004.

14. David Reimers, *Still the Golden Door?* (New York: Columbia University Press, 1985).

15. Calavita 1998, 103–6.

16. Linda Bosniak, "Nativism the Concept: Some Reflections," *Immigrants Out! The New Nativism and the Anti-Immigrant Impulse in the United* States, ed. Juan Perea (New York: New York University Press, 1997), 280.

17. Hing 1993, 36.

18. Keith Aoki, "No Right to Own?: The Early Twentieth-Century 'Alien Land Laws' as a Prelude to Internment," *Boston College Law Review* 40(37) (1998): 40–45.

19. Aoki 1998, 40–42.

20. Letti Volpp, "Obnoxious to Their Very Nature: Asian American and Constitutional Citizenship," *Citizenship Studies* 5(1) (2000): 58–60.

21. Aoki 1998, 43.

22. Ibid.

23. See Krikorian 1998. The use of temporary contract workers is not new. Another example is the aforementioned Bracero Program (1951–64), which instituted the formal recruitment of temporary farm workers from Mexico. See Reimers 1985, 41–51.

24. Saskia Sassen, *Losing Control? Sovereignty in an Age of Globalization* (New York: Columbia University Press, 1996), 59–64.

25. Ibid., 59.

26. See Leo Chavez, "Immigration Reform and Nativism: The Nationalist Response to the Transnational Challenge" in *Immigrants Out!*, ed. Juan Perea (New York: New York University Press, 1997), 61–77.

27. Hing 2004, 110.

28. See Krikorian 1998. High-tech computer programmers and physical therapists are two such in-demand specialty occupations.

29. Ibid.

30. See Paul Ong, ed., *The State of Asian Pacific America: Transforming Race Relations* (Los Angeles, CA: Asian American Public Policy Institute and UCLA Asian American Studies Center, 2000), 179–80; see also U.S. Department of Labor, Office of Inspector General, "The Department of Labor's Foreign Labor Certification Programs: The System Is Broken and Needs to

Be Fixed (May 22, 1996), report no. 06–96–002–03–321. Available at http://www.oig.dol.gov/public/reports/oa/pre_1998/06-96-002-03321s.htm. Last verified on May 21, 2004. Studies indicate a wide discrepancy between the wages declared by employers in visa applications and the actual wages earned by migrant employees.

31. See chapter 4 of *Servants of Globalization.*

32. The Department of Labor and the Immigration and Naturalization Service are two government bodies assigned to implement the Labor Certification Program. Information on this program is available at http://www.ows.doleta.gov/foreign/perm.asp. Last verified on February 4, 2004.

33. Schedule B enumerates the occupations that qualify for a petition of waiver to participate in the labor certification process for permanent employment in the United States. These jobs are not sufficiently filled by U.S. workers, and they include various low-wage service occupations, including domestic work. See Section 656.11, in http://www.access.gpo.gov/nara/cfr/waisidx_01/20cfr656_01.html. Last verified on February 4, 2004.

34. See Hing 1993, 19–36.

35. Ibid., 198.

36. See Sucheng Chan, *Asian Americans: An Interpretive History* (Boston: Twayne Publishers, 1991), 146; Hing 1993, 198–99.

37. See Hing 1993, 199.

38. Cited in Dorothee Schneider, "Symbolic Citizenship, Nationalism, and the Distant State: The United States Congress in the 1996 Debate on Immigration Reform," *Citizenship Studies* 4:3 (2000): 265.

39. Hing 1993, 40.

40. In other words, the migration of immediate family of U.S. citizens, for instance foreign spouses, is not considered against the annual quota limit of immigrant entries.

41. Hing 1993, 40.

42. Ibid.

43. Bill Ong Hing, *Defining America Through Immigration Policy* (Philadelphia, PA: Temple University Press, 2004), 98.

44. See Sarah Vaughan, "Immigrant Visa Waiting List at 3.6 Million," *Center for Immigration Studies Bulletin* 28 (1997), available at http://www.cis.org/articles/1997. Last verified on February 4, 2004. In 1997, the two largest migrant ethnic groups waiting to unify with permanent resident family members in the United States were Mexicans and Filipinos, totaling approximately 1.6 million people. A significant number of these individuals were unmarried adult children of U.S. citizens and the children of legally permanent residents.

45. See Vaughan 1997; and Trucios-Haynes 2002.

46. See U.S. Department of State, Bureau of Consular Affairs Visa Services, publication no. 62, vol. 8, *Visa Bulletin* (Washington, DC, October 2003), available at http://travel.state.gov/visa_bulletin.html. Last verified on February 4, 2004.

47. U.S. Department of State, Bureau of Consular Affairs Visa Services, publication no. 56, vol. 8, *Visa Bulletin* (Washington, DC, April 2003), available at http://travel.state.gov/visa_bulletin.html. Last verified on February 4, 2004.

48. Ibid.

49. Ibid.

50. Hing 1993, 198.

51. See Vaughan 1997.

52. See U.S. Department of State, Bureau of Consular Affairs Visa Services 2003b. Priority is given to individuals petitioned on July 22, 1989.

53. Trucios-Haynes 2002, 990–98.

54. Ibid., 991.

55. Ibid.

56. See Bureau of Citizenship and Immigration Services, Immigration and Naturalization Service, *Fiscal Year 2001 Statistical Year Book*, Table 3: Immigrants Admitted by Region and Country of Birth, Fiscal Years 1989–2001. Available at http://www.immigration.gov/graphics/index/htm. (This figure includes quota and non-quota immigrants.)

57. Steven A. Camarota, "5 Million Illegal Immigrants: An Analysis of New INS Numbers," *Center for Immigration Studies Bulletin* 28, available at http://www.cis.org/articles/1997. Last verified on February 4, 2004.

58. See chapters 4 and 5 of *Servants of Globalization* for extensive discussion of transnational mothering.

59. See chapter 5 of *Servants of Globalization*.

60. U.S. Department of Labor offers a Labor Certificate Program. See http://www.ows.doleta.gov/foreign/perm.asp. Last verified on February 4, 2004.

61. See Alejandro Portes and Ruben Rumbaut, *Ethnicities: Children of Immigrants in America* (Berkeley: University of California Press, 2001); Alejandro Portes and Ruben Rumbaut, eds., *Legacies: The Story of the Immigrant Second Generation* (Berkeley: University of California Press, 2001); and Alejandro Portes, ed., *The New Second Generation* (New York: Russell Sage Press, 1996).

62. See Hing 1993, 76–78, for a description of the predominately male pre-1965 Asian immigrant community and the role of immigration law in excluding workers' families from reunification.

63. Evelyn Nakano Glenn, "Split Household, Small Producer, and Dual

Wage Earner: An Analysis of Chinese-American Family Strategies," *Journal of Marriage and the Family* (February 1983): 35–46.

CONCLUSION

1. See R. W. Connell, *Gender* (Cambridge: Polity Press, 2002), 88; Mahon 2002.

2. See Kristine Baber and Katherine Allen, *Women and Families: Feminist Reconstructions* (New York: Guilford Press, 1992); Berk 1985; Coltrane 1996; DeVault 1991; Hays 1996; Lorber 1994; Presser 1994; Risman 1999; and Barrie Thorne, "Feminism and the Family: Two Decades of Thought," in *Rethinking the Family: Some Feminist Questions*, ed. Barrie Thorne and Marilyn Yalom, rev. ed. (Boston: Northeastern University Press, 1992), 3–30.

3. Hochschild 1989.

Aganon, Marie. 1995. "Migrant Labor and the Filipino Family." In *The Fil-ipino Family: A Spectrum of Views and Issues*, ed. Aurora Perez, 79–96. Quezon City: University of the Philippines, Office of Research Coordination.

Agence France Presse. 1995a. "Ramos: Overseas Employment a Threat to Filipino Families." *Philippine Inquirer* (May 26).

———. 1995b. "Ramos Says Pinay OCWs Threaten Filipino Families." *Philippine Star* (May 26).

Aguiling-Pangalangan, Elizabeth. 1995. "The Family Under Philippine Law." In *The Filipino Family: A Spectrum of Views and Issues*, ed. Aurora Perez, 12–26. Quezon City: University of the Philippines, Office of Re-search Coordination.

Aoki, Keith. 1998. "No Right to Own?: The Early Twentieth-Century 'Alien Land Laws' as a Prelude to Internment." *Boston College Law Review* 40(37).

Appadurai, Arjun. 1996. *Modernity at Large: Cultural Dimensions of Glob-alization*. Minneapolis: University of Minnesota Press.

Arao, Danilo A. 2000. "Deployment of Migrant Workers Increasing." *Ibon Facts and Figures* 23:8 (April 30): 8.

Asis, Maruja. 1995. "Overseas Employment and Social Transformations in Source Communities: Findings from the Philippines." *Asian Pacific and Migration Journal* 2/3: 327–46.

———. 2001. "Philippines: The Return Migration of Filipino Women Mi-grants: Home, But Not for Good." In *Female Labour Migration in South-East Asia: Change and Continuity*, 23–91. Bangkok: Asian Re-search Centre for Migration and Institute of Asian Studies.

Baber, Kristine, and Katherine Allen. 1992. *Women and Families: Feminist Reconstructions.* New York: Guilford Press.

Bakan, Abigail, and Daiva Stasiulis, eds. 1997. *Not One of the Family: Foreign Domestic Workers in Canada.* Toronto: University of Toronto Press.

Basch, Linda, Nina Glick Schiller, and Cristina Szanton Blanc. 1994. *Nations Unbound: Transnational Projects, Postcolonial Predicaments, and Deterritorialized Nation-States.* New York: Routledge.

Battistella, Graziano, and Maria Cecilia Astrado-Conaco. 1996. *Impact of Labor Migration on the Children Left Behind.* Manila: Episcopal Commission for the Pastoral Care of Migrants and Itinerant People.

Berk, Sarah Fenstermaker. 1985. *The Gender Factory: The Apportionment of Work in American Households.* New York: Plenum.

Bernard, Jesse. 1981. "The Good Provider." *American Psychologist* 36(1): 1–12.

Bosniak, Linda. 1997. "Nativism the Concept: Some Reflections." In *Immigrants Out! The New Nativism and the Anti-Immigrant Impulse in the United States,* ed. Juan Perea, 279–99. New York: New York University Press.

Bourdieu, Pierre. 2001. *Masculine Domination.* Stanford, CA: Stanford University Press.

Bureau of Labor and Employment Statistics. 2002. "Remittances from Overseas Filipino Workers by Country of Origin Philippines: 1997—Fourth Quarter 1999." In *Pinoy Migrants, Shared Government Information System for Migration.* Available at *http://cmisd-web.dfa.gov.ph/ pinoymigrants.*

Butler, Judith. 1990. *Gender Trouble.* New York: Routledge Press.

Cabreros, Mac. 1997. "Edukasyon ng mga anak ng OFWs nassaskipisyo" (Education of children of OFWs suffer [sic]). *Abante* (June 23): 5.

Calavita, Kitty. 1998. "Gaps and Contradictions in U.S. Immigration Policy: An Analysis of Recent Reform Efforts." In *The Immigration Reader: America in a Multidisciplinary Perspective,* ed. David Jacobson, 92–110. Malden, MA: Blackwell Publishers.

Camarota, Steven A. 1997. "5 Million Illegal Immigrants: An Analysis of New INS Numbers." *Center for Immigration Studies Bulletin* 28. Available at http://www.cis.org/articles/1997. Last verified on February 4, 2004.

Cancian, Francesca, and Stacey Oliker. 2000. *Caring and Gender.* Thousand Oaks, CA: Pine Forge Press.

Castillo, Gelia T. 1993. *Where Food and Population Meet: The Filipino Household Among Other Households.* Diliman, Quezon City: University of the Philippines Press and Center for Integrative and Development Studies.

Center for Women's Resources. 1989. *Is the Traditional Filipino Family Still Surviving?: The Women's Perspective on the Family Code.* Quezon City: Center for Women's Resources.

Chan, Sucheng. 1991. *Asian Americans: An Interpretive History.* Boston: Twayne Publishers.

Chavez, Leo. 1997. "Immigration Reform and Nativism: The Nationalist Response to the Transnational Challenge." In *Immigrants Out!*, ed. Juan Perea, 61–77. New York: New York University Press.

Cheng, Lucie. 1999. "Globalization and Women's Paid Labor in Asia." *International Social Science Journal* 160 (June): 217–28.

Chin, Christine. 1998. *In Service and Servitude: Foreign Domestic Workers and the Malaysian Modernity Project.* New York: Columbia University Press.

Choy, Catherine. 2003. *Empire of Care: Nursing and Migration in Filipino American History.* Durham, NC, and London: Duke University Press.

Colen, Shellee. 1995. "'Like a Mother to Them': Stratified Reproduction and West Indian Childcare Workers and Employers in New York." In *Conceiving the New World Order: The Global Politics of Reproduction*, ed. Faye Ginsburg and Rayna Rapp, 78–102. Berkeley: University of California Press.

Coltrane, Scott. 1996. *Family Man: Fatherhood, Housework, and Gender Inequity.* New York and Oxford: Oxford University Press.

Coltrane, Scott, and Justin Galt. 2000. "The History of Men's Caring." In *Care Work: Gender, Labour and the Welfare State*, ed. Madonna Harrington Meyer, 15–36. New York and London: Routledge Press.

Connell, R. W. 1987. *Gender and Power.* Stanford, CA: Stanford University Press.

———. 1994. *Masculinities.* Berkeley: University of California Press.

———. 2002. *Gender.* Cambridge: Polity Press.

Conroy, Martin. 2000. *Sustaining the New Economy: Work, Family, and Community in the Information Age.* New York: Russell Sage Foundation Press; and Cambridge, MA: Harvard University Press.

Constable, Nicole. 1997. *Maid to Order in Hong Kong: Stories of Filipina Workers.* Ithaca, NY: Cornell University Press.

Corporal, Lynette L. 1998. "OFW's Kids Emotionally Troubled." *Manila Standard* (August 18): 1.

Cunningham, Mick. 2001. "Parental Influences on the Gendered Division of Housework." *American Sociological Review* 66 (April): 184–203.

Dalisay, Grace Aguiling, Roberto Mendoza, John Benedict Santos, and Anita Echevaria. 1996. *Luto ng Diyos: Mga Kuwento ng Buhay Mag-asawa.* Manila: De La Salle University Press.

Daly, Mary, and Jane Lewis. 2000. "The Concept of Social Care and the Analysis of Contemporary Welfare States." *British Journal of Sociology* 51:2 (June): 281–98.

Department of Social Welfare and Development. 1993. *Coping Capabilities of Solo Parents and Spouses of Overseas Workers.* Manila: Department of Social Welfare and Development.

DeVault, Marjorie. 1991. *Feeding the Family: The Social Organization of Caring as Gendered Work.* Chicago, IL: University of Chicago Press.

Diokno-Pascual, Maitet. 2001. "The Burdensome Debt." Unpublished paper. Available at the Freedom from Debt Coalition. Quezon City, Philippines.

Donato, Katherine. 1992. "Understanding U.S. Immigration: Why Some Countries Send Women and Others Send Men." In *Seeking Common Ground: Multidisciplinary Studies of Immigrant Women in the United States,* ed. Donna Gabbacia, 159–84. Westport, CT: Greenwood Press.

Ehrenreich, Barbara, and Arlie Hochschild, eds. 2003. *Global Woman: Nannies, Maids, and Sex Workers in the New Economy.* New York: Metropolitan Books.

Epstein, Cynthia Fuchs. 2000. "Border Crossings: The Constraints of Time Norms in the Transgression of Gender and Professional Roles." Paper presented at the American Sociological Association meeting, Washington, DC, August.

Feliciano, Myrna. 1994. "Law, Gender, and the Family in the Philippines." *Law and Society Review* 28: 547–61.

Fenstermaker, Sarah, and Candace West. 2002. "'Doing Difference' Revisited: Problems, Prospects, and the Dialogue in Feminist Theory." In *Doing Gender, Doing Difference: Social Inequality, Power, and Resistance,* ed. Sarah Fenstermaker and Candace West, 205–16. New York: Routledge Press.

———, eds. 2002. *Doing Gender, Doing Difference: Social Inequality, Power, and Resistance.* New York: Routledge Press.

Fenstermaker, Sarah, Candace West, and Don H. Zimmerman. 2002. "Gender Inequality: New Conceptual Terrain." In *Doing Gender, Doing Difference: Social Inequality, Power, and Resistance,* ed. Sarah Fenstermaker and Candace West, 25–40. New York: Routledge Press.

Fernandez, Susan. 1997. "Pamilya ng OFWs maraming hirap" (Many hardships in the families of OFWs). *Abante* (January 27): 5.

Folbre, Nancy. 2001. *The Invisible Heart: Economics and Family Values.* New York: New Press.

Foucault, Michel. 1979. *Discipline and Punish.* New York: Vintage Books.

Gamburd, Michelle. 2000. *A Kitchen Spoon's Handle.* Ithaca, NY: Cornell University Press.

Gerson, Judith, and Kathy Peiss. 1985. "Boundaries, Negotiation, Consciousness: Conceptualizing Gender Relations." *Social Problems* 32(4): 317–31.

Gibson, Katherine, Lisa Law, and Deidre McKay. 2001. "Beyond Heroes and Victims: Filipina Contract Migrants, Economic Activism, and Class Transformation." *International Feminist Journal of Politics* 3(3): 365–86.

Giddens, Anthony. 1984. *The Constitution of Society.* Cambridge: Polity Press.

———. 1991. *Modernity and Self Identity: Self and Society in the Late Modern Age.* Stanford, CA: Stanford University Press.

Glenn, Evelyn Nakano. 1983. "Split Household, Small Producer and Dual Wage Earner: An Analysis of Chinese American Family Strategies." *Journal of Marriage and the Family* 45 (February): 35–46.

Goddard, V. A. 1996. *Gender, Family and Work in Naples.* Oxford and Washington, DC: Berg.

Guzman, Rosario Bella. 2001. "The Economy Under Arroyo: Crisis and Bitter Pills." *Birdtalk: Economic and Political Briefing* (July 18): 1–18.

Hays, Sharon. 1996. *The Cultural Contradictions of Motherhood.* New Haven, CT: Yale University Press.

Heymann, Jody. 2000. *The Widening Gap: Why America's Working Families Are in Jeopardy—and What Can Be Done About It.* New York: Basic Books.

Heyzer, Noeleen, Geertje Lycklama á Nijeholt, and Nedra Weekaroon, eds. 1994. *The Trade in Domestic Workers: Causes, Mechanisms, and Consequences of International Labor Migration.* London: Zed Books.

Hing, Bill Ong. 1993. *Making and Remaking Asian America Through Immigration Policy, 1850–1990.* Stanford, CA: Stanford University Press.

———. 2004. *Defining America Through Immigration Policy*. Philadelphia, PA: Temple University Press.

Hochschild, Arlie. 1976. *The Managed Heart*. Berkeley: University of California Press.

———. 1995. "The Culture of Politics: Traditional, Post-modern, Cold Modern, Warm Modern Ideals of Care." *Social Politics* 2(3): 331–46.

———. 2000. "The Nanny Chain." *American Prospect* 11(4). Available from http://www.prospect.org/print/V11/4/hochschild-a.html. Last verified on February 4, 2004.

———. 2003. *The Commercialization of Intimate Life: Notes from Home and Work*. Berkeley: University of California Press.

———, with Anne Machung. 1989. *The Second Shift: Working Parents and the Revolution at Home*. New York: Avon Books.

Hondagneu-Sotelo, Pierrette. 1994. *Gendered Transitions: Mexican Experiences of Migration*. Berkeley: University of California Press.

———. 2001. *Doméstica: Immigrant Workers Cleaning and Caring in the Shadows of Affluence*. Berkeley: University of California Press.

———, and Ernestine Avila. 1997. "'I'm Here, But I'm There': The Meanings of Latina Transnational Motherhood." *Gender and Society* 11(5): 548–71.

Ibon. 1996. "Mirrors of the Social Crisis." *Ibon Facts and Figures* 19(7): 2–4.

———. 1997a. "In the Cycle of Debt." *People's Policy and Advocacy Studies Special Release* (September): 8.

———. 1997b. "The Creditors' Conspiracy." *People's Policy and Advocacy Studies Special Release* (September): 9.

———. 1997c. "The Neo-Liberal Prescription." *People's Policy and Advocacy Studies Special Release* (September): 16.

———. 1998. "The Export Strategy." *Ibon Facts and Figures* 21(13 and 14) (July 15 and 31): 5–7.

———. 2000a. "Debt Curse." *Ibon Facts and Figures* 23(21 and 22) (November 15 and 30): 8.

———. 2000b. "National Budget: People's Budget?" *Ibon Facts and Figures* 23(21 and 22) (November 15 and 30): 2–5.

———. 2000c. "Teachers of the New Millennium." *Ibon Facts and Figures* 23(8) (April 30): 2–5.

John Paul VI, Pope. *Pastoral Constitution on the Church in the Modern World, Gaudium et Spes*. Pasay City, Philippines: Paulines Publishing House.

Kanlungan Center Foundation. 2000. *Fast Facts on Labor Migration*. Quezon City: Kanlungan Center Foundation.

Krikorian, Mark. 1998. "Captive Workers: A Disturbing Trend in Immigration Policy," *Center for Immigration Studies Bulletin* 3. Available at http://www.cis.org/articles/1998. Last verified on February 4, 2004.

Lamont, Michele. 2000. *The Dignity of Working Men: Morality and the Boundaries of Race, Class, and Immigration*. Cambridge, MA: Harvard University Press; and New York: Russell Sage Foundation.

Lan, Pei-chia. 2003. "Political and Social Geography of Marginal Insiders: Migrant Domestic Workers in Taiwan." *Asian and Pacific Migration Journal* 12(1–2): 99–125.

Lindio-McGovern, Ligaya. 2003. "Labor Export in the Context of Globalization: The Experience of Filipino Domestic Workers in Rome." *International Sociology* 18(3): 513–34.

Liwag, Maria Emma Concepcion, Alma S. dela Cruz, and Maria Elizabeth Macapagal. 1999. *A UNICEF and Ateneo Study: How We Raise Our Daughters and Sons: Childrearing and Gender Socialization in the Philippines*. Quezon City: United Nations Children's Fund and Ateneo Wellness Center.

Lorber, Judith. 1994. *The Paradoxes of Gender*. New Haven, CT: Yale University Press.

Lugo, Leotes Marie T. 2002. "Search for Greener Pastures Continues." *Business World* (March 15–16).

Mahon, Rianne. 2002. "Child Care: Toward What Kind of 'Social Europe'?" *Social Politics* 9: 343–79.

Manalansan, Martin, IV. 2003. *Global Divas*. Durham, NC: Duke University Press.

Marchand, Marianne H., and Anne Sisson Runyan. 2000. "Introduction. Feminist Sightings of Global Restructuring: Conceptualizations and Reconceptualizations." *Gender and Global Restructuring: Sightings, Sites, and Resistances*, ed. Marchand and Runyan, 1–22. London and New York: Routledge.

Martin, Susan, et al. 2002. "U.S. Immigration Policy: Admission of Highly Skilled Workers." *Georgetown Immigration Law Journal* 16(619).

Medina, Belen. 2001. *The Filipino Family*. 2d ed. Diliman, Quezon City: University of the Philippines Press.

Meerman, Marije. 2001. *The Chain of Love*. Netherlands: VPRO-TV.

Mellor, Jennifer. 2000. "Filling in the Gaps in Long Term Care Insurance."

*Care Work: Gender, Labour and the Welfare State*, ed. Madonna Harrington Meyer, 202–16. New York and London: Routledge.

Mendoza, A. M., Jr. 1992. *The Record of a Non-Confrontational Debt Management Approach, State of the Nation Report.* Diliman, Quezon City: University of the Philippines Press and the Center for Integrative and Development Studies.

Milkman, Ruth, Ellen Reese, and Benita Roth. 1998. "The Macrosociology of Paid Domestic Labor." *Work and Occupations* 25(4): 483–507.

Mission, Gina. 1998. "The Breadwinners: Female Migrant Workers." *Women's International Network* 15A.

National Commission for the Role of Filipino Women. 1995. *Philippine Plan for Gender-Responsive Development 1995–2025.* Manila: National Commission on the Role of Filipino Women.

National Statistical Coordination Board. 1999. *Men and Women in the Philippines: A Statistical Handbook.* Manila: National Statistical Coordination Board.

Ofreneo, Rene E. 1995. *Philippine Industrialization and Industrial Relations,* State of the Nation Reports 12. Diliman, Quezon City: University of the Philippines Press and the Center for Integrative and Development Studies.

Ong, Paul, ed. 2000. *The State of Asian Pacific America: Transforming Race Relations.* Los Angeles, CA: Asian American Policy Institute and UCLA Asian American Studies Center.

Ong, Paul, Edna Bonacich, and Lucie Cheng, eds. 1994. "The Political Economy of Capitalist Restructuring and the New Asian Immigration." In *The New Asian Immigration in Los Angeles and Global Restructuring,* ed. Paul Ong, Edna Bonacich, and Lucie Cheng, 3–35. Philadelphia, PA: Temple University Press.

Parreñas, Rhacel Salazar. 2001a. *Servants of Globalization: Women, Migration, and Domestic Work.* Stanford, CA: Stanford University Press.

———. 2001b. "Transgressing the Nation-State: The Partial Citizenship and 'Imagined (Global) Community' of Migrant Filipina Domestic Workers." *Signs: Journal of Women in Culture and Society* 26(4): 1129–54.

Perez, Aurora, ed. 1995. *The Filipino Family: A Spectrum of Views and Issues.* Quezon City: University of the Philippines, Office of Research Coordination.

Pesigan, Arturo M., Ruben N. Caragay, Marilyn Lorenzo, and Victoria A. Bautista. 1992. *Assessments of Primary Health Care in the Philip-*

*pines*. State of the Nation Reports 3. Diliman, Quezon City: University of the Philippines Press and the Center for Integrative and Development Studies.

Pessar, Patricia. 1999. "Engendering Migration Studies." *American Behavioral Scientist* 42(4): 577–600.

Pope John Paul IV. *See* John Paul IV.

Portes, Alejandro, ed. 1996. *The New Second Generation*. New York: Russell Sage Foundation Press.

Portes, Alejandro, and Ruben Rumbaut. 2001. *Ethnicities: Children of Immigrants in America*. Berkeley: University of California Press.

———, ed. 2001. *Legacies: The Story of the Immigrant Second Generation*. Berkeley: University of California Press.

Presser, Harriet. 1994. "Employment Schedules Among Dual-Earner Spouses and the Division of Household Labor by Gender." *American Sociological Review* 59 (June): 348–64.

Philippine Tonight Staff. 1993. "'Sleeping Beauty' Gets Raped . . . While Her Mom Works as DH in Hong Kong." *Philippine Tonight* (July 16).

Potuchek, Jean L. 1997. *Who Supports the Family? Gender and Breadwinning in Dual-Earner Marriages*. Stanford, CA: Stanford University Press.

Pratt, Geraldine. 1997. "Stereotypes and Ambivalence: Nanny Agents' Stereotypes of Domestic Workers in Vancouver, B.C." *Gender, Place, and Culture* 4: 159–77.

———. 1999. "From Registered Nurse to Registered Nanny: Discursive Geographies of Filipina Domestic Workers in Vancouver, B.C." *Economic Geography* 75: 215–36.

Principe, June, Corazon Garcia, Cersencio Viernes, Carlos Asuncion, and Trinidad Flores. 1999. *Technology and Home Economics for Secondary Schools*. Rev. ed. Quezon City: FNB Educational, Inc.

Rafael, Vicente. 1997. "Your Grief Is Our Gossip: Overseas Filipinos and Other Spectral Presences." *Public Culture* 9: 267–91.

Rai, Shirin. 2002. *Gender and the Political Economy of Development*. Cambridge: Polity Press.

Ramirez, Mina and Alfonso Deza. 1997. "When Labor Does Not Pay: The Case of Filipino Outmigration." *Occasional Monograph* (Manila: Asian Social Institute) 9: 12.

Rapp, Rayna. 1982. "Family and Class in Contemporary America: Notes Toward an Understanding of Ideology." In *Rethinking the Family*, ed. Barrie Thorne and Marilyn Yalom, 168–87. New York: Longman.

Raymundo, Corazon. 1993. "Demographic Changes and the Filipino Family." In *The Filipino Family and the Nation: A Collection of Readings on Family Life Issues and Concerns*, ed. University of the Philippines College of Home Economics, 16–32. Quezon City: University of the Philippines.

Reimers, David. 1985. *Still the Golden Door?* New York: Columbia University Press.

Republic of the Philippines. 1986. *The 1986 Constitution of the Republic of the Philippines*. Manila: Republic of the Philippines.

———. 1987. *The Family Code of the Philippines*. Manila: Republic of the Philippines.

———. 1998. *The 1998 Regional Social and Economic Trends, Region VI (Western Visayas)*. Makati City: National Statistical Coordination Board.

Risman, Barbara. 1999. *Gender Vertigo: American Families in Transition.* New Haven, CT: Yale University Press.

Ruddick, Sarah. 1982. "Maternal Thinking." In *Rethinking the Family: Some Feminist Questions*, ed. Barrie Thorne and Marilyn Yalom, 76–94. New York: Longman.

Santamaria, Francis. 1992. "Problems Regarding Family Relations and Children of Migrant Workers." In *Filipino Women Overseas Contract Workers: At What Cost?*, ed. Ruby Palma Beltran and Aurora Javate de Dios, 69–72. Quezon City: Goodwill Trading Company.

Sassen, Saskia. 1996. *Losing Control? Sovereignty in an Age of Globalization.* New York: Columbia University Press.

———. 2000. "Women's Burden: Counter-Geographies of Globalization and the Feminization of Survival." *Journal of International Affairs* 53(2) (Spring): 503–34.

Schneider, Dorothee. 2000. "Symbolic Citizenship, Nationalism and the Distant State: The United States Congress in the 1996 Debate on Immigration Reform." *Citizenship Studies* 4(3): 255–74.

Sempio-Diy, Alicia V. 1993. "The Philippine Constitution and the Filipino Family: 'The Family Code.'" *The Filipino Family and the National Collection of Readings on Family Life Issues and Concerns*, ed. University of the Philippines College of Home Economics, 1–15. Quezon City: University of the Philippines.

Stacey, Judith. 1996. *In the Name of the Family*. Boston, MA: Beacon Press.

Structural Adjustment Participatory Review International Network (SAPRIN). 2002. "The Policy Roots of Economic Crisis and Poverty: A

Multi-Country Participatory Assessment of Structural Adjustment."
Washington, DC: SAPRIN: 152. Report available online at http://
www.saprin.org/global_rpt.htm. Last verified on February 4, 2004.

Suarez-Orosco, Carola, and Marcelo Suarez-Orosco. 2001. *Children of Immigration*. Cambridge, MA: Harvard University Press.

Tadiar, Neferti. 2002. "*Himala* (Miracle): The Heretical Potential of Nora
Aunor's Star Power." *Signs* 27: 703–42.

Tamayo, William. 1995. "When the 'Coloreds' Are Neither Black Nor Citizens: The United States Civil Rights Movement and Global Migration." *Asian Law Journal* 2(1).

Thorne, Barrie. 1992. "Feminism and the Family: Two Decades of Thought,"
in *Rethinking the Family: Some Feminist Questions*, ed. Barrie Thorne
and Marilyn Yalom. Rev. ed. Boston: Northeastern University Press.

———. 1995. "Symposium: On West and Fenstermaker's 'Doing Gender,'"
*Gender and Society* 9: 497–99.

Toledo, Lorie. 1993. "Overseas Job vs. Family Stability." *People's Journal*
(December 15): 4.

Tronto, Joan. 2002. "The 'Nanny' Question in Feminism." *Hypatia* 17(2)
(Spring): 34–51.

Trucios-Haynes, Enid. 2002. "Temporary Workers and Future Immigration
Policy Conflicts: Protecting U.S. Workers and Satisfying the Demand
for Global Human Capital." *Brandeis Law Journal* 40(967): 990–98.

U.S. Department of Labor, Office of Inspector General. 1996. "The Department of Labor's Foreign Labor Certification Programs: The System Is
Broken and Needs to Be Fixed." Report no. 06–96–002–03–321 (May
22). Available at http://oig.dol.gov/public/reports/oa/pre_1998/06-96-
002-321s.htm. Last verified on May 21, 2004.

U.S. Department of State, Bureau of Consular Affairs Visa Services. 2003a.
*Visa Bulletin*, publication no. 56, vol. 8. Washington, DC, April. Available at http://travel.state.gov/visa_bulletin.html. Last verified on February 4, 2004.

———. 2003b. *Visa Bulletin*, publication no. 62, vol. 8. Washington, DC, October. Available at http://travel.state.gov/visa_bulletin.html. Last verified on February 4, 2004.

U.S. Immigration and Naturalization Service. 1997. *1995 Statistical Yearbook*. Washington, DC: Government Printing Office.

———. *1998–2001 Statistical Year Book*, Table 3: "Immigrants Admitted by
Region and Country of Birth, Fiscal Years 1989–2001." Available at

http://uscis.gov/graphics/exec/whereis/query.asp. Last verified on February 4, 2004.

Valenzuela, Abel. 1999. "Gender Roles and Settlement Activities Among Children and Their Immigrant Families." *American Behavioral Studies* 42(4) (January): 720–42.

Vaughan, Sarah. 1997. "Immigrant Visa Waiting List at 3.6 Million." *Center for Immigration Studies Bulletin* 28. Available at http://www.cis.org/articles/1997. Last verified on February 4, 2004.

Volpp, Letti. 2000. "Obnoxious to Their Very Nature: Asian Americans and Constitutional Citizenship." *Citizenship Studies* 5(1): 57–70.

Yeoh, Brenda, and Shirlena Huang. 1998. "Negotiating Public Space: Strategies and Styles of Migrant Female Domestic Workers in Singapore." *Urban Studies* 35(3): 583–602.